# survivor guilt

## a self-help guide

APHRODITE MATSAKIS, Ph.D.

New Harbinger Publications, Inc.

## Publisher's Note

*This publication is designed to provide accurate and authoritative information in regard to the subject matter covered. It is sold with the understanding that the publisher is not engaged in rendering psychological, financial, legal, or other professional services. If expert assistance or counseling is needed, the services of a competent professional should be sought.*

Distributed in the U.S.A. by Publishers Group West; in Canada by Raincoast Books; in Great Britain by Airlift Book Company, Ltd.; in South Africa by Real Books, Ltd.; in Australia by Boobook; and in New Zealand by Tandem Press.

Copyright © 1999 by Aphrodite Matsakis, Ph.D.
New Harbinger Publications, Inc.
5674 Shattuck Avenue
Oakland, CA 94609

Cover design © 1999 by Lightbourne Images
Text design by Tracy Marie Powell

Library of Congress Catalog Card Number: 98-68755
ISBN 1-57224-140-3 Paperback

New Harbinger Publications' Website address: www.newharbinger.com

01    00    99

10    9    8    7    6    5    4    3    2    1

First printing

This book is dedicated to all who suffer and all who will suffer as the result of human cruelty, human error, the inevitability of death, and other tragic events beyond their control.

*Suffering is the sole origin of consciousness.*

—Fyodor Dostoyevsky,
*Notes from the Underground*

# Contents

**Acknowledgments**                                                    x

**Introduction**                                                       1

**Part 1**    Understanding Survivor Guilt

1    What is Guilt                                                     19

2    Existential Survivor Guilt                                        39

3    Content Survivor Guilt                                            57

4    Causes and Circumstances                                         85

5 ·  Psychological Consequences of Survivor Guilt                    119

**Part 2**    The Healing Process

6    Healing From Survivor Guilt                                      155

7    Remembering                                                      175

8    Mentally Reconstructing Your Critical Event                      189

**9**    Exercises for Coping with Guilt                                    219

**Appendix A**   Getting Help: Survivor Groups and
Therapy Programs                                        235

**Appendix B**   Resources                                               247

**Appendix C**   Deep Breathing Techniques and
Muscle Relaxation Exercises                    263

**Appendix D**   Self-Assessment: Depression and                271
Post-Traumatic Stress Disorder


**References**                                                              275

# Acknowledgments

I would like to acknowledge Farrin Jacobs, for her excellent organizational suggestions and other editorial revisions, and the staff at New Harbinger Publications, for their support during the writing of this book. I would also like to thank Peter Valerio, M.A., C.P.C., for his insights into survivor guilt, and Fernando Gutierrez for all his support.

Most of all, however, I would like to thank my psychotherapy clients and others who trusted me enough to share their stories and their struggles as they attempted to heal their wounds and reclaim their lives. The massive emotional, and often financial and physical, losses some of these individuals sustained as the result of their traumas or life stresses were sometimes unbelievable. The fact that they nevertheless desired to overcome their pasts and lead productive, loving lives filled me with respect and humility and inspired me to write this book in hopes that it would help, to whatever extent possible, alleviate some of the pain and open the doors to hope and renewed faith in life.

# Introduction

*How come they shot you, Abale? Why not me?*

—Words spoken by Yitzhak
Rabin's wife after his murder
(Ben Artz-Pelossof, 1996)

It had been two years since Duane had seen his brother, Patrick. Duane missed his brother so much he offered to pay Patrick's airfare to come visit on the Fourth of July. At first Patrick was reluctant: he was in the midst of completing an important project. But when Duane insisted, Patrick consented. Yet he would not accept the offer of an airline ticket. He said he'd drive instead.

En route to see his brother, Patrick was killed in a highway accident.

"If I hadn't forced Patrick to visit me, he would have never been in that crash. When he said 'no' at first, I should have taken it as a sign that he shouldn't make the trip," says Duane. Duane also feels guilty for not insisting that Patrick fly instead of drive. "I should have forced him to accept the ticket. Then none of this would have happened."

Duane's father feels guilty too, since he had suggested to Duane and Patrick that they make more of an effort to keep the family close by seeing each other more often. Duane's mother feels guilty as well. She knew that Patrick didn't like driving. Yet the accident had nothing to do with Patrick's feelings about driving. In fact, the accident had not been Patrick's fault at all. Nevertheless Patrick's mother feels responsible for her son's death. She is certain that if only she had stopped her son from driving, he'd be with her today.

Duane and his parents are not delusional. In their minds, they know they did not kill Patrick. But in their hearts, they feel responsible for his death. They tell themselves that if only they had paid for Patrick's airline ticket or had never suggested that Patrick visit at all, Patrick would still be alive. They assume responsibility for his death even though they did not actually kill him and did not even intend to kill him.

This type of thinking is the logic of survivor guilt, and it can plague anyone who has managed to stay alive while another (or others) has died, anyone who has suffered fewer injuries than another, even anyone who has been spared certain hardships due to favorable economic, social, or psychological circumstances. Survivor guilt is not a mental illness. In many cases, it stems from a deep love for another person or from a spiritual identification with other human beings and an altruistic desire to give of one's self, even to the point of self-sacrifice (Campbell 1988). For example, Andrew developed malaria during his tour of duty in Vietnam. At times the malaria was so severe he could barely walk straight. But loyal marine that he was, he tried to keep his malaria hidden from his officers so that he wouldn't be forced to leave his squad and be sent to the rear for medical treatment. Eventually the malaria progressed to the point that Andrew could barely function. Realizing that if he stayed with his squad, he would be a liability to them, he did not protest when a helicopter was sent to fly him to the nearest hospital.

For weeks, Andrew was in delirium from fever. When he recovered, he was sent back to his squad, only to find that most of the original men in his squad had been killed in an ambush. The ambush occurred 24 hours after he was evacuated to the hospital.

Afterward, Andrew fought with renewed vigor and rage. His fury was fueled not only by his grief at the loss of his friends but also by his intense guilt at having survived when others in his squad had died. Furthermore, he was convinced that if he had been with his squad during the fateful ambush, he could have helped to save their lives. "There were a lot of inexperienced guys in my squad. This was my second tour in 'Nam. If I had been there, maybe I could have stopped them from making some stupid mistake. If I couldn't have saved them, at least I could have died with them," Andrew says.

To this day, Andrew has nightmares in which his dead friends call out his name and beckon him to join them. "I don't know if they're condemning me for not being with them when they got overrun or not," Andrew sobs in his therapy session. "But I do know this: I belong with them. I should be dead. In fact I'd be better off dead because at least I'd have some peace of mind. There's not a day of my life when I don't think about those guys and feel terrible for not being there to help them when they needed me. I also feel as if I'm living on borrowed time!"

Andrew's wife and children love him very much. But Andrew pushes them away. He doesn't feel he deserves their love. When he has sex with his wife, he remembers his dead friends who can never enjoy love or sex again. Sometimes Andrew denies himself sexual relations with his wife to avoid that horrible guilt feeling. Other times his guilt turns into either a deep depression during which he wants to be left alone or angry outbursts at his family.

Last year, Andrew's son graduated from college. Andrew debated whether he should attend the graduation ceremonies. He was afraid the guilt he would feel about having such a fine son (when others in the squad never even had the chance to get married) would cause him to get angry or become obviously depressed. Either way, he would ruin the graduation ceremony for his family.

After considerable thought, Andrew decided not to attend the ceremonies.

# Survivor Guilt: A Normal Reaction to Loss

People experience many forms of guilt. You can feel guilt about being less competent than others or guilt about having sexual or aggressive thoughts. You can also feel guilt about the opposite conditions, for example, guilt about outdoing or outshining others, or perhaps even about not being sexual or aggressive enough. Many people feel guilty about committing a crime or another misdeed or about not meeting social expectations. Survivor guilt can include those and other types of guilt, but it is unique in that it comes from having remained alive or uninjured in a circumstance in which another person (or persons) died or was physically or psychologically injured.

Survivor guilt is not a neurosis or sign of mental or emotional derangement. In fact, it can be a reflection of the deepest kind of love one human being can have for another: the wish to spare another person agony and death, even at the price of one's own happiness, health, or very life.

For example, Derrick married his high-school sweetheart, Ruby. He adored her. At thirty-five, Ruby developed breast cancer and died. Derrick feels he killed Ruby because he couldn't make enough money to support the family himself. After their second child, Ruby had to take on several part-time jobs to make ends meet. Many nights she came home tired, only to start baking pies and pastries to sell to a local bakery. Derrick is convinced that the overwork had caused the cancer.

Derrick tries to be a good father, but he feels that if his children were destined to have only one parent, it should have been Ruby. In his view, Ruby was a better person than he is. Unlike him, she never complained about the work she had to do. Also, she was more educated, more religious, and less selfish. He wonders why she got cancer and he didn't.

Not a day goes by when Derrick doesn't review the events leading to Ruby's death; he wonders if they chose the right doctor or made the right medical decisions, or if he did everything he could to help save Ruby.

After she died, there were times Derrick felt lonely for female companionship. Once in a while, he went on a date. Yet today, at fifty-five, he lives alone, celibate, and full of remorse. He still wishes that he had died instead of Ruby.

Survivor guilt is not a sign of "loving too much," being "overly dependent," or being "masochistic." It is a totally normal reaction to being in a circumstance in which someone you care about loses his or her life, is injured, or comes into some form of suffering that you somehow have managed to escape.

Survivor guilt has two aspects: The first aspect, *existential survivor guilt*, is guilt over having fared better than others. The second aspect of survivor guilt, called *content survivor guilt*, refers to feeling guilty about something you did, thought, or felt in order to survive a certain stressful or traumatic situation.

## *The Scope of Survivor Guilt*

Although survival guilt is usually thought of with respect to situations in which someone dies or is injured, I'm taking the liberty of extending the concept to situations in which people become aware that others are suffering from economic, social, or psychological disadvantages (because of race, religion, disability, economic background, or family history) that they have somehow managed to escape due to accident of birth or some other piece of good fortune.

For example, Lisa had a natural talent for science. But since Lisa's parents were immigrants from a country where education for women was not a priority, Lisa only finished high school. After Lisa married, she had the opportunity to go to college but chose not to so that she wouldn't outshine her husband, who didn't have a college education. Lisa did encourage her daughter, Esperanza, however, to go to college, and Esperanza obtained an advanced degree in biology.

By the time she was a mother herself, Esperanza was the chair of many important scientific committees and was being asked to present papers all over the world. Esperanza, however, got little joy from all her achievements and all the recognition she received. In fact, she felt guilty for doing so well, because her mother, who was perhaps equally intelligent, had never had the chance to develop her talents. Every time Esperanza was given an award for a scientific discovery, she wanted to hide and cry. Outside she smiled, but inside she was tortured with guilt.

Extending the definition of survivor guilt to include those types of situations may be somewhat controversial and may be refuted by some mental health professionals. However, in my thirty years of experience as a therapist, I have seen many clients struggle with their guilt for having experienced less discrimination or harassment or having more money, education, family support, social clout, or other advantages than others. Some have stayed in marriages or other relationships that did not meet their needs partially because they felt guilty about leaving a partner from an economically or politically disadvantaged or socially stigmazed group. Others have overextended themselves financially or in other ways because they felt guilty about having more money, talent, or prestige than someone else.

Of course, many people feel twinges of guilt when confronted with someone who is poorer, less healthy, or less blessed than they are. However, when the guilt feelings are stronger than mere twinges and come to motivate much of a person's behavior, stunt a person's growth, poison a person's ability to enjoy life, or contribute to the development of an addiction, depression, or anxiety disorder or to serious emotional, vocational, or relationship problems, then that guilt might legitimately be seen as a form of survivor guilt.

# Secrecy and Guilt

If you suffer from survivor guilt, part of your torment comes from feeling that you could have prevented the death, injury, or mistreatment of another person or that you should have suffered those hardships yourself. Another part of your torment is feeling that you must keep the guilt, and perhaps the circumstances that gave rise to the guilt, a secret. You fear that if your guilty secret was disclosed, you would be ostracized. People would look down on you and despise you for what you had done and you might be left loveless, friendless, and perhaps even jobless.

Yet by keeping your guilt a secret, you may feel like an emotional hypocrite and fear you can never be truly intimate with another person because you could never share your secret with anyone—even a spouse, partner, family member, or best friend.

You may also spend a considerable amount of time and energy trying to keep the guilt hidden from yourself. When that guilty feeling attacks you or memories of what you feel guilty about pop into your mind, you might try to push the memories away by discounting them or trivializing them. "That happened years ago. It doesn't bother me anymore," you might tell yourself. However, the sadness and guilt you feel inside lets you know that the guilt is very much alive, no matter how long ago the stressful event that caused the guilt took place.

Survivor guilt, like any other type of guilt, doesn't go away when it is hidden. In fact, left unexamined, the guilt festers and grows and can invade many aspects of your being. According to Bazyn (1977), trying to repress guilt is a device that "aggravates our feelings of guilt so that they overwhelm us."

Outside of certain religious organizations and spiritual groups, guilt is often a taboo subject. Even among mental health professionals and medical workers, the subject of guilt tends to be avoided. Indeed, much of pop psychology is oriented toward helping people get rid of their guilt, for in today's society, to be guilt-ridden is not fashionable. There is so much emphasis on being free of "guilt trips" that some people feel guilty about feeling guilty, as if feeling guilty is a sign that they have failed to make therapeutic progress. However, guilt is a normal part of human suffering (Kollbrunner 1996).

# Coping with Survival Guilt

The feelings of sadness you have may never go away. Like Andrew, who thinks about his dead army buddies every day, you may find yourself thinking about the person you lost frequently for much of your life. However, the way you think about and interpret the events that gave rise to your survivor guilt may be fraught with thinking errors and illogical conclusions. You may never stop feeling guilty about what happened and your role in it. However, it is highly possible that you do not need to feel as guilty as you do now. It's also quite possible that you have underestimated the contributions you did make toward helping the victim in the situation.

This book can not eliminate all of your guilt feelings. (That would be an impossible task!) Rather, the goals are to help you bring your guilt feelings out in the open and to help you examine them in depth with an eye to catching any thinking errors you have made that may have caused you to exaggerate or distort your role in the outcome of the unhappy events of your life. Looking at your guilt is a courageous step; most people would rather not think about what they did, felt, or thought that resulted in their feeling guilty. This book allows for a rational reexamination of your guilt. It is not a complete treatment guide for all the issues involved in your particular trauma or stressful event. It will help you put your thinking in accord with reason, rather than superstition, fantasies, or distorted views of reality. As you change how you think about what happened, some of the feelings you have about what happened may also change—for the better. You will be better able to identify what you are genuinely guilty of, as opposed to what you erroneously have concluded you are guilty of. You will also be able to find some ways of putting some of the guilt behind you and using the remaining guilt for constructive purposes.

It bears repeating that healing from survivor guilt, or any other form of guilt, does not mean eliminating the guilt. Rather it means putting the guilt into perspective and "shifting" it, from guilt about the past to guilt about how you might be cheating or hurting yourself or others as the result of that past guilt. Once you become aware of how your survivor guilt has affected your life, you will be better able to make conscious choices and value decisions in your life.

# Whom This Book Is For

Anyone who has been in a natural catastrophe, such as a fire, flood, hurricane, or tornado, or who has experienced a man-made catastrophe, such as a vehicular accident, physical or sexual assault, crime, political terrorism, or war, can suffer from survivor guilt. Indeed, survivor guilt is a common occurrence among persons who have been through a traumatic or life-threatening experience. (Appendix E defines the term *trauma*.)

In homes where there was physical or sexual abuse, someone who escaped the abuse or feels he or she was abused less than others may also develop survivor guilt. Furthermore, family members who witness or know about the mistreatment of another family member, even if they are not abused themselves, can suffer from intense survivor guilt.

People who feel they could have helped prevent the death or injuries of others, even if circumstances made it impossible for them to be of assistance, can also develop survivor guilt. Andrew developed survivor guilt following the deaths of members of his squad. He feels guilty that he wasn't with them when they were ambushed by the enemy. Yet at the time he was so weak with malaria that even if he had been with his buddies, he could not have helped them. In fact, his presence may have harmed them, because they would have had the additional responsibility of trying to protect a sick comrade from attack. Yet he still suffers from survivor guilt.

In a parallel manner, military nurses and medical staff who were not sent to the front lines often develop survivor guilt for not having been able to help wounded soldiers. Needless to say, survivor guilt among medical staff on the front lines of battle, in emergency rooms back home, and among firefighters, rescue workers, police, and paramedics is a major mental health issue. As Kubany (1997) points out, people whose vocational role involves caring for and protecting others may experience a form of survivor guilt when there is a death or injury among those in their charge. People in such positions often mistakenly equate *failure to prevent* death or injury with *causing* the death or injury (Shovar 1987).

Survivor guilt is one of the most common—and devastating—feelings experienced by parents who lose a child or by anyone who loses a loved one to suicide or homicide. When a suicide or homicide occurs, it is not just the immediate family but members of the victim's social circle, church, twelve-step program, group therapy, school, sports team, or recreational group who can develop tremendous feelings of survivor guilt.

Survivor guilt can also occur in situations that do not involve trauma, such as the normal death or illness of a parent, spouse or partner, or beloved friend. People who have a family member or close friend with an alcohol or drug addiction or an eating disorder can also develop survivor guilt, as can members of minority groups when they overcome certain societal and personal obstacles and achieve more economic security, social acceptance, and other rewards that have been historically denied to their minority group. On the job, workers who witness co-workers being harassed or verbally abused may experience survivor guilt, especially if the targeted co-worker is suspended, fired, or denied privileges accorded to most other employees. In therapy and recovery groups, it is not uncommon for people making noticeable strides in mastering their addiction or mental health problem to feel survivor guilt toward fellow members of their group who are not progressing at all, progressing less rapidly than themselves, or somehow doing worse.

This book is not a complete trauma- or stress-processing book. Please refer to the Cautions section at the end of this chapter for a more complete description of the limitations of this book.

## How to Use This Book

Pop psychology would have us believe that feeling guilty is old-fashioned, a relic from the past, and that by adopting the proper attitude, all guilt feelings can be made to easily disappear. This book will not attempt to delude you into thinking that you can erase your survivor guilt, or any other form of guilt, simply by completing a few written exercises. Nor will this book at any point trivialize your guilt by giving you platitudes such as "If life gives you lemons, make lemonade." There is no magic formula that will erase all your guilt feelings or your grief for people you have lost or those you have seen harmed.

What this book does attempt to do is explain what survivor guilt is and what causes it. It also attempts to explain other types of guilt people can experience in order to help you differentiate your survivor guilt from other types of guilt. You will be guided in identifying the ways your survivor guilt affects your life, including your relationships, your self-concept, and your career, and in examining your survivor guilt more rationally.

The healing process is presented step by step, with journal-writing exercises to help you gradually uncover the guilt and explore the circumstances that led up to that guilt, as well as subsequent events that may have contributed to your survivor guilt.

The book is divided into two parts. Part 1, "Understanding Survivor Guilt," explores different types of guilt and the consequences of survivor guilt. Chapter 1, "Types of Guilt," provides an overview of various types of guilt that frequently coexist with survivor guilt. Understanding the various kinds of guilt will increase your awareness of how they can compound the weight of survivor guilt. This understanding is necessary for a keener understanding of survivor guilt.

Chapters 2 and 3, "Existential Survivor Guilt" and "Content Survivor Guilt," describe the two types of survivor guilt. The causes and various aspects of each of these types of survivor guilt are explored in detail, and self-assessment exercises for each are provided.

Chapter 4, "Causes and Circumstances," describes the various types of survivor guilt. A number of situations can give rise to survivor guilt, such as trauma, normal bereavement, physical illness, addiction in the family, and emotional abuse in the family or workplace. This chapter also explores survivor guilt that can result from social and financial success or from progress in therapy or a recovery group.

Chapter 5, "Psychological Consequences," presents some of the manifestations of survivor guilt both within the individual and in relationships. This chapter shows how unresolved survivor guilt can contribute to the development or exacerbation of substance abuse, eating disorders, clinical depression, paranoia, anger, suicidal feelings, and certain physical or somatic symptoms. This chapter also discusses anniversary reactions and the effects of survivor guilt on relationships. An exercise to help you assess the effects of survivor guilt on your personality and on your relationships is provided.

Part 2, "Healing from Survivor Guilt," begins with chapter 6, "The Healing Process," which describes the process of healing from survivor guilt and the various obstacles that can seriously impede, or totally prevent, healing from occurring. Some of these obstacles include survivor guilt itself, feelings of worthlessness, fear of punishment, and unresolved grief, as well as fear of change.

Before healing can occur, you need to remember what happened and your role in it, at least in part. Chapter 7, "Remembering," discusses difficulties in remembering and provides suggestions for stimulating your memory of the past. Cautions to be observed in the remembering process are clearly outlined and need to be respected.

Chapter 8, "Reconstructing Your Critical Event Mentally," guides you in recording the event or series of events that gave rise to your survivor guilt. However, you will not simply be writing down what happened: you'll also be examining how you felt and what you thought during those crucial moments. In addition, you'll be asked to remember what you did not think, feel, or do and to consider if these might be sources of guilt. The first few exercises in this chapter will help you separate your survivor guilt from other types of guilt and from other emotional issues. Additional exercises will help you form a more rational view of what happened. You will be provided with a Thinking Errors Sheet, which outlines some of the thinking errors common to those who experience survivor guilt, and asked to evaluate your view of what happened during your traumatic or stressful events.

All the intellectual or mental analysis in the world, however, may not erase some of your guilt feelings. Chapter 9, "Accepting and Coping with Guilt," is designed to help you accept and cope with the guilt that still remains. Chapter 9 identifies some standards of recovery from survivor guilt and provides a questionnaire that can help you assess how far you've come in dealing with your survivor guilt and what areas you may need to examine and consider in greater depth

The appendixes provide information on getting help, recovery resources, relaxation and meditation methods, and self-assessment guides for post-traumatic stress disorder and clinical depression.

## *How to Read This Book*

You need to read this book and work on the written exercises slowly, at your own pace. I suggest that you set a time limit on the amount of writing you do, writing no more than thirty minutes at a time. There may be times when you want to write more; feel free to do so, but keep the cautions listed on the following page in mind and stop at the first sign of becoming overwhelmed, anxious, or preoccupied.

You can use this book as part of an ongoing therapeutic program, either with a trained professional or in a self-help or other recovery program. As you work on your survivor guilt in a therapeutic setting, your increased awareness of its impact on your inner life will only help you in your goal of improving your self-esteem, your relationships, and your ability to make contributions to your family and community. The greater your commitment toward some guilt-processing work either with a therapist, a support group, or a recovery program, the more you can benefit from this book.

## The Value of Writing

You might be asking yourself, "Why bother doing all this writing? What good does it do to put on paper what I already know? Why can't I just think or talk about the topics in this book? Why do all the work of writing everything down?"

Writing, like any form of expression, is healing. Writing about troubling experiences and the troubling aspects of your relationships helps you to see them more clearly and gives you a sense of mastery over the experience. Once you put something on paper, you may make connections you were not aware of and get in touch with feelings you haven't experienced before. You may feel more guilt or more grief before you come to be aware of your guilt and the losses and experiences that gave rise to it. The intensification of your feelings of guilt and grief is painful in the short run but healing in the long run because unresolved guilt is an obstacle to moving on with your life. Getting in touch with your guilt may be the beginning of making plans and decisions for your future.

Research shows that just writing down some painful experiences is helpful. Like being in group therapy, writing helps boost your immune system and helps keep your body healthy (Pearlman 1996).

This book contains several questionnaires and written exercises. The more honest and complete you are in completing this work, the more you'll learn about yourself and the more you can help yourself change in the ways you want to.

Working through this book is a process: you will reread, reevaluate, and expand on your work as you go along. For that reason, you need to keep a journal that contains all of the writing you do in completing the exercises. You may already keep a personal diary, or you may decide to begin one after you've begun to heal, but right now you need to make a separate "healing journal" for the work you do in this book.

I recommend that you buy a three-ring binder, some dividers, and some loose-leaf paper. Since you will be asked, as you work through the book, to go back, reread, and add to the writing you've done for previous exercises, using a loose-leaf notebook will enable you to add sheets as necessary. You will also be asked to write on a number of specific topics, including the event that precipitated your survivor guilt. The dividers will make each topic distinct and easy to find later on.

## *Cautions*

This book is not a complete trauma-processing or stress-, anxi-ety-, or anger-management program. You will need to seek help else-where (in other self-help books or in treatment with a trained mental health professional) for managing feelings and other reactions to the events you will be concerned with in this book. This book is limited to cognitive or intellectual analysis of stressful and traumatic events with a focus on guilt; it is not a total treatment program.

For some people, guilt serves as a type of glue that holds them together, just as for others, it is their anger that helps them maintain their sanity. For some, guilt is a protection against a psychotic break-down or an outbreak of aggressive, or even murderous, behavior. If thinking about dealing with your guilt frightens you, because you fear that you might become suicidal or homicidal or that you might "lose your mind," then you need to consult with a trained mental health professional before reading this book.

You need to monitor your reactions to this book since portions of it may bring to the surface painful memories and strong reactions you were not aware existed. Caution is needed even if you've been in therapy or a twelve-step program in which you discussed painful incidents in your past. Readers who have been repeatedly trauma-tized need to be especially cautious, since some traumatic memories may not have come forth yet and may be triggered into awareness by material in this book. Should this occur, I recommend that you seek professional help.

If, during the reading of this book or at any other time during the healing process, you experience any of the following reactions, seek professional help immediately; do not continue to read this book without first consulting your physician or counselor.

- Hyperventilation, uncontrollable shaking, or irregular heartbeat

- Feelings that you are losing touch with reality, even tempo-rarily, for instance, having hallucinations or extreme flash-backs of certain traumatic or stressful events

- Feeling disoriented, "spaced out," unreal, or as if you might be losing control

- Extreme nausea, diarrhea, hemorrhaging, or other physical problems, including intense, new, or unexplained pains or an increase in symptoms of a preexisting medical problem, for example, blood-sugar problems if you are diabetic or wheezing if you suffer from asthma

- Self-mutilation or the desire to self-mutilate
- Self-destructive behavior such as alcohol or drug abuse, self-induced vomiting, or overspending
- Suicidal or homicidal thoughts
- Memory problems

Also call for help if you are having so much emotional pain, anxiety, or anger that you fear you are going to die. Mild anxiety is to be expected, but extreme anxiety or despair needs professional attention as soon as possible.

If you are unable to contact a mental health professional and are truly frightened, go to the emergency room of a local hospital. Meanwhile, do the following:

- Stop reading this book (or doing whatever healing work you are engaged in) and focus on something else.
- Touch a physical object.
- Talk to someone right away.
- Avoid isolating yourself or taking alcohol, drugs, or other mood-altering substances.
- If you are angry, try expressing it in a safe way, by talking to a trusted friend, punching a pillow, or tearing up a telephone directory, for example.
- Do something pleasurable and relaxing: take a hot bath, go for a long walk, listen to your favorite music, pet the cat.

Even if you feel certain you do not need professional help, if you experience any of the negative reactions listed, take a break from reading this book and follow one of the suggestions.

Keep in mind that having a strong reaction to thinking about your survivor guilt (and other guilt that may be associated with your survivor guilt) and the effects of such guilt on your life or taking a long time to work on your survivor guilt does not make you a "failure." Developing symptoms as a result of reading this book or being in therapy does not reflect an inability to heal or a hidden unwillingness to heal. Instead, your reactions probably reflect the degree of stress or trauma you endured, which was not under your control. Your reactions have nothing to do with strength of character or intelligence. If you need to stop at any time and take a breather, whether for a day or a few weeks, you can always come back later and examine the past.

There are people, however, who have been so severely traumatized that they may be better off not thinking about the past. The memories of some family-abuse survivors, combat veterans, torture victims, prisoners of war, and concentration camp survivors may be better left buried. If you fall into one of these categories or find that the reactions listed above occur so frequently and intensely that the "healing" process is making your life unlivable, you should concentrate your efforts on finding relief from your survivor guilt and other symptoms, rather than trying to understand the trauma or improve your relationships. (If you're unsure, see chapter 7, "Remembering," for a more complete discussion of who should not read this book and who should postpone following the suggestions made in this book.)

This book is not for people suffering from any form of schizophrenia or multiple-personality disorder. If you suffer from panic disorder, clinical depression, manic-depressive illness, or another major psychiatric problem in addition to a post-trauma reaction, you need to be under the care of a trained professional. If your manic-depressive illness or clinical depression is severe, reading this book is not recommended, since bringing up painful topics will be of little benefit to you. If you have one of these conditions, your priority is to be able to resume normal functioning, not to explore the past.

Similarly, if you have a psychiatric disorder that varies in intensity and you are in a phase in which your suffering from the disorder is intense or at a peak, do not read this book until you have stabilized and until your physician and therapist give you permission to do so. Even if you do not suffer from a psychiatric problem, if you are experiencing severe stress in your everyday life, either in your relationships or in your work, you may want to put this book aside until the crises in your present life subside and you have the psychic energy to undertake the kind of emotional work outlined in this book.

Although the healing process involves confronting and managing numerous strong feelings, it is beyond the scope of this book to offer anything more than the briefest suggestions on anger management, grief work, or any kind of issues regarding identifying and coping with feelings. Managing trauma-based feelings or feelings arising from situations of extreme stress belongs to the realm of trauma-processing work or traditional group or individual therapy. You will need to consult with a trained mental health professional for assistance in these areas. You can also avail yourself of the numerous self-help books on these topics, some of which are listed in appendix B.

It is also beyond the scope of this book to offer guidance to survivors of family violence or sexual assault in confronting their abusers. The issue of confronting an abusive family member or another assailant is one that needs careful consideration and planning. Books such as *The Courage to Heal Workbook* by Laura Davis (1990) should be consulted in deciding whether or not or how to confront an abuser.

# A Final Note

As you work through this book, you need to keep several things in mind: Despite considerable recent interest and research on the effects of trauma and severe stress on human beings, professional interest in these areas has historically been relatively sparse compared with research and study of other problems. Consequently, our knowledge of the effects of overwhelming stress on human beings is limited, and sometimes the results of research studies are conflicting. Most of the suggestions in this book are based on clinical experience, in combination with whatever research exists.

There are no guarantees that any of the suggestions made will radically transform your life, improve your relationships, or enhance your job performance. In the case of relationships, change requires the efforts of two people. If there is any guarantee in reading this book, it is that you can work to better understand your survivor guilt and exert more mastery and control over how you treat yourself and how you function in relationships and work settings.

Remember, however, that this book is only a beginning guide to understanding your survivor guilt and improving your self-esteem. No self-help book, regardless of its quality, is a substitute for counseling or other forms of in-depth help. You will probably need the assistance of a caring friend, a qualified mental health professional, or perhaps even a spiritual advisor in understanding and meeting the challenges survivor guilt has thrust upon you in your efforts to improve your abilities to love, work, and play.

Some of the writing exercises and suggestions may be helpful; others may not be. If a particular writing exercise does not apply to you or doesn't offer you insight or relief, it doesn't mean you don't have the "right answer" or that you aren't trying hard enough. What helps one person may not help another.

# Part 1

# Understanding Survivor Guilt

# 1

# What Is Guilt

*Guilt matters. Guilt must always matter.*
*Unless guilt matters the whole world is meaningless.*

—Archibald MacLeish, *JB*

*Guilt* is an English word that originally meant "debt" (Ayto 1990). The *American College Dictionary* (1996) defines guilt as the "fact or state of having committed an offense or crime" or a "conscious violation of moral or penal law." Robertson (1994) defines guilt as an "uncomfortable feeling resulting from the commission or contemplation of a specific act contrary to one's internalized standards of conduct." In Freud's view, guilt was pain generated by the conscience in order to change a person's behavior (Freud 1961). The concept of guilt also involves an expectation of fear of being disapproved of or being punished (Campbell 1978, Bowles 1978).

Although there are many possible definitions of guilt, in this book Edward Kubany's definition will be used. Kubany, a cognitive behavioral psychologist who has worked extensively with abused women and combat veterans, defines guilt as a negative feeling state that is triggered by the belief that one should have thought, felt, or acted differently (1994). Many situations in life can create guilt feelings. The death, injury, or insult of another or any type of traumatic experience is a breeding ground for guilt.

While survivor guilt is the focus of this book, it's important to be aware of other sources of guilt, because your experience of survivor guilt may be compounded by their presence. Sometimes the various kinds of guilt you experience are not related, but when they are, your overall experience of guilt is intensified. At such times, your guilt feelings can overwhelm you, making you feel unable to cope with them. As a result you may try to ignore them, or you may let them dominate your life. However, trying to ignore guilt is only a temporary solution. Strong guilt feelings, like any other feelings, are bound to emerge, no matter how hard you try to suppress them.

# Types of Guilt

The first step in understanding and resolving guilt feelings is to be able to break down your big burden of guilt into smaller pieces by separating the feelings into the various types of guilt and examining each type of guilt. In order to do this, you need to be able to distinguish the different forms of guilt.

## Infantile Guilt

"All upbringing is a cultivation of the sense of guilt on an intensive scale," writes Paul Tournier (1977, 10). According to Anna Freud (1996), guilt begins in our childhood when we are completely dependent on our parents and other adults for our well-being. Since our survival depends on pleasing our caretakers, when they scold or become angry with us, we fear that we will be abandoned or neglected. Along with that fundamental fear comes guilt at not having pleased the parent or caretaker.

Sigmund Freud used the term *infantile guilt* to describe guilt you felt as a child when you were reprimanded or rejected by your parents or other caretakers. This type of guilt motivated you to change your behavior in order to avoid parental scolding or neglect. Through direct teaching as well as parental admonitions, you probably learned the morale and rules of your household and society. In Freudian terms, you *internalized* your parent's or caretaker's value system and expectations and automatically felt guilty when you violated parental or societal norms. Even when your parents or caretakers weren't around to scold you, you probably scolded yourself for disobeying their rules. For example, studies of two-year-olds have shown that even when their mothers were not around, they called themselves "naughty" and "bad" for having violated a household rule (Aronfreed et al. 1971).

Sigmund Freud further postulated that as people grew older they could transfer their infantile guilt from their parents and caretakers to other authority figures, such as teachers, clergy persons, work supervisors or superiors, political figures, or others with religious, political, economic, or vocational status or power. Hence even a sixty-year-old man could feel guilty about not meeting the expectations of someone in an authority position. Psychologically, the man feels as if his supervisor has the power not only to harm his professional standing but to obliterate him. This fear not only of being scolded or shamed but also of being annihilated stems back to infancy and childhood, when being judged as deficient in some way could have led to being rejected and neglected, which could have led to death itself.

Infantile guilt involves fear of losing the esteem and love of other people (Tournier 1977) and evokes a fear of physically dying or being psychologically obliterated as the result of displeasing others. An adult whose life is organized around avoiding the criticism of others, especially authority figures, may be suffering from infantile guilt. Infantile guilt can lead to "people-pleasing," which refers to putting aside one's own needs and desires in order to give precedence to the needs and desires of others.

When infantile guilt guides people's lives, they may have difficulty recognizing their own needs or talents and discovering their own convictions. Infantile guilt can compound survivor guilt in instances when an individual's failure to obey or please an authority figure resulted in the death or injury of another. For example, Tyrone was raised in a strict household where he learned that children were supposed to obey their parents no matter what. In the military, he'd learned to obey commanding officers. However, while he was in battle, Tyrone balked one day when his commanding officer ordered him to fire at a group of supposed enemy soldiers in the distance. Based on reliable sources, including information from other soldiers, Tyrone thought the soldiers were Americans, not the enemy.

Tyrone refused to fire, only to discover that the commanding officer had been right: the soldiers in the distance were indeed armed enemy troops. During the resulting firefight, some of Tyrone's comrades were killed. Tyrone's guilt for having stayed alive was compounded by his infantile guilt at disobeying an authority figure (his commanding officer).

Infantile guilt provides the basis for two other types of guilt: guilt about failing to meet specific parental expectations and guilt: about failing to meet societal expectations.

## Failure to Meet Parental Expectations

As an adult, you may experience feelings of infantile guilt for failing to please an authority figure or a person who is otherwise important to you. But you might also feel guilty for not living up to the specific expectations placed upon you by your parents or caretakers. So if your father was a meticulous gardener and instilled in you the value of maintaining a garden of the highest quality, as an adult, you might feel guilty when you allow the weeds to take over your garden. Somewhere in the back of your mind your father's voice reminds you that you have failed to complete your gardening duties.

In some cases survivor guilt can be intensified by guilt for not having lived up to certain parental expectations. For example, Infon bought his son a motorcycle for his twenty-first birthday. Two weeks later, his son was in a motorcycle accident that lead to nine months of hospitalization and several surgeries. Not only does Infon blame himself for his son's pain because he bought him the motorcycle, but he is also experiencing some infantile guilt because in purchasing his child an expensive gift he violated two of his father's admonitions. The first admonition was against "spoiling children" by giving extravagant gifts. The second was against spending money for luxury items under almost any circumstances. Infon's father firmly believed that every extra penny should be saved for the future, and in his own life, he spent money only on necessities.

Every time Infon went to see his son at the hospital, he could hear his father's voice saying, "Spending money on fancy cars and toys is foolishness. See, I told you so. I warned you that it was wrong to spend money on expensive items and luxuries. If you'd saved your money for the future, like I taught you to do, this would never have happened."

Camry, a military nurse, also suffers from double guilt. She was on the front lines nursing a wounded soldier when the enemy attacked again. A bullet grazed her face and killed a soldier next to her. She then used the soldier's corpse as a shield against the continued fire. To this day, decades later, she feels she should have died with the soldier.

But Camry also suffers from guilt for violating her father's beliefs about respecting the dead. Her father had been a soldier during World War II. He had served under a general who insisted that his troops respect not only their own dead but also enemy dead.

Soldiers under this general were harshly punished if they mutilated the bodies of the dead. Camry's father had instilled in all his children the value of consecrating the remains of the dead. As a result, Camry feels as if she betrayed her father and all that he stood for when she used the corpse for protection.

## ✍ Self-Assessment for Infantile Guilt and Guilt Stemming from Failure to Meet Parental Expectations

The purpose of this writing exercise is to help you bring out into the open the kinds of messages you were given during your formative years. You may have received these messages from parents or other caretakers, such as grandparents, aunts and uncles, or other significant people who were directly involved in taking care of you and trying to teach you "right from wrong."

Often people are not aware of why they feel guilty about a certain matter because they haven't had the opportunity to examine early messages about how they "should" be or act or how "good" people should be or act. This exercise will help you put into words the kinds of values you were expected to embody as a child. Later on, when you are asked to describe the situation that caused you to experience survivor guilt, you will refer back to your responses to this exercise in order to see how your early experiences with guilt interact with your survivor guilt.

On a fresh piece of paper in your journal, write the heading "Early Should Messages." Think of all the "shoulds" you learned about how you ought to be during the first twelve years of your life. On your paper, draw three columns. In the first column, list as many shoulds as you can remember. Include those shoulds you heard from your parents, neighbors, friends, family members, teachers, religious instructors, and the media.

In the second column, list the source of the should—where you learned it or who taught it to you. In the third column, describe what happened to you when you did not live up to this particular should. For example, were you verbally chastised, rejected, hit, or made to feel ashamed? Were you threatened with abandonment or some other punishment?

Look over your list of shoulds and notice if any of the shoulds contradict one another. For example, suppose your mother told you you should stand up for yourself and fight with bullies in school, but your grandfather told you that fighting was a sin. Or perhaps one of your caretakers gave you a double message. For instance, suppose your grandfather told you that fighting was a sin but that letting one-self get beat up was a sign of being a "sissy" and a disgrace to the family.

On another piece of paper, write "Shoulds Contradictions." Once again draw three columns. In the first column, list any discrep-ancies you found between what the various people who were impor-tant in your early life taught you about how to behave, think, or feel. In the second column, describe how you coped with the contradictory shoulds you heard growing up. In the third column, describe what happened to you as the result of how you coped with the contradic-tory shoulds.

For example, if your mother taught you to fight bullies and your grandfather taught you to turn the other cheek, perhaps you lied to your grandfather when you fought back or perhaps you lied to your mother when you walked away from fights. Or maybe you didn't tell either of them how you responded to bullies and tried to carry the burden of being threatened at school all by yourself. Did you lie, steal, pretend, run away, hurt yourself, or hurt others as a result of the contradictory messages? If so, please describe in detail.

It's important to identify the ways you responded to such pres-sures in order to see if you are still using these coping methods to deal with any guilt you are experiencing today.

## Failure to Meet Societal Expectations

Your parents and caretakers aren't the only source of the demands to meet certain standards. Society also places pressures on people. Regardless of how independent anyone thinks he or she might be, he or she can probably be made to feel guilty for not living up to cultural expectations placed upon them.

For example, many women in Western culture feel guilty about not being slender enough, even if they grew up in homes that paid no particular attention to female body size. Because the culture tends to measure the worth of a man by the size of his bank account, men who are unemployed or who are burdened with financial hardships tend to experience guilt for not being financially successful. Even men who grew up in homes that valued spiritual matters over the acquisition of material goods can experience some level of guilt for not living up to the cultural expectation that, as men, they should have a job, a home, a car, and plenty of money in the bank.

"In everyday life," writes Tournier, "we are continually soaked in this unhealthy atmosphere of . . . criticism" (1977, 15). Sometimes the criticism is "keen and outspoken, sometimes silent" but it is "not less painful for being so. We are all sensitive to it, even if we conceal the fact" (13).

Guilt derived from failing to meet societal expectations complicates survivor guilt. For example, Maureen is overweight and feels guilty about not meeting societal expectations that she be slender. When her daughter was sexually abused by her husband's brother, Maureen experienced survivor guilt in that she wished she could have been abused in her daughter's place. "She was a young girl who had everything to look forward to. I'm an overweight middle-aged woman with nothing ahead of me. If someone had to be raped, it should have been me," she sobbed in session.

Maureen's survivor guilt was exacerbated by her guilt about her weight. Even though her eating habits and body size had nothing to do with her daughter's molestation, in her mind they did. Maureen confused the two guilts—her guilt over her appearance and her survivor guilt. She concluded that her overeating and overweight somehow caused the rape of her daughter. She felt that if she had been thinner she might have married a different man, one who didn't have a brother who was a child molester.

Maureen's therapist pointed out that while it was true that Maureen might have married a different man if she had been thinner, this would not have prevented her daughter from getting hurt. Maureen might have married a man who was a child abuser himself or who had a nephew or father or friend who was a pedophile. Only if Maureen had witnessed her daughter being abused or in some other way had been aware that her daughter was being hurt and, instead of helping her daughter, chose to go food shopping or on an eating binge, then and only then could her eating problems be related to her daughter's rape. Furthermore, Maureen needed to remember that it was not she or her overeating, but a pedophile, who had violated her daughter.

## ✍ Self-Assessment for Guilt Stemming from Failure to Meet Societal Expectations

The expectations you feel others have of you can exert a powerful influence on your life. It's important to be aware of what you feel others or society expect of you. The greater your awareness, the greater the possibility that you can decide for yourself which of these expectations you feel you want to strive toward and which you choose to reject as personal goals.

On a fresh page in your journal, write the heading "What Others Expect of Me." Then answer the following questions as honestly as you can:

What do you feel society expects of you in terms of appearance, intimate relationships, family relationships, financial status, community obligations, or political involvement?

Try to identify at least three expectations in each category. For example, under intimate relationships, you might write, "I feel society expects me to be married and to enjoy spending my leisure time with my spouse. Society expects me to be sexually faithful to my spouse and to make my spouse happy. If my spouse is unhappy and wants to leave me, society says that means that I failed."

Review the expectations you listed for each category and, on a separate page, describe how you feel or what you do when you feel you've failed to meet these expectations.

## Childhood Omnipotent Guilt and Superman/Superwoman Guilt

*Childhood omnipotent guilt* is a well-documented tendency of young children to think that the world revolves around them and that they control everything that happens. Young children think that if they wish something it might come true. For example, when children become frustrated with a parent or sibling, they often think or say, "I hate you! I wish you were dead!," which is a perfectly normal expression of aggression for a child. But, if for some reason that parent or sibling subsequently becomes ill, dies, or leaves the family, the child may think that he or she caused it to happen. This is called *magical thinking*, because hating a parent, sibling, spouse, or friend, or even wishing another person dead, does not cause harm unless the aggressive wish is acted upon.

No matter how old or how mature you are, a part of you—consciously or unconsciously—may still be engaging in magical thinking or seeing yourself as omnipotent. If someone you know commits suicide, the child in you may feel that your hostility killed that person because you sometimes harbored hostile feelings toward him or her.

But hating people doesn't kill them or make them sick. Angry, hateful feelings and wishes in themselves cannot cause the physical death, suicide, illness, or injury of another, with one important exception: if you have severely or continually maltreated someone, and then that person commits suicide or acquires an illness or injury directly related to your treatment, some of your guilt may be appropriate. If not, some of the guilt you are experiencing may fall into the category of childhood omnipotent guilt.

In adolescence and adulthood, childhood omnipotent guilt can be transformed into a type of guilt called *superman* or *superwoman guilt*. In order to cope with a traumatic or extremely stressful situation, people can come to believe they have superhuman qualities. The more helpless and powerless people feel in a life-or-death situation, the greater the need for superhuman powers. One theory is that during traumatic conditions, people tend to revert to childlike thinking, including the tendency toward childhood omnipotent guilt (Krystal 1971).

Kubany (1994) , Opp and Samson (1989), and others have found that survivors of traumatic circumstances often experience guilt and feelings of failure for not knowing what no human being could have known and for not having abilities that are beyond human capability. Examples are medical staff who feel guilty for not being able to save everyone, parents who feel guilty for not being able to protect their children from all illnesses and harm, soldiers who feel guilty for not having been able to protect their comrades from injury during unexpected enemy assaults, and relatives of seriously ill persons who feel guilty for not knowing the outcome of certain medical procedures.

If you suffer from superman/superwoman guilt, then you are telling yourself, "I'm in charge of all the variables for life and death" and "I knew things would happen before they did" (Opp and Samson 1989, 162).

## ✍ Self-Assessment for Childhood Omnipotent Guilt

You may be experiencing childhood omnipotent guilt and not be aware of it. The following questions are designed to help you determine the extent to which childhood omnipotent guilt is a part of your emotional life.

In your notebook, write the heading "Childhood Omnipotent Guilt" and answer the following questions as honestly as you can. Remember, you're answering these questions for yourself, and nobody can read what you have written unless you choose to share your answers.

1. Have you ever wished for the injury, illness, mistreatment, or death of a friend or relative? List five instances when you made such wishes.

2. Did harm come to any of the people you wished to be harmed?

3. If harm did come to them, explain how your wishing the harm caused it to happen. Assume you are presenting the case to a jury of reasonable adults. What evidence could you present that would indicate that your wishing caused each of these individuals to be injured or die?

4. If you hadn't wished harm on them, what is the probability that they might have come to harm anyway at that time or some other time?

5. Have you ever wished for positive things to happen to others? List five examples of times you have wished for others to enjoy life, good health, prosperity, or other forms of well-being or happiness. In which of these instances do you feel your wishing made these positive results occur? If you were presenting a case to a jury of reasonable adults, what evidence could you present that would indicate that your wishing caused each of these people to have an improved life?

6. Write three or four sentences about how childhood omnipotent guilt or superwoman/superman guilt has caused you to feel responsible for events by ascribing magical powers to yourself.

## Religious Guilt

Sin and guilt are the themes of many major religions. People are often taught to feel guilty for failing to adhere to the tenets of their faith or to expected forms of worship; this can lead to *guilt of doing*. Furthermore, some faiths espouse the notions of original sin and people's inherent guilt. According to some Christian beliefs, all people are born evil and are therefore guilty unless they are redeemed through faith; this can lead to *guilt of being*.

### Guilt of Doing

Guilt of doing involves the sense that you cannot live up to a certain religious or spiritual ideal because of something you did wrong or something you failed to do right. Religious guilt frequently coexists with survivor guilt. For example, it is not uncommon for soldiers to experience guilt of doing for violating the religious code of "thou shalt not kill." Some domestic violence survivors, such as battered women and physically or sexually abused children, are coerced into committing cruel or sadistic acts such as lying, stealing, committing sexual acts (including prostitution), or killing animals or people, as in cult abuse. People who are victimized in these ways can suffer from severe religious guilt, which is often at the core of their survivor guilt.

In some cases, people who have lost a loved one to suicide or homicide attribute the death of this loved one to their having violated a tenet of their faith. For example, Randy still suffers from survivor guilt over the suicide of his daughter some fifteen years ago. However, his survivor guilt is compounded by his religious guilt for having an adulterous affair during his marriage. On some level, he feels that the death of his daughter is divine payback for violation of his marriage vows. Another example is Esther, whose teenage son was killed by a mugger. When Esther is honest with herself, she feels the mugging was a form of punishment for leaving the religion of her childhood and converting to another faith.

Another type of religious guilt involves rejecting your previous religious and spiritual beliefs and traditions due to a traumatic event. For example, parents of children who have died as the result of illness, murder, or suicide may have stopped believing in God because their prayers were not answered. People trapped in natural disasters, such as fires or floods, or man-made disasters, such as violent or abusive homes, may abandon their religious beliefs when their God does not provide them the help and rescue they need.

However, there can be guilt in abandoning your religious or spiritual beliefs, especially if family members or significant others are critical of this change. Hence people who reject their faith as the result of a severe trauma may feel guilty about not being able to believe what they used to believe or not attending services as they used to.

## ✍ Self-Assessment for Religious Guilt (Guilt of Doing)

The purpose of this exercise is to help you identify and understand your religious values. If you are a member of an organized religion, some of these values are available in written form, or you may hear them articulated when you attend meetings of your religious group. Even if you are not a member of an organized religious group now, you may have been raised to believe in a certain religion; although you no longer formally adhere to that religion, some of the values may still be important to you or may still influence you. It's often the case that even though certain religious values have been rejected, they become part of the psyche, especially if others who are important to you still adhere to those values.

You may have changed faiths or adopted spiritual values that are not unique to or particularly identified with any religious group. Regardless of the origin of your religious or spiritual values, it's important to be aware of these values, because they can form the basis of guilt when you transgress them.

Open up your journal and on a fresh piece of paper, write the heading "My Religious/Spiritual Values" at the top of the page. Then answer the following questions:

If you belonged to an organized religion as a child, what values were you taught? How did that religion define "right" and "wrong" or "good" and "evil"? You may need several pages to answer this question, or you may simply make a list of the values of your religion.

Looking back over what you have written, ask yourself which of those values you truly believed in? All of them? Some of them? None of them?

Were you ever scolded or chastised for not obeying one of the rules of the religion or for violating one of the religion's codes? What value or code did you violate? At the time, how did you feel about being chastised? Did you feel guilty, or not? If you felt guilty, how guilty did you feel? Just a twinge of guilt? A moderate amount of guilt? Profound guilt?

Were you conflicted about your guilt? In other words, did a part of you feel guilty while another part of you felt justified or not guilty at all?

What happened when you felt guilty? Did your mood change? Did your attitude toward yourself or others change? Did your lifestyle or daily habits change? Did you become angrier or more destructive to yourself or others? Did the guilt result in any changes that, in retrospect, you see as positive?

At the time, were you given means to make amends for your errors, were you punished in some manner, or both? How did you feel about being punished or making amends at the time?

How do you feel about being scolded or punished today, years later? If your religion provided a means of atonement, how do you think that affected you? Did punishments or means of atonement help relieve any guilt you were experiencing in the past? Did the feeling of relief carry into the present?

If you have changed religions or adopted a different spiritual approach to life, what would you say are the values of your new spirituality or religious outlook? How do you feel when you violate one of these values? Is it part of your current spiritual or religious program to punish yourself in some way or make amends in some manner? If so, please describe in detail.

As the result of the stresses or traumas you have experienced, have you come to doubt some of the tenets of your faith and perhaps reject your faith altogether? If this is the case, do you feel guilty about having moved away from your original faith? Write two or three sentences about any such feelings of guilt.

Do your close friends or family members accept your change in beliefs or withdrawal from your original faith? How does their response to your change affect your sense of guilt?

## Guilt of Being

Religious guilt can also arise from the sense that you cannot live up to your religious and spiritual beliefs because of what you are—vulnerable and, according to some faiths, by nature sinful. This type of religious guilt is the *guilt of being*. In the Judeo-Christian tradition, the guilt of being derives from the notion of original sin. In other religions—for example, Islam—there is no parallel to the idea of original sin (Swanson 1995).

While guilt of being can originate from religious ideas about the inherent sinfulness of being human, it can also arise from being the emotional scapegoat in a family or group. Usually one child or family member is selected. However, in some families, more than one person can be placed in the role of scapegoat. There can be so much emotional and verbal abuse of the family scapegoats that they can easily begin to feel they should never have been born. This sense of guilt about being is even greater if those who are being emotionally scapegoated are also being physically or sexually abused.

Family scapegoats who become the objects of frequent or ongoing verbal or other forms of abuse need to develop coping strategies to survive, some of which may be dysfunctional. For example, abused people with little support and no way out may start to drink, use drugs, overeat, lie, or steal. Sometimes they have memory problems and make frequent mistakes. These behaviors then become the object of criticism by the other family members, and the scapegoated person may criticize himself or herself as well. The self-criticisms and the criticisms of others lead to guilt of doing, which only reinforces the scapegoat's fundamental feeling of guilt of being.

Another important factor in such situations is the humiliation involved in being the recipient of verbal, physical, or sexual abuse. The awareness of being used and that others have power over your body, emotions, and thoughts erodes integrity, which can make you feel like a thing, not a person. This vulnerability to the verbal and other forms of attack to others can create a sense of powerlessness and worthlessness that can lead to a sense that you don't deserve to live and a feeling of guilt at simply being alive.

One woman writes: "I've been criticized from the day I was born. My mother told me she was ashamed to have such an ugly child. My dad wasn't happy with me either. I felt I shouldn't have been born. I never should've existed. I felt guilty for being alive—for breathing, eating, sleeping, having fun, working, anything. Even today I can feel guilty about anything I do, even going to church or doing good deeds, because I feel like I shouldn't have been born.

"To try to steal a little peace and happiness, I lied a lot about what I did and where I went. I stole money, too, to feed my drug addiction. Of course the family caught me lying, stealing, and drinking, which only gave them more cause to hate me and criticize me. I couldn't argue with them because, of course, it was wrong to do those things. But even if I never told another lie and was the holiest person in the world, I would still be guilty in their eyes—guilty for being me or just for being.

"I've cleaned up my act somewhat. No more drinking, stealing, or lying. But I slip sometimes, and when I do, I'm scared that doing just one little wrong thing will cause my family to reject me. Then I'll be an outcast. It's like they're all watching me, waiting for me to make a mistake. I know I'm exaggerating the feeling of being watched, but it's also true that they look and judge me, more than they do others. I'm not imagining that they are looking and judging. They are. And they only see the bad, not the good. I can feel the negative energy coming toward me and it destroys me. I don't even have the energy to fight back. I shrivel up. Then that makes me feel guilty for taking up room in the world, guilty for just being alive."

## ✍ Self-Assessment for Religious Guilt (Guilt of Being)

Use a fresh sheet in your journal and write "Guilt of Being" as the heading. Answer the following questions in your journal as completely as possible.

1. Have you ever felt guilty not for any particular characteristic you have or for something you've done (or not done) but simply for being alive?

2. Describe in detail the circumstances when you first began experiencing guilt of being. Be careful to remember pressures or stresses imposed by others. For example, when was the first time you had this feeling? Did the idea come from within you or from somewhere outside of yourself, perhaps an organization, a book, a media presentation, or another person?

3. Did anyone ever tell you that you didn't deserve to be alive? Who? How often did that person invalidate your existence? Did you believe that person? If so, did you believe that person entirely or only partially? Did that person harm you in other ways—emotionally, physically, financially, or socially?

4. Did your guilt of being start as part of a trauma, or was it made stronger by being involved in a life-threatening experience? If you'd never been involved in this trauma, do you think you'd feel guilty about being alive? If so, why? Did this feeling of guilt of being originate as part of the teaching of a religious or spiritual group with which you were, or are, affiliated?

## Shadow Guilt

Related to religious guilt, but somewhat different, is shadow guilt. According to psychologist Carl Jung, the human personality has many parts. One part of our personality—the person we present to the world—is called *persona*. This part has learned socially acceptable traits and knows how to modify certain instincts and desires in order to fit into society and not be punished for breaking societal rules.

Another part of the personality, however, is called the *shadow*. The shadow is the reservoir of many of our desires and feelings that we, or society, feel are unacceptable. Hence the shadow contains lust, greed, vanity, aggressiveness, pettiness, selfishness, capacity for violence and evil, and all those parts of us that are "bad"—instincts that should definitely not be acted upon. Also contained in the shadow are qualities that are not considered "evil" but are socially undesirable: for example, vulnerability in men and aggressiveness in women.

According to Tournier (1977), even though the shadow is usually repressed and even if we do not act on the impulses and desires in the shadow, we are aware that we have secret desires and temptations that we, or others, judge to be immoral. Our awareness of our shadow, however vague, unclear, or confused, breeds a sense of guilt. "In an existential sense . . . man feels guilt with regard to himself . . .

because there are within him obscure forces, impulses, and inhibitions which neither his will nor his intelligence or his knowledge can master" (48). In addition, no matter how much we suppress our shadow, the primitive urges and feelings contained in it continue to emerge. They are very powerful.

One way to handle the shadow is to deny it exists but to satisfy it by watching other people act as if motivated by their shadow. That's one reason why movies with lots of sex, violence, and other sometimes socially unacceptable behavior are so popular—people release their shadow urges by watching others act out those urges. People also often admire those who act out or who are thought to act out their shadow. For example, a recent study concluded that voters "secretly" want presidents and elected officials to be adulterous and have sexual escapades (Morin 1998).

However, people who've been in stressful life circumstances leading to the death, injury, or debasement of others have often encountered the shadow not in movies or in distant political figures but in real life. They may have seen people act out their shadows and may have been in situations in which they were forced to act out their shadow or where their shadow urges were activated.

Anyone who has been the victim of sexual assault, war, or other forms of violence has seen people who are acting out shadow urges. Anyone who has been exposed to injustices based on prejudice due to race, gender, sexual orientation, religion, or disability, and anyone who has grown up in a home where there is emotional or other types of abuse or where one or more family members suffer from an alcohol, drug, or food addiction, has seen people whose shadow selves are damaging not only their own lives but the lives of others. Those who have been forced to abuse another person, lie, steal, cheat, or go against their own moral standards in order to save their own life or the lives of others were forced to act out parts of their shadow.

Even if you were not forced to betray your values during your stressful experiences, if you have ever felt vengeful or murderous toward those who hurt you or someone you loved, you have met your shadow. Having self-destructive thoughts is also a part of the shadow personality, and people coping with survivor guilt frequently have thoughts of suicide, self-mutilation, and self-abasement.

Even if you've never acted on a shadow impulse, you may experience shadow guilt, because when you are honest with yourself, you realize that no matter how hard you try, you can not eliminate the shadow part from your being, and because you sense that the shadow, although repressed, has the potential to erupt and cause havoc in your life. The fantasies and desires of the shadow, whether they be of sloth, murder, greed, lust, or self-aggrandizement, "defy the censorship of our will. It is another self which is in us, which we cannot stifle, and which we fear will be discovered" (Tournier 1977, 47–48).

## ✍ Self-Assessment for Shadow Guilt

On a fresh piece of paper in your journal, write the heading "Shadow Guilt" and answer the following questions to the best of your ability. Since shadow guilt is related to religious guilt, some of your answers to the following questions may be similar to those for the questions on religious guilt.

1. Have you ever lusted for or had sexual fantasies about someone whom you were told you should not desire sexually?

2. Have you wanted more than your share of money, food, recognition, power, or some other commodity?

3. Have you ever wanted to act selfishly and think only of yourself?

4. Have you ever stolen anything or wanted to steal something?

5. Have you ever been petty or manipulative or thought about being petty or manipulative?

6. Have you ever injured or killed or thought about injuring or killing another living being?

7. Have you ever injured or killed another living being and enjoyed the sense of power involved or fantasized about how enjoyable killing and maiming might be?

8. Have you told a lie or felt like lying?

9. Have you ever thought about cutting or mutilating yourself or about killing yourself?

10. Have you ever injured yourself physically or attempted suicide?

Look over your responses to these questions, then answer the following question: have you felt or do you feel guilty for answering "yes" to any of the questions? Write two or three sentences about your experience of guilt for each of the questions you answered "yes" to.

# True Guilt vs. False Guilt

Infantile guilt, religious guilt, and childhood omnipotent guilt result from not measuring up to societal expectations. Carl Jung and Paul Tournier contrast these types of guilt, which they label *false guilt*, with *true guilt*, which stems from not meeting standards you have set for yourself. True guilt involves letting yourself down, whether in the form of not taking care of yourself, not developing your talents, allowing others to mistreat you, or not pursuing your personal dreams. False guilt derives from "fear of social judgment and the disapproval" of others (Tournier 1977, 69), but true guilt derives from not being faithful to yourself.

For example, Toni's husband insisted that she have her tubes tied when she was twenty-one. They already had two children. He didn't want more children, but she did and she wanted to retain the capacity to have children. When she suggested he have a vasectomy, her husband refused. He pressured her until she relented. "I didn't want to do it. I felt I was too young to get my tubes tied. But my husband made me feel guilty about not doing what he wanted. I went along because I wanted to be a good wife," explains Toni.

"Today I feel guilt toward myself for doing what he wanted instead of what was important to me. We separated soon after I got my tubes tied, and many of the men I met wanted to marry a woman who could have a family. Of course, I couldn't have any more children, so it was hard for me to find a new life partner. But even if I had remained married to my ex-husband, I would still be mad at myself today for not sticking up for what I wanted."

Men as well as women can be pressured by a significant other into actions they don't want to take. Bill, for example, accepted a high-paying but high-pressure job at his wife's insistence. "I didn't want that job but thought I'd feel too guilty if I didn't do what she wanted. What's worse, I gave into her on other important issues, too. Maybe they weren't important to her, but they were to me. I believe compromise is necessary for a good marriage, but I was doing all the compromising. Sure I'm still married, but I lost my self-respect."

Bill and Toni feared the guilt involved in disappointing someone they loved and, quite possibly, incurring their spouse's anger and rejection. In this respect, they were guided by false guilt when they acquiesced to their spouse's demands. However, today they feel the pangs of true guilt, a guilt based on not acting on their true convictions and not standing up for themselves.

True guilt is widespread, for few people are always faithful to themselves. In fact, true guilt can be as repressed as the shadow or other antisocial impulses, because to acknowledge the ways in which we have let ourselves down can be excruciatingly painful. When we are true to our inner callings and personal convictions, we run the risk of being criticized or even ostracized by others. In some cases, being true to ourselves can cost us our lives or the lives of those whom we love. On the other hand, to not be true to ourselves and to not actualize our dreams has another penalty: living under the weight of true guilt.

Yet some people find themselves in situations in which there is massive pressure to abandon their own beliefs and conform to others. The resulting spiritual or moral guilt can intensify any feelings of survivor guilt, depression, and a host of other trauma-related disorders. This topic will be explored more fully in chapter 4, "Content Survivor Guilt."

## ✍ *Self-Assessment for True Guilt*

This exercise may be difficult to complete. In many ways, true guilt is perhaps one of the most painful types of guilt you can experience, because it doesn't involve others betraying you: it involves you betraying yourself. However, keep in mind that few people are free enough from economic necessity, family obligations, and social pressure to be true to themselves *all the time*. It is entirely normal to give in to pressures to act a certain way rather than follow the desires of your heart or conscience.

On a fresh piece of paper, write the heading "True Guilt vs. False Guilt." Try to be as honest as you can be. Remember, nobody needs to see your responses but you.

Think of at least three instances when you gave in to pressures outside of yourself and acted against your own self-interest, your own development, or your own moral values. Describe each instance in detail. Pay special attention to the kinds of pressures being placed upon you by others or by circumstances. Be sure to include one or two sentences for each instance describing how you reacted to your decision to give in to these pressures. For example, did you punish yourself in some way? Did you try to harm those who pressured you in some way and then feel guilty about that? Did you try to put the incident out of your mind?

In your present-day life, are you acting against your values or your own growth? How is any guilt you are experiencing about your behavior affecting your self-esteem, your emotional health, your physical health, your personal relationships, your family life, or your career? Write two or three sentences about each aspect of your life that is affected by your true guilt.

Look over your answers to these questions and compare them with your answers to the "Early Shoulds Messages" exercise earlier in this chapter. Do you see any similarities in how you respond to feelings of guilt? Can you list at least three ways your response to guilt today is similar to your responses as a child or young adult? Can you list at least three ways your responses to guilt today are different from your responses as a child or young adult?

# 2

# Existential Survivor Guilt

*The tornado destroyed almost every home in the neighborhood
except mine. Six people died. The people next door lost their
baby and everything they owned.*

*The night after that tornado hit our town, my wife and
I had the best sex we'd had in years. Is there something wrong
with me? Why am I glad I'm okay when others around me are
hurting? And how can I enjoy sex so much when my
neighbors are living in shelters and planning funerals?*

—Mitchell, tornado survivor

Everyone has to deal with the types of guilt discussed in chapter 1.
However, in times of stress, such as the loss of a loved one, or in
times of trauma, such as a natural or man-made catastrophe, people
are subject to survivor guilt as well.

There are two types of survivor guilt: existential survivor guilt
and content survivor guilt. *Existential survivor guilt* refers to feelings

you have about staying alive in situations where others died or about being less injured or harmed than others. *Content survivor guilt,* which will be addressed in chapter 3, refers to guilt feelings about something you did, thought, or felt in your efforts to stay safe and protect yourself from psychological or physical harm. Both types of survivor guilt are forms of self-blame.

At the end of this chapter, a questionnaire is provided to help you assess whether you suffer from existential survivor guilt. However, before you complete this questionnaire you should read this chapter. The more knowledge you have, the better you will be able to assess and understand your own degree of survivor guilt.

# Asking Why

Survivor guilt involves asking the existential question of why you suffered less than someone else or why you lived while others died. You may be sincerely confused about why you fared better than someone else and the meaning of your good luck, or your very survival. Survivor guilt forces you to ask questions about the meaning of your existence and the meaning of life itself, questions that many people avoid thinking about because of their seriousness and complexity. Such questions bring to the fore ethical and spiritual issues over which theologians, philosophers, writers, artists, intellectuals, and religious leaders of many different schools of thought have debated for centuries.

Asking such questions and trying to answer them to your satisfaction can create anxiety, self-doubt, and doubts about the values of your family, your immediate social circle, and society at large. The fact that survivor guilt can lead to such a deep penetrating look at life is one reason why people might try to suppress that guilt. To experience the guilt is to give rise to a host of spiritual, existential, and moral questions that have no easy answers. The sheer weight and complexity of such questions can make you want to avoid the subject.

You might also want to avoid the subject because when you try to talk to others about your survivor guilt and any existential and religious issues raised by it, you may not always receive a warm reception. In our society, others tend to become highly anxious or threatened by discussions about such serious matters. As Marin (1981) observes, our society has a limited capacity to deal with the psychological and ethical problems that stem from being in situations that give rise to survivor guilt. Hence, individuals with survivor guilt may find themselves isolated, only able to share their questions and concerns with therapists, religious or spiritual leaders, or a few trusted friends.

## *Changing Places with the Dead*

Although the purpose of this book is to help you understand and ease your survivor guilt, I don't want to leave the false impression that survivor guilt is a form of neurosis. It is *not* a form of mental illness that needs to be obliterated in order for you to have the life you want. In fact, quite the opposite is true. Survivor guilt stems from one of the noblest emotions known to human beings: the love of one person for another. That other person could be a relative or beloved other, or it could be a complete stranger.

There are countless examples of how people risk their lives for someone they don't know, for example, in wars and in emergency situations. Books could be filled recounting the stories of people who spontaneously, without any thought, rush to the aid of another person, even at the risk of losing their own life. Joseph Campbell (1988) writes of the willingness of some people to sacrifice their own lives for another, or for a cause in which they deeply believe. We call these people heroes.

The willingness to risk your life for someone else or a cause can stem from a deep identification with that person or from a keen awareness that, as human beings, we are all connected. In a parallel manner, survivor guilt includes a deep identification with the dead (Kolb 1983). It also includes the wish to exchange places with the dead or with the person who suffered more than you, as well as the feeling that you should have died or suffered in the person's place (Williams 1978). This wish may express itself in dreams in which you replace or join someone who has died. The feelings you have in the dream may include horror and dread at seeing yourself dead. However, if your dream is a survivor guilt dream, you will also experience comfort, peace, and perhaps even joy at having replaced or joined someone who has died, especially if that person is beloved to you.

For example, Doris, an emergency room nurse, has a recurring dream in which she frantically runs around an operating room trying to save someone's life. But no matter how hard she works, her patient dies. As she goes to cover the dead person's face with a sheet, she sees that it is her own face she is covering. "I feel that with every patient who died, I died too, so to finally see myself die, was a relief. In the dream, I'm taken aback when I see that it's me who's dead, not someone else. But I'm only petrified for a split second. Within a minute, I'm no longer afraid; I feel glad. At last. It's over. The horrible guilt is over," Doris explains.

Vietnam combat veterans sometimes dream about replacing their dead comrades. In some dreams, they envision their names on the Vietnam Wall. In other dreams, their dead comrades jump out of their graves, or the Wall, and ask them to join them in the land of the dead. There is fear and apprehension in these dreams, but there is also a profound sense of peace. "At least in my dreams I'm where I belong—with the guys who died over there," a veteran explains.

Survivors of mass catastrophes have reported similar dreams and fantasies. For example, Kubany and Manke (1995) report the dream of a survivor of the bombing of Hiroshima in which dead relatives of the survivor come out of their grave and offer her flowers, which she interprets as an invitation to join them in death. A survivor of the Armenian genocide of the 1920s in Asia Minor reports that her husband, who died as a result of the war, came to her in a dream and asked her to join him in the land of the dead.

## Magical Thinking

Survivor guilt is not just compassion for those who have suffered more than you. It is also a way of saying, "If I had suffered more, you would have suffered less." Such thinking may not be logical, but it makes emotional sense. It can be a defense against the pain you felt at seeing others hurt. It also reflects the very human wish not to see those you love or care about suffer.

Survivor guilt hearkens back to notions about making sacrifices to the gods to assure a desired outcome. History is full of examples of peoples who practiced the custom of sacrifice. Typically they sacrificed grain, animals, and even children or young people to the gods in order to ensure good weather, victory at war, protection from disease, and fertility. Sacrifices were also made as a form of repentance for sin or various kinds of wrongdoings.

Suicide can also be seen as a form of self-sacrifice. In some instances, a motivation for suicide is the wish to join the dead or to atone for whatever you did, thought, or felt, which you feel contributed to the death or injury of others.

For example, in Shakespeare's play, *The Tragedy of Antony and Cleopatra*, Mark Antony, a Roman leader, falls in love with Cleopatra, the queen of Egypt. When Mark Antony is told that Cleopatra is dead, he kills himself in sorrow. However, Cleopatra isn't really dead. She sent a message to Antony telling him she was dead in order to test his love for her and woo him back into her arms. When

Cleopatra hears that Antony committed suicide as the result of her lie, she arranges to commit suicide herself, by having herself bitten by poisonous asps. As she prepares for death, she is joyous, for she is certain she will be reunited with Antony in the next life. While Cleopatra certainly had several motives for committing suicide, survivor guilt was among them.

The logic behind these thoughts and self-destructive actions is that by punishing yourself (or perhaps even killing yourself) you can undo the damage, or at least keep bad things from happening again. But, of course, the world doesn't really work that way.

Nevertheless, when the desire for things to have turned out differently is strong and when the pain of the losses involved is deep, it can be a relief to continue to feel guilt and act in ways that harm yourself or block you from achieving full happiness and growth. As illogical as it might sound, feeling guilty and acting in a self-punishing manner can help you maintain the illusion that if only you suffer hard enough or long enough, you can change or atone for the past. You keep feeling guilty and denying yourself (or actively hurting yourself), hoping that this time the sad ending will turn into a happy ending. Of course, this wish does not come true. Furthermore, if you attribute the lack of a happy ending to your personal failings, sins, or limitations, then your self-esteem is decreased even further and your survivor and other types of guilt can easily be intensified.

The fact that survivor guilt can function as a form of wishful thinking doesn't mean that you lack sincere remorse or genuine caring for the individual who has died or was harmed. Indeed, sometimes using self-punishment and survivor guilt as a means of rewriting history is not a conscious process. It stems from a belief in the magical and a wish that through your power, even the power of self-hate and self-punishment, you can bring about a desired outcome—in this case, a reversal of certain tragic events.

## Honoring the Dead

Oftentimes survivor guilt serves as a way of honoring the dead by ensuring that the event doesn't lose its meaning (Opp and Samson 1989).

If you suffer from survivor guilt, you may feel you should not go on with life, or at least not enjoy success or happiness. You may secretly be giving up a part of your life as a tribute to the person who suffered. For example, you may have given up an activity that gave you joy or you may feel you aren't entitled to have children, an intimate relationship, good friends, or professional success, because it would be disrespectful to those who died or suffered.

"My husband and son died in the car crash," explains a widow. "Even though it was years ago, I feel I shouldn't go out socially or ever remarry, or have more children. I know that being a recluse and staying home won't bring them back from the dead. I also know that my husband and son would want me to go on with my life, but I feel that doing so would dishonor their memory and I just won't do it. My guilt and my grief are the only things I have left. My guilt and my grief bind me to them. I can't give these feelings up. I was in that car crash. I should have died too."

Survivor guilt can also feel like a means of preserving the memory of the dead. For example, Andrew, the combat veteran who acquired malaria, was sent to the rear for treatment, and returned to the front lines only to discover that his squad had been annihilated by the enemy during his absence. He has frequent nightmares about the dead. He came to therapy seeking relief from these dreams because they made it difficult for him to work the next day and made him irritable around his family. Several types of dream therapy were attempted. None of them worked. Finally Andrew came to the conclusion that he didn't want the dreams to stop:

"In a way I want to have the nightmares. I want the flashbacks. I want to see those guys' faces. I want to remember, because if I don't remember, who will? The average citizen? I'll take the guilt. I'll take the grief. If feeling guilty is the price I have to pay for keeping their memory alive, that's fine. That's nothing compared to what they sacrificed."

Similarly, Tanya doesn't want to give up her guilt feelings about her mother's heart attack, in order to keep her mother close. "I know it wasn't my fault Mom died, but my mind keeps harping on the fact that I didn't push her to go to the doctor soon enough. To me, feeling guilty is a way of being close to her. Rehearsing in my mind the conversation we had about whether or not she should go to the doctor and where I didn't insist hard enough that she make an appointment makes me feel guilty, very guilty. But it also brings me comfort. That conversation was the last conversation I had with her before she died. I don't want to give her up. So I'll cling to that memory, and the guilt that goes with it. I want to keep her memory alive, in my mind and in my heart, in every way possible. And if guilt is the price I have to pay, I consider the agony of that guilt to be far less weighty than the agony of losing one more memory of her."

Combat veterans and others who have been involved in political or domestic struggles in which the dead have not received proper recognition by others or by society at large often feel that if they "forget" the dead, these dead will be completely forgotten and once again dishonored, as they were during the trauma. In writing about Holocaust survivors, Yael Danieli writes that the "hearts of the survivors have served as the graveyards for the known and the nameless dead of the Holocaust who were turned into ashes and for whom no graves exist" (1994, 4). As Danieli explains, for some Holocaust survivors, to complete the grieving process would feel like repeating the crimes committed by the Nazis, who wanted the deaths of the Jews and their other victims to be invisible and forgotten. Instead, the survivors remain in a continuous state of mourning for those who did not receive proper burial."

People who have suffered through such losses find it easier to work through their survivor guilt and grief if they can establish a time and place to mourn and involve others in the grieving. Solutions include establishing some kind of memorial, either in the form of a building, a work of art or writing, or making an audio or videocassette describing what happened so that the dead can be honored and not forgotten (Williams 1987, Danieli 1994).

## A Defense against Grief and Powerlessness

If you are in a twelve-step program, group or individual counseling, or another kind of healing or growth program, you may have found yourself at a "stuck point" or "plateau" in your recovery and personal growth. Perhaps you have overcome an addiction, compulsion, or other self-defeating behavior only to discover that you seem to have an undefined internal block that prevents you from enjoying your accomplishments thus far, and making further therapeutic progress, or enjoying life's pleasures. For example, you may be having difficulty enjoying the improved self-esteem that is now yours due to all your hard work in therapy or other recovery program. It's as if you cleared the ground to plant a rosebush and spent time watering the rosebush and fertilizing the soil; however, when the flowers start to bloom, you avoid the rosebush and don't take time to enjoy its beauty.

Some mental health professionals view this kind of "stuckness" as a form of masochism, wherein clients seem to somehow enjoy suffering and punishing themselves by denying themselves the good things in life. However, I see it as a result of unresolved survivor guilt and the grieving that goes hand in hand with it. Counselors with a Freudian orientation often talk about "resistance" in therapy. By this they do not mean the client is resisting getting better because the client wants to suffer. Rather the idea is that the client can't move forward because to do so would bring to the surface an awareness of some painful event or painful emotion that he or she tries not to remember.

Survivor guilt and grieving and the incidents that gave birth to them are painful and wrenching experiences. No wonder people try not to think about them. These people aren't trying to avoid making progress: they are trying not to be devastated and shattered by the pain of grieving. Staying "stuck" in survivor guilt can help many people deflect experiencing grief and can forestall the pain of the grieving process. Many people cling to attitudes and habits in their lives that are self-limiting or self-punishing because to give up these manifestations of survivor guilt would mean facing the raw truth of their powerlessness as well as facing the true extent of their sorrow.

In this sense, survival guilt is a defense against grief and powerlessness. As Opp and Samson (1989) point out, guilt helps some (not all) people avoid the pain of accepting that the negative outcome of a particular event was beyond their control. "Feeling helpless," they write, "is more painful than feeling guilt" (160).

The tendency to experience survivor guilt as a means of avoiding feelings of helplessness has been found among combat veterans (Opp and Samson 1989), Holocaust survivors (Krystal 1971), and traumatized children (Terr 1983).

# Survivor Guilt and the Grieving Process

Grieving is perhaps one of the most difficult aspects of human existence. Emotionally, grieving is such a challenge that most people tend to avoid it at all costs.

In many respects, it's easier to feel guilty than to feel sad. When you feel guilty, you can retain some sense that you had some power in the situation. Perhaps you did have some control, but not enough to save the life, prevent the injury, or rescue a person from mistreatment. Nevertheless, feeling as if you had some power is better than feeling absolutely powerless, which is one of the dominant emotions involved with grieving.

When you are grieving, you feel like a collapsed balloon. The pain of loss engulfs you and you feel vulnerable, defenseless, and weak. And you hurt. You hurt so much you feel like you are dying inside. You never thought it was possible to suffer so. You'd give anything, pay any price, to end the suffering of remembering what you lost and may never have again. If you are to be healed, you need to grieve. However, if the prospect of grieving overwhelms you or you don't have the time, place, or social support to grieve, it may seem safer, and easier, to feel guilty.

In her landmark book, *On Death and Dying*, Dr. Elizabeth Kubler-Ross (1981) explains that the grieving process consists of five stages: denial, anger, bargaining, depression, and acceptance. Not only those who are dying but anyone who suffers major losses in life usually experiences the five stages of grief.

These stages do not always occur in precise order. A person can be in more than one stage at a time, and the length of the time spent in each stage varies from person to person, as does the depth of feeling. Throughout the five stages, feelings of fear, despair, disorganization, guilt, anxiety, and even adrenaline surges may be experienced (Staudacher 1987, 1991).

In some cases, survivor guilt is a means of avoiding the grieving process. In other instances, survivor guilt can be viewed as being "stuck" at the third stage of grief: the bargaining stage.

## Denial

In the first stage, denial, the loss and its aftermath are not acknowledged. For example, a father in denial about his son's death continues to set aside money for his son's education and acts as if his son were still alive; an abused wife in denial believes the abuse never happened.

Similarly, people who have seen others injured or die, whether in a car accident, war, or hurricane or other disaster, can easily go into denial regarding the injuries and deaths they observed. They might even feel they were dreaming instead of living real life. Some individuals deny the reality of the deaths or injuries around them by unconsciously hoping for miraculous resurrections.

This stage often keeps not only grief but also feelings of guilt hidden.

## Anger

Once your denial is cracked, expect to be flooded with anger. You may be angry at life for giving you such hardships. If you are religious, you may be angry at the deity of your understanding. If you were in a situation in which others were injured or died, you may be angry at the individuals and institutions involved. You may be furious at the human error, indifference, or malice that caused the suffering.

If were unable to help, you may be angry at your powerlessness. If you made any mistakes, you may forget the positive contributions you made and instead be furious at yourself for your errors. At times, you may be angry that you were ever born and that you have to go on living when you have to carry so much loss and guilt.

## Bargaining

The bargaining stage of grief is similar to survivor grief in that it is characterized by fantasies of "what if" and "if only." It is also characterized by excessive and irrational self-blame. If you were carelessly driving a car that caused a ten-vehicle crash on a highway, killing a dozen people, then you might have a right to hold yourself responsible and feel guilty. Similarly, if you killed or abused others, then you need to take responsibility for your actions. However, you also need to ask yourself why you were driving carelessly or why you killed or abused others.

However, it's more likely that you didn't purposely cause the misfortune or its aftereffects. Continuing to punish yourself for the what-ifs and if-onlys is the essence of survivor guilt. It serves little purpose other than to wear you down and perhaps ultimately destroy you. If part of your survivor guilt involves wishing you were dead or as injured as another, then survivor guilt itself may serve as an efficient tool for your own self-destruction.

## Depression

There are many kinds of depression: among them are the normal fluctuations in mood experienced by almost everyone; clinical depression requiring medication and psychotherapy; and the depression associated with the grieving process. You may be experiencing this last type. If so, remember that this is a normal response to an extremely stressful situation.

If you are grieving a loss, whether that loss be of someone's life, someone's health, or someone's emotional, physical, or financial well-being, you are under severe stress. Not only are you coping with your everyday feelings and needs, but you are also coping with your grief, as well as the reactions of others. You may also be making complex arrangements for the reordering of your life and obtaining medical, legal, and other help for yourself and others involved in the events leading to the death or injury. At the same time, you are also suffering the loss of yourself as you once were, the disruption to your marriage, family life, or career caused by the tragic incident and its aftermath.

Depression is a natural response to all these stresses and losses. Even though the depression associated with the grieving process is temporary, it can still be intense and painful. You can expect all the symptoms associated with clinical depression: difficulty concentrating, low self-esteem, changes in your eating and sleeping habits, feelings of futility and hopelessness, or various physical problems such as backaches, headaches, vomiting, or constipation.

Extreme fatigue, and its opposite, physical agitation, are also common to depression. You may find every little task an overwhelming burden, see little hope for yourself or your situation, feel tired all the time, and receive little or no pleasure even from people or events that normally would please you.

(Appendix D, "What Is Depression," can help you ascertain whether you are suffering from clinical depression, which is more serious and longer lasting than the depression associated with grief.)

## *Acceptance*

Acceptance is the final stage of grief. After you have passed through the other stages, you will feel less depressed and enraged about your losses. You will simply accept them and the emotional toll they have taken on you, your family, and any others involved. Acceptance does not mean that you are happy, but rather that you have stopped fighting your own limitations and the reality of what has happened to you.

You can compensate to some extent for what you have lost. However, part of acceptance is realizing that whatever compensations you arrange for yourself are partial, at best. There is no way to restore what you have lost. In the acceptance stage, you accept those losses. You accept your pain. You learn to be as kind and loving to yourself as you would be to a wounded child who is in the process of healing, but you realize that even your self-love cannot take away all the pain.

This major issue of undergoing the grieving process belongs to the realm of grief work and is not covered in this book. The following books offer information and guidance about grieving: *On Death and Dying* (Kubler-Ross 1981), *Men and Grief: A Guide for Men Surviving the Death of a Loved One* (Staudacher 1991), *Beyond Grief: A Guide for Recovering from the Death of a Loved One* (Staudacher 1987), and chapter 9, "Stage Two: Understanding Grief and Sorrow," in *I Can't Get Over It: A Handbook for Trauma Survivors* (Matsakis 1996).

# The Repressed Part of Survivor Guilt: Gratitude

It is difficult to accept that you might be grateful that it was someone else who suffered and not yourself, but survivor guilt does involve gratitude. "It sounds heartless," some people will openly admit, "but if someone had to die, I'm glad it was someone else, not me." Yet some people can't accept the idea that, on some level, they are glad they were not the one who died, was injured, or was otherwise harmed.

However hard this feeling is to face, it is nothing more than an expression of the natural and vital instinct for self-preservation. Yet this part of survivor guilt can generate a considerable amount of guilt and internal confusion. It's difficult to be grieving for the suffering of someone else while at the same time rejoicing in your own relative good fortune. For example, Paul and his wife, Karen, were driving home one night when their car was struck by a truck. Karen was severely injured, but Paul was not. Paul wondered why he was spared injury while his wife had to endure numerous surgeries and much pain. "It should have been me. And if it couldn't have been me, why couldn't the injuries at least have been divided equally between us?" Paul asked others.

Paul meant what he said. He sincerely wished he could have suffered in place of his wife or at least borne half the pain. On the other hand, he was glad he had been spared Karen's ordeal. He didn't know if he could take being bedridden for months like Karen had. The very thought of enduring the kind of pain she had was unimaginable.

Most of the time Paul didn't think much about how grateful he was that he hadn't been injured. The minute such a thought would pop into his mind, he would quickly dismiss it. He found such a thought unacceptable. After all, he loved Karen. She was his wife and he was a dedicated husband. However, every time Karen moaned in pain and every time appointments had to be made with doctors, physical therapists, or surgeons, Paul found himself secretly sighing with relief that he didn't have to tolerate all these medical procedures.

Paul felt guilty about being grateful he wasn't hurt, just as guilty as he felt about not having been injured. It's this terrible contradiction, between wishing you could suffer for the other and being grateful that you've been spared the suffering, that makes survivor guilt very difficult to deal with and talk about openly.

Just as often as people think, "Thank goodness it wasn't me," they may look at their loved ones and think, "Thank goodness it wasn't one of them." When Jill found out her neighbor's son was slipping into alcoholism, she couldn't help thinking, "If someone's son has to be a drunk, I'm glad it's my neighbor's son, not my son." She felt a little guilty for thinking that way, but she couldn't help it. She really felt guilty when her cousin's son was shot to death. "I looked at my son and said, 'Thank God it wasn't you.'"

"'But what about cousin Billy. Don't you care about him?' my son said.

"Sure I care about Billy, but I care about my son more. It's natural, I suppose, but I feel guilty about it. What my son said made me feel guilty, but I was already feeling guilty. Like it's selfish and heartless of me to be glad that my son is alive."

# Survivor Guilt and Responsibility Guilt

If you held a position of responsibility during the traumatic event, you may have developed an extra strong sense of survivor guilt as the result of being technically responsible for the welfare of others. Kubany (1996) stresses that individuals such as parents, teachers, squad leaders, airline pilots, head nurses, and others who have obligations toward others tend to feel responsible for negative outcomes affecting those others, because they confuse their assigned responsibility with being accountable for any negative events.

Hence, if a fire station chief sends out staff to fight a fire and three firefighters die as a result, there is a high probability that this chief will feel a keener sense of guilt than other employees who don't have such a responsible role. Chiefs are responsible for taking care of their staff—training them, making sure they have the right equipment, and otherwise enabling them to do their job as safely and effectively as possible. But chiefs are not responsible for causing giant uncontrollable fires or unforeseen events that cause harm. Yet chiefs, or others in responsible positions, tend to feel accountable for such events because of their designated responsibilities, and to confuse designated responsibility with accountability (Kubany 1996).

"If I hadn't been such a dedicated firefighter, that young trainee of mine would never have lost the use of his legs," says Vince, a firefighter. "The station got a call about a huge fire downtown, and I had to take all my men, even the new guy, Fernando. Fernando had been through all the training and was very skilled, but I warned him not to do the more dangerous and heavy work because he was still new.

"When we got to the blaze, there were people screaming everywhere. Apparently two women were trapped on the third floor. It looked hopeless, because the fire was too intense. But I decided to try anyway. I got the ladder rigged up and started climbing up to get the women. I didn't think I would succeed, but I had to try.

"Before I got on the ladder, I turned to Fernando and told him to stay with the hoses and not try to prove he was a hero, because, inexperienced as he was, he could hurt himself as well as the person he was trying to save. But he didn't listen to me. The minute my back was turned, he grabbed a ladder and tried to help out, only to fall and break his legs. That boy is in a wheelchair now. If I hadn't tried to be heroic, he would never have tried to be heroic too. His not ever walking again—that's on me."

"I'll always be the squad leader," says Jim. "I left Vietnam twenty years ago, but in my bones I still feel responsible for my men. I felt responsible for my squad while I was their leader. When one of them got hurt or killed, I felt it was my fault, even if they got themselves killed driving drunk while they were off duty. I figured I should've warned them more about acting crazy.

"Even after I left Vietnam because I got wounded and was flown back home, whenever I found out that one of the guys died or got wounded on the field, I felt guilty. I should have been there to instruct and protect them. I should have never left them, even though I had no choice because I was wounded so bad I couldn't do my job.

"When it comes to survivor guilt, logic makes no difference. A squad leader is responsible for his men. That's it. No exceptions. Even now, when some of them call me about their nightmares and flashbacks, I feel like I have to be there for them, even though listening to them talk about their problems makes me depressed and I end up having night sweats, anxiety attacks, flashbacks, and nightmares too. Sometimes I just want to hang up the phone and never see or talk to those guys again, because listening to them brings back all the guilt, and all the pain. But I can't cut myself off from them, no matter how much talking to them damages me. In my heart, they are still my men. I'm their squad leader and I'm responsible for them—'till the day I die."

An example of role-related survivor guilt is that of Wang Dan, the Tiananmen Square protest leader. He helped organize the Tiananmen Square demonstrations for democracy in China. His idea for a hunger strike brought millions of Chinese to the square. However, on the night of June 3, 1989, hundreds and according to some estimates, thousands, of Chinese civilians were shot to death by the Chinese army (Sun 1998). Almost ten years later, in 1998, Wang Dan stated that he will always feel guilt over the hundreds who died in the Army crackdown. Wang Dan is experiencing survivor guilt.

In retrospect he can see that he made some mistakes in planning the demonstration that may have contributed to the deaths. However, he does acknowledge that "the main responsibility was not ours, the main responsibility was with the government who actually did the killing (Sun 1998, A3). Nevertheless, his sense of survivor guilt is profound.

Survivor guilt related to role is especially strong among parents and grandparents. Human beings, both male and female, are biologically wired to respond to the helplessness and dependency of their young, and when a child dies or is injured, regardless of the cause, the survivor guilt can be enormous. For example, Sarah was sitting by her living-room window watching her husband show their baby daughter the roses twining on the fence when suddenly a dog jumped over the fence and attacked the child. Though Sarah was a pediatric nurse who had seen many injuries and illnesses, she became immobilized at the sight of her own child being harmed and was unable to call for help. Fortunately her husband was able to ward off the dog before the child was killed.

The child required numerous plastic surgeries to restore her face. Sarah, however, required many years of therapy to deal with her self-recriminations for her temporary paralysis, which, she feels, resulted in her daughter's face being scarred.

## ✍ Self-Assessment for Existential Survivor Guilt

This questionnaire will help you determine whether you suffer from survivor guilt. As you read this questionnaire and those that follow, keep in mind the recommendations listed in the "Cautions" section of the introduction. If at any point you begin to hyperventilate or gag, feel faint or dizzy, or begin to experience hallucinations, flashbacks, or out-of-body experiences, stop immediately and follow the instructions in that section.

Since survivor guilt is not a psychiatric diagnosis, there is no official way to determine if you have it. However, if you find that you answer "yes" to two or more of the following questions, there is a high probability that you have experienced or are experiencing some degree of survivor guilt.

1. Do you feel guilty because you made it out of a situation alive and others didn't?  No

2. Do you feel guilty because you were less injured or less damaged than others?  No

3. Do you feel guilty because you have more social or financial advantages than others?  Yes

4. Are you confused about why you escaped emotional pain, financial distress, illness, or social disgrace or humiliation when others had to suffer these hardships?  Yes

5. Have you ever wished you could bear the suffering of another, or others, whether it be physical, mental, emotional, or financial?  Yes

6. Do you frequently wish you could die so you could join the dead?  Yes

7. Do you ever feel that you should have died and someone else should have lived? In other words, do you ever wish you could exchange places with someone who has died?  Yes

8. Do you believe that the dead person would have had a better life than you or had more to live for?  Yes

9. Do you feel the dead are luckier than you are because they have no more pain and suffering whereas you have inner torment?  Yes

10. Do you dream of the dead or the injured?  _____

11. Do you ever fantasize being able to relive the past and have certain tragic events end happily?  _____

12. Are there certain events that you will never talk about because you feel you will be punished if you disclose what happened?

_____

13. Does thinking about the death or injury of another ever make you feel depressed, even to the point of suicide?  _____

14. Do you ever feel as if you've lost your soul or have no conscience?  _____

15. Do you have frequent thoughts about people who have died or were injured?  _____

16. On some level do you still find it impossible to believe that someone you loved or knew is dead or was severely injured?  _____

17. If you were active in a religious community or a certain faith, has your guilt caused you to leave that community or faith? _____

18. Do you have periods of intense grieving or intense rage about incidents that make you feel guilty? _____

19. Do you suffer from an alcohol or drug addiction, an eating disorder, a gambling addiction, or some other addiction or compulsion? _____

20. Do you find yourself becoming emotional or weeping when you watch sad movies but relatively unemotional and unfeeling when you see someone in pain or attend a funeral? *Yes* _____

21. When you hear of a natural disaster, such as a hurricane, earthquake, or tornado, occurring in another city or country, do you feel glad your city escaped the natural catastrophe but then feel guilty for feeling glad that others were harmed instead of you? *Yes* _____

22. When you hear of someone being mugged, raped, or killed, do you feel glad it wasn't a member of your family or a friend but then feel guilty for feeling grateful that the people you love weren't harmed? *Yes* _____

23. Do you think more about a person or people who are dead than those who are alive? *Yes* _____

24. On a gut level, are you truly living for yourself or are you living for someone who died? *I think sometimes I live for someone else.*

25. Do you feel like a "cheat" in that someone died so that you could live? *Yes* _____

26. Do you engage in high-risk activities in hopes of getting yourself killed? *Sometimes* _____

27. Do you feel obligated to live for a person or people who are now dead? *Sometimes* _____

28. When you feel your life is a failure, do you feel you have failed a person or people who are now dead? _____

29. Do you feel you don't deserve to live? _____

30. Do you feel you should have died along with another person or people during a particular traumatic or stressful event? _____

31. Do you find yourself trying to control your family members, friends, and other people you value in an effort to keep them safe from harm? _____

32. Do you find yourself avoiding jobs, career opportunities, or personal relationships where you would have to assume responsibility for the well-being or safety of others? _____

33. Do you find yourself sabotaging any personal or job-related opportunities or successes? Do you tend to quit school (or some other educational endeavor) just before graduating? To leave jobs at the point at which you might be promoted? To end relationships at the point at which the other person is beginning to truly know and love you or, the converse, at the point at which you are truly beginning to know and love the other person? _____

# 3

# Content Survivor Guilt

*I lay crumpled on my living room floor, alive, but not alive.
I didn't know who I was or why I existed. My husband hadn't
hit me this time: he had only yelled at me, but it didn't make
any difference. After nine years of abuse, his slightest action
against me had the same effect as being whipped with his belt.
I was weak, so weak.*

*I heard the baby crying upstairs, but I didn't have the
strength to go to her. I knew she was safe, because he was
gone, but that didn't mean she didn't need me.*

*There were many times the children called for me but
I was too depressed and drained to go to them. Today, fifteen
years later, one of them is on antidepressants and the other one
is a hundred pounds overweight. To me, their problems are my
fault. I failed as a mother because I couldn't tend to them
properly. My husband, now ex-husband, with all his beatings
and manipulations and demands on my time, made it nearly
impossible for me to be the kind of mother I should have been.*

*I fought him the best I could. Nevertheless, I failed my
kids. The guilt I have about all that is a sword that cuts me
in two and nobody, no therapist or minister, can talk me out
of it. It makes me feel I should have never been born and*

*that my kids should never have come into being either.*
*We would have all been better off never existing at all*
*than suffering what we suffered.*

—Lisa, domestic violence survivor

The previous chapter concerned itself with one aspect of survivor guilt: existential survivor guilt. This chapter explores another aspect of survivor guilt: content survivor guilt.

# What Is Content Survivor Guilt?

*Content survivor guilt* refers to guilt that is the result of something you did to keep yourself safe or stay alive (Williams 1987). It can be guilt over coping mechanisms, such as denial, rationalizing, lying, and stealing, or it can be due to having certain thoughts or feelings during a trauma or stressful ordeal. It can be broken down into a host of other types of guilt, including negligence guilt, competency guilt, moral or spiritual guilt, demonic or atrocity guilt, superman/super-woman guilt, and catch-22 guilt.

Many times, during stressful events people do things to protect themselves that they later regret because these actions violated their personal code of ethics or the moral code of their family or society. However it is quite unlikely that most of these people would have behaved in the same way in nonstressful conditions. The classic example is that of soldiers who kill and maim in time of war. Killing is their military duty; however, it violates the code of "thou shalt not kill" that is found in certain religions. For some soldiers, "thou shalt not kill" is as deeply ingrained as their commitment to follow military orders. As a result, some soldiers feel guilty for killing, even though they did so in the line of duty. If they had not participated in trying to destroy the enemy, they would have been considered traitors or cowards and may have felt guilty for contributing to the injuries or deaths of their comrades in that way.

Similarly, people who live in abusive households or who are trapped in prostitution, forced labor rings, ritual abuse cults, or other types of hostage situations are sometimes forced into shoplifting or other unethical or illegal acts in order to avoid being beaten or to forestall the abuse of another person or pet. Even though they were coerced into violating their own moral standard, they can feel tremendous guilt about committing such acts. This is a form of content survivor guilt in that it involves feeling guilty about doing something in order to stay alive or preserve one's safety or sanity.

# Causes of Content Survivor Guilt

Faced with danger, people can find themselves acting, thinking, or feeling like a different person—a person they don't like and aren't proud of. All such acts, thoughts, and feelings are part of content survivor guilt. Content survivor guilt tends to be especially strong in people who feel they acted in a cowardly manner or who denied help to those in need, made mistakes that caused the death or injury of others, or found themselves acting with more violence, brutality, and sadism than they thought possible. Yet they may have acted in these ways as a form of physical, emotional, or mental self-preservation.

## *Feeling Like a Coward*

A woman who hid in the bathroom while her husband was verbally abusing her son feels guilt for not having protected her son. She let her son fend for himself because she feared that if she intervened, her husband would punish her with verbal abuse and financial restrictions and limit her visits with her family. Also, had she tried to intervene, her husband might have become so angered that he might have gone on to verbally abuse the son more viciously, for example, by calling him a "sissy" or a "girl" for having a woman try to defend him. Her involvement could also have triggered an act of physical violence, if not immediately, at some later point in time. She chose to act in the most reasonable, least risky manner, yet she feels like a coward.

Rape victims who don't put up a fight because they fear being harmed for resisting often then feel guilty for "giving in." But they didn't "give in" because of cowardice or a character deficiency. They might have had a freeze reaction or they might have made a quick assessment that it was safer to acquiesce than to fight back. Had they resisted and been beaten or injured in other ways, they might have felt guilty for not having "known better" and not having been able to predict that the rapist would become even more violent. (Fight/flight/freeze reactions are discussed in more detail in a later section of this chapter.)

## Ignoring Requests for Assistance

A woman and her elderly father were attacked by a mugger. The woman and her father began to run, but the father tripped and fell. The father called out for help. When the daughter turned around, she saw the mugger stabbing her father mercilessly in the chest. Her father continued to cry for help. For a moment, she considered running back to answer her father's call. Instead she turned around and ran for help.

Today she feels like a coward. She also feels "heartless" for not answering her father's call. Yet she knew she wasn't strong or skilled enough to fend off the attacker. If she had rushed to her father's aid, not only would she have been unable to save her father, but there was a high probability that she would have been harmed or killed also. By running away while she could, there was at least a chance of obtaining help for her dad.

A rescue worker ignored a trapped car-accident victim's cries for help because he could predict that the car would explode momentarily. Within seconds, the car exploded into flames. It's obvious to all that the rescue worker would not have had time to cut the victim out of the car before the explosion. Had he tried to save the victim, he would have caused two deaths, his and the victim's. Rationally, he knows that he had little choice but to do what he did, unless he wanted to throw away his life. Emotionally, however, he suffers from survivor guilt for "letting someone die."

## Making Mistakes

Making mistakes during a stressful or traumatic situation is also a major cause of survivor guilt. For example, it has been found that killing Americans by accident in friendly fire incidents was a top source of combat-related guilt in Vietnam veterans (Brende 1991). Doctors, nurses, and medical staff who, under extreme duress, make mistakes that hurt their patients or cause them to die suffer from extreme survivor guilt. Yet on the front line in wartime or in the midst of a natural catastrophe, it's easy for anyone to make mistakes, even trained professionals.

## Inappropriate Thoughts and Feelings

During times of stress or trauma, people also have thoughts and feelings that they didn't expect to have and that they judge as inappropriate at best and "bad" or "evil" at worse. For example, upon hearing that her brother was hospitalized for a tumor, Sally thought, "Oh good. I get the television all to myself." Within seconds, she felt guilty for having such a thought and even more guilty when she realized how automatically the thought came to her.

In some situations, people care so much about another person or feel so responsible for that person's well being, they may wish that person dead so that they can be free of the responsibility. Bernice, an abused teenager who ran away from a home where most of her brothers and sisters were being abused, felt extremely guilty for leaving the others behind. She felt so protective of them that at times she wished they would die so she wouldn't feel she had to go home to do what she could to help keep them safe. Bernice felt she was a horrible person for wishing her brothers and sisters dead.

Bernice failed to realize that she didn't really want her brothers and sisters to die: what she truly wanted was freedom from the burden of feeling she should return to a situation that was hellish for her in order to protect them from harm. She felt powerless and helpless to help them except by sacrificing herself. Had she felt other options were available to save her brothers and sisters, most likely she would never have wished for their deaths.

People exposed to dead people or severely injured or mutilated bodies sometimes find themselves looking at the bodies with objectivity and curiosity. "It was really interesting to see what the inside of a stomach looked like, or what human brains looked like," police, rescue workers, medical staff, soldiers, and others sometimes say. Later on, they may feel guilty for looking at the body without emotion.

"I should have been feeling bad for the person who was dead, not looking at them like I was doing a science experiment," explains Michael, a rescue worker. Yet the objectivity and the emotional calmness with which many people confront the dead and dying is a way of distancing from the pain and death of others as well as from the truth about their own vulnerability to illness or injury and the inevitability of their own death.

## *Guilt over Coping Methods*

In *Courage to Heal*, authors Bass and Davis (1988) write about some of the methods survivors of sexual abuse developed to cope with the abuse. These include minimizing, rationalizing, denying, forgetting, making jokes, being super-busy, escaping, lying, stealing, overworking, gambling, overindulging in sex, developing a mental illness or an addiction, self-mutilation, and suicide attempts. These coping methods are common among many types of trauma survivors, not only sex abuse survivors. They are also common among people who have survivor guilt. These coping tactics may have been necessary to ensure emotional and physical survival or to maintain the ability to keep on functioning. Yet when people reflect on how they acted or felt during their trauma or stressful event, they may feel tremendous guilt for having used any of these coping mechanisms. This guilt can exist even when they did not *consciously choose* to engage in the coping mechanism.

## Minimizing and Denial

*Minimizing* means reducing the severity of the event, its impact, or its meaning. For example, the mother of a child with a 105-degree fever is minimizing when she thinks to herself, "My child isn't that sick." The friend of a rape victim is minimizing when he or she thinks, "What's a little rape compared with losing a parent?"

Trauma survivors sometimes minimize the impact and meaning of other people's traumas. Hence combat soldiers can wonder what incest survivors are "complaining about" by thinking that incest is "nothing" compared with the horror of war. Incest survivors, in turn, can wonder what combat soldiers are "complaining about." Some point out that whereas soldiers fought for their lives in danger zones for one to four years, they may have fought for their lives and were subject to assault for ten to fifteen years, if not longer.

*Denial* means acting as if the event never happened. "Denying is turning your head the other way and pretending that whatever is happening isn't, or what has happened didn't" (Bass and Davis 1988, 42). Both minimizing and denial serve to protect people from the emotional shock of the event as well as from their own feelings of helplessness and powerlessness to make things better or to avert an insult, injury, or death. In such instances, minimizing and denial can also reflect the inability to handle the intense feelings of anxiety, fear, and grief that would be involved in directly facing the event or trauma.

For example, a husband whose wife complains of a lump in her breast might minimize the possibility that the lump is malignant by saying, "It's just a cyst. You get them all the time. They come and go. Don't worry about it," or "It's not that big. Even if it is cancer, it can't be that bad." Or he might even deny the existence of the potentially life-threatening lump by saying that he can't see it or feel it. Even if a physician verifies the reality of the lump, the husband may insist that the physician is in error.

"It's plain as day. There is no lump," a distraught husband may argue with his wife's doctor. Later on, when it becomes obvious that the lump is cancerous, the husband is overwhelmed with guilt for his minimization and denial. He feels he failed his wife by minimizing and denying the possibility of cancer. Two factors contributed to his minimizing and denial. The first was his fear of being unable to pay the medical bills involved in treating cancer. The second reason was even more important: He feared his wife's death. He simply could not conceive of life without her. Ironically, it was his very love and need for his wife that prompted his minimization and denial.

Minimization and denial can also serve to protect people from the responsibility of having to make a decision about a course of action. In times of stress or trauma, decisions about what to do or not do are often complex. Sometimes every option seems inadequate, morally dubious, or fraught with risks and pain. One solution is to avoid the necessity of having to make a decision by minimizing or denying the reality of the situation that is calling for a response.

People who use minimizing or denial as coping mechanisms sometimes feel like "cowards" later on. Upon closer examination, however, the coping mechanisms may not reflect cowardice but a fear for one's safety and survival, or a sincere confusion about the significance of the event.

For instance, in work situations, you might see a co-worker being mistreated, but you minimize or deny the mistreatment for two reasons: First, you may want to avoid the emotional pain involved in feeling compassion for your co-worker, especially if you are already experiencing personal stress in other areas of your life. Becoming emotionally involved with the co-worker's pain could put you on overload and cause you to become less efficient and productive. Second, if you support the co-worker and this becomes evident, the person who is harassing your co-worker may well begin to harass you as well.

Arnie observed his boss upbraid the office manager on how she was making copies of two pieces of paper. The boss changed his directions to her at least a dozen times. By the end of three hours, the office manager was weeping and the boss's face was glowing with glee at her suffering.

Arnie dismissed the incident by viewing it as the boss simply having a bad day. He assumed the incident would not repeat itself. At this point, he was not necessarily minimizing, because he didn't have enough information to assess the situation. In the weeks to come, the boss denigrated the office manager at staff meetings, ridiculed her physical disability in front of guests, and made frequent public comments about how he'd like to be rid of her. It was obvious to other office staff that the office manager was being harassed. However, Arnie viewed the situation as a "minor personality conflict" between the office manager and his boss.

In time, the office manager had a mental breakdown and resigned. Afterward, Arnie felt guilty for minimizing the events and not intervening on her behalf. "I could have at least said something at those staff meetings where she was being humiliated. Or I could have documented the abuse in case she ever went to court. But instead I did nothing. I was a coward. I was afraid of losing my job because my boss had hinted to me that anyone who didn't go along with his policies could expect a poor evaluation and a possible removal. I looked around for other jobs, but there were none, so I knew I had to stay there and I couldn't stay there if the boss got on my back like he did the office manager's.

"Today I feel guilty because I didn't stand up for what was right. The boss just gave me a promotion, and I feel guilty about it. I feel like it's contaminated with the blood of the office manager. A wimp like me doesn't deserve a raise!"

Minimizing and denial are common defenses against the reality of emotional, physical, or sexual abuse in any setting, especially in families. The victims may deny or minimize their abuse in order to lessen the pain and make their lives tolerable. At the same time, the perpetrators of the abuse also tend to deny or trivialize the abuse. Judith Herman writes, "After every atrocity one can expect to hear the same predictable apologies: it never happened; the victim lies; the victim exaggerates; . . . the more powerful the perpetrator . . . the greater his prerogative to name and define reality" (1992, 8).

However, it is not just victims and the perpetrators who use minimization and denial—but the bystanders as well. The bystanders can include other family members, neighbors, and friends. For example, Irene recalls seeing her older brother hold her younger brother down and yank his arms. "They're just roughhousing," Irene thought. Even when her younger brother needed medical care after a few "roughhousing" incidents, Irene still viewed the abuse in her home as a case of "boys will be boys" rather than what it was: sibling abuse.

Today, she feels guilty for not having helped her younger brother. "How could I have been so blind? So stupid? So dumb? If I had done something, maybe my younger brother wouldn't be so insecure today," she says. She forgets how much she needed to believe that her family was perfect and how much she feared her older brother would turn on her.

Similarly, mothers who see their boyfriends, husbands, uncles, or other male relatives inappropriately fondling their small daughters may minimize the violations they are witnessing. "He's just cuddling with her," "He's just trying to calm her down," or "He doesn't mean anything by it," a woman might think. These are all forms of minimizing. Instances of total denial are also possible. Mothers can walk into a situation where they see their daughters (or sons) being sexually or otherwise violated and then deny that they saw anything extraordinary occurring. (This type of denial could also be a form of dissociation, which is discussed later in this chapter.)

If, at a later date, the protective shield of denial is shattered, victims and bystanders can feel ashamed and guilty about not having seen the abuse for what it was and taken appropriate action. For victims, the guilt stems from feeling that they let themselves down by not acknowledging the abuse. For bystanders, the survivor guilt stems from the realization that if only they hadn't minimized or denied what was going on, they might have been able to help the victim. (The section on fight/flight/freeze reactions later in this chapter can provide further insight into the causes of denial and minimization.)

## Rationalizing

*Rationalizing* means using rational ideas to make excuses for someone who is being abusive, or using logical thoughts as a way of excusing your own unwillingness to act in a manner that would help preserve the safety, integrity, or life of another. In the preceding example, Arnie was rationalizing when he tried to figure out why his boss was harassing the office manager and made excuses for the boss by thinking that the boss was "having a hard day." Irene, who observed her older brother physically abuse her younger brother, would have been rationalizing if she decided that her older brother needed to get rid of pent-up energy because he was taking some difficult courses at school.

Like minimizing and denial, rationalizing functions as a defense against acknowledging a painful reality and your own powerlessness or restricted ability to rectify matters. When confronted with a stressful or traumatic circumstance in which all of your options seem inadequate to solve the problem and involve great emotional or physical costs or even risks to your own life, rationalization offers a way out. Instead of agonizing over which of several unacceptable and frightening choices you could select, you ease the impact of the problem by finding a way to explain it. This helps free you from the dilemma of deciding how to respond when all possible responses are unacceptable or ineffectual.

## Escapism: Being Superbusy or Developing an Addiction

*Escapism* can involve being superbusy, developing an addiction to a substance, gambling, or sex, or becoming involved in other escapist activities, such as taking long vacations; it is a way of managing the anxiety associated with being in a stressful or traumatic situation. People become workaholics, develop substance abuse problems or other forms of addiction, or engage in escapist activities in an attempt to reduce their pain and to preserve their sanity. While these might not be the most constructive choices, sometimes they are the only choices people feel they have other than self-mutilation, suicide, or insanity. There may be other options, but they are not known, are not available, or are too costly. Nevertheless, people can suffer great survivor guilt for having used one of these coping methods during a crisis or traumatic circumstance. "My sister was being hit in front of my eyes, and all I was thinking about was getting enough binge foods," a woman says.

The guilt is even greater if the person was engaging in the escapist activity when the victim was in special need. "I was working late at the office, as usual, when my daughter Diane committed suicide. If I had gone home at five or six o'clock, like most people in my office do, I'd have found her and taken her to a hospital. But no, compulsive worker that I was, I had to finish the project I was working on. My workaholism killed my daughter. I'm sure of it, and I'll never forgive myself for it," says one father.

This father had begun working late in order to escape a domestic situation wherein his wife verbally abused one of their daughters. He had tried to intervene several times, but his wife had berated him so severely, he eventually withdrew from the mother-daughter arguments. Since he couldn't stand to be in the home when his wife was punishing his daughter, he took up sports as an escape, and then work.

To this day, he feels guilty about his escapism and overwork. Yet these activities in themselves did not cause the suicide. Most suicides are highly complex matters. In this suicide, the mother's abusiveness toward her daughter as well as the father's inability to protect his daughter from his wife were obviously contributing factors. But they were not the sole factors leading to the girl's death.

Part of the father's healing involved looking at why he could not stand up to his wife. The reasons included fear of his wife's criticisms and the need to preserve his ability to function so he could provide for the family. "Whenever I fought with my wife about the ways she mistreated our daughter, my wife would insult me to the core. I was so devastated by her comments, I couldn't fight back. Then at work the next day I was half a man. I was afraid I couldn't function if I kept on arguing with my wife. I had to keep my job, didn't I?" the father explains.

## Dissociation: Forgetting, Spacing Out, Tuning Out

People often suffer from survivor guilt because they "spaced out," "tuned out," or "forgot" during an event or series of events that led up to or involved the injury or harm of another person. In psychological terms, these experiences of "spacing out" and "forgetting" are called *dissociation*.

Have you ever been driving to a familiar place and missed the exit on the highway because your mind was somewhere else? Have you ever left your keys or wallet somewhere by accident because you were stressed out or "on overload"? Have you ever forgotten to meet someone or do something because, at the time, you were preoccupied with other important matters? Such experiences are common to everyone. They are minor forms of dissociation wherein certain parts of reality are overlooked and other parts are focused on intently.

Without dissociation, we could not study for tests or even watch a movie, because any concentrated activity requires paying attention to one part of reality and blocking out another. Many people who have lived through severe stress or trauma wish they could dissociate from the situation so they could simply have a little peace. To truly dissociate involves not only temporarily forgetting or dimming the memory of the event, but also diminishing feelings and anxiety about the event.

Dissociation is a normal reaction to trauma. It's just as common a reaction to extreme stress and trauma as are clinical depression and post-traumatic stress disorder. During dissociation, your feelings become disconnected from your experience. You feel distant from what is going on around you, almost as if you're an observer rather than a participant in your own life. Amnesia about all or part of a specific traumatic event may also develop.

These forms of emotional and mental shutdowns are to be expected under conditions of extreme stress or trauma. Emotionally, most people can't tolerate living in a constant state of extreme feeling, whether that emotion be grief, panic, or anger. Physiologically, the body can't remain in a constant state of alertness without reprieve. The usual response to being in a prolonged state of emotional and physiological overload is a slowing down of all systems—emotional, mental, and physical.

In many cases, dissociation can be a lifesaver. For example, the ability to dissociate helps medical workers, rescue workers, firefighters, and police officers to focus on the task at hand by allowing them to ignore their emotions. Dissociation also helps children in homes where there is physical or sexual abuse to bear unbearable conditions.

Dissociation often occurs in intolerable situations when there is no other way out. If you cannot flee physically, dissociation permits you to flee in other ways. However, people who have dissociated or tuned out often feel guilty for being in this state, because they feel this state prevented them from correctly assessing the difficulties at hand and from taking action to help themselves or others.

"My dad yelled at my mom all the time. He said some very mean things to her, but I didn't hear them. Well, not exactly. I did hear what he was saying, but I don't remember the exact words and I blocked out the emotional significance of the words. I didn't react with anger and hurt. I was like a blob. My dad was calling my mom all kinds of names, and to me it was as if he was discussing the weather. I feel I betrayed my mother by not being present and appreciating the full impact of what was happening to her. Even if I couldn't have stopped my dad's rages, at least I could have reacted and felt something. Instead I felt nothing and I feel guilty about that," says Carlos.

As Carlos's reaction illustrates, true dissociation can involve not only a blocking of information or memories, but also a numbing of the emotions associated with that information or those memories. Similarly, veterans may not recall a firefight or may be confused or vague about the specifics of a battle, and also report that they cannot remember their feelings at the time or that they have few feelings about the event today.

### Self-Harm:   Mental Illness, Self-Mutilation, or Suicide Attempts

Developing a mental illness, self-mutilation, and suicide attempts are ways of coping with the stress involved in being a situation in which someone is being or can be harmed. They often reflect the intensity of the stress, rather than the person's personal strength, moral character, or love and concern for the victim or potential victim. In addition, people who become mentally ill, self-injurious, or suicidal are probably also being harmed themselves or lack sufficient inner resources, external supports, or financial or other means to bring about the resolution to the stressful situation. We are only human, and given enough stress, we are all vulnerable to developing a mental illness or such a severe depression that we want to harm ourselves.

"Here I was, in the mental hospital with a depression when my nephew needed me. I had no right to be mentally ill when he was going through so much. If I had been well, I could have been there to guide him. Instead, he turned to drugs and alcohol. That's my fault," says a distraught uncle. Yet the uncle did not will himself to become mentally ill, and there were other influences on the nephew besides the absence of an uncle that caused him to develop an addiction.

# Types of Content Survivor Guilt

Existential survivor guilt refers to the guilt you feel because you are alive, healthier, or otherwise better off than someone else. Content survivor guilt refers to guilt about the content or substance of what you did, including what you thought or felt. There are several types of content survivor guilt.

## Competency Guilt

*Competency guilt* involves feeling guilty for not having acted as efficiently or wisely as you think you should have. In truth, you may have not been functioning at your best or meeting your personal performance standards during the time you were being stressed or, if you were traumatized, during the trauma. You need to take into account the bigger picture—the fact that you were operating under conditions of trauma or extreme stress.

As Kubany (1996) points out, different decision-making rules apply during trauma than during everyday life. In the first place, trauma is usually both unexpected and chaotic. Even though your senses are hyperalert, there is usually so much going on during a trauma, and at such a rapid pace, that no one person can accurately observe all that is taking place. A whole team of people would be needed to obtain a total view of the situation and come up with a list of viable options and an effective action plan. If, for instance, you are held up by an armed mugger, you may find yourself focused on his gun, not his face or his clothing. You may or may not see that there is another bandit with him, or that there is a police officer one block away. Such information could influence what you decide to do or not do. But all the information necessary for the best decision possible isn't available because of the tendency, under conditions of trauma, for there to be selective attention to the most life-threatening aspect of the situation. So in the mugging situation, your attention is on the gun—because that gun has the power to destroy you—not on other aspects of the situation.

In the second place, during trauma, time is precious. You do not have the luxury of brainstorming alternatives and carefully examining all the options available before you make a decision. If you are running away from a rapist or a mugger or have only a few seconds to escape from a fire or flood, you may not be able to think of all your options and carefully select the best one. You have to act right away, or risk dying or being injured or the deaths or injuries of others. You also have to act (a) without having the time to ask the opinions of people who may know more than you about what to do; (b) at a time when your mind may not be functioning at its best due to the terror and the stress; and (c) at a time when strong emotions, such as fear and panic, take over and you have no choice but to feel them and try to make a good decision in spite of them.

Some conditions of extreme stress are not unexpected or chaotic but are chronic and long-term in nature. Unlike during an unexpected traumatic event, the stress you experienced may have been fairly predictable. For example, if you were tending to a sick parent or child, after the initial shock, the illness may have become a routine part of your life. However, the fact that your stress was somewhat predictable doesn't make it less stressful. The very fact that someone is ill or in danger of being hurt, injured, or mistreated can put you in a state of emotional overload.

You were probably subject to work overload as well as emotional overload. In most stressful situations an important source of the stress is the sheer number of tasks that need to be performed. For example, if you have parents who are ill, you may have extra responsibilities such as preparing meals for them, cleaning their home, taking them to the doctor, coordinating their appointments, picking up their prescriptions, and so on. These extra responsibilities, in addition to your regular load of responsibilities, can fragment your energies, making it difficult to focus clearly on all the factors involved and impairing your ability to make sound decisions, not only for them but for yourself and your family.

Your awareness that your functioning powers are impaired creates yet another stress; a vicious cycle begins wherein the stress creates more stress, making you feel less and less able to cope. Even though you may be trying to be as responsible and helpful as possible, your mental, emotional, and physical powers are, to one degree or another, weakened, which makes it harder for you to think logically and rationally. In addition, there are usually so many matters to attend to that it can become hard to think clearly and make accurate predictions about the best course of action.

Competency guilt has also been called "I-should-have-done-more guilt" (Williams 1987). Underlying your belief that you should have done more are several assumptions: that you could have done more; that what you did do in the situation was ineffectual or unhelpful; that people can control their physiological and emotional reactions; and that under conditions of stress and trauma, people, including you, could be and should be operating at peak performance.

In reality, under stress, people cannot always control their physiological and emotional reactions. Nor can they force themselves to remember accurately or think quickly and rationally. It is a myth that our performance under conditions of stress or trauma "should be and can be perfect" (Williams 1987, 151). By focusing on what you think you should have done, you may overlook the positive contributions you made by what you did do.

## *Negligence Guilt*

Closely related to competency guilt is *negligence guilt*, or the guilt that can result from some form of negligence in performing your assigned duties or executing your designated role.

Do you feel guilty because you were negligent in your duties and someone died or was injured as a result? For example, if you are a parent, did you fail to check with your pediatrician before you gave your child the medication that nearly caused your child's death? If you are a nurse or medical professional, did you forget to monitor your patient's blood-sugar level only to find that patient in a diabetic coma? If you work in an office or a factory, did you fail to document instances of harassment of a co-worker as you had promised because you were too tired or too busy with other job responsibilities? Regardless of your vocation, were you taking a break, eating, smoking marijuana, or drinking when you should have been tending to your duties?

As with competency guilt, it is important to examine your negligence guilt in the context of the larger picture. Sometimes negligence is the result of the stress or trauma itself. For example, if you work in an environment where a co-worker is being harassed, the stress of that situation may compel you to take additional breaks or days off.

Similarly, if you are a medical professional who works long hours or with many complex cases, you may indulge yourself in a way that appears like negligence but more truthfully is a means to replenish yourself emotionally or physically so that you can continue to function in a demanding environment.

An important question to ask yourself is, What prompted the negligence? Was it a sincere desire to cause harm or abdicate responsibility, or was it instead a misguided, but nevertheless sincere, effort to reduce stress or to meet some of your legitimate needs? Were you truly negligent or were you simply not trained or inadequately trained for the task at hand?

## Hindsight Bias

Kubany (1994, 1996) defines *hindsight bias* as the tendency to think you were more capable than you actually were during a difficult time or to think that you knew things while you were under stress that you only realized after the stress was over. For example, people under stress tend to evaluate what they did or didn't do based on the information they have about the outcome of the stressful event or options they thought of long after the stressful event was over, rather than on the information they had and options they thought of during the time of the event itself.

A father and mother allowed their three daughters to go to the beach with a favorite aunt and uncle. During the vacation at the beach, the uncle raped one of the daughters. Several years later, the daughter revealed this rape to her parents. After the rape was disclosed, the parents learned from other sources that this particular uncle was a known child abuser. However, he had cleverly hid the information from his family, even his wife.

The parents feel guilty. They feel they should have known the uncle was a pedophile. Yet at the time, they had no knowledge of this uncle's sexual history, and what they did know about this uncle was that he was very kind and generous with their daughters and appeared to be a devoted family man.

A similar example is that of a nurse who administered medication to a child who then had a severe allergic reaction. The nurse feels she should have known the child was allergic to the medication, yet she had no information about the child's allergies, neither was there any evidence that this child was allergic. The nurse's intention in administering the medication was to alleviate the child's suffering, not to harm the child. Yet her hindsight bias has resulted in a deep and abiding sense of guilt.

## Catch-22 Guilt

Stressful life events, especially if they are traumatic, are often lose-lose situations, or catch-22s, in which all the choices available are unacceptable or involve a violation of personal ethics. No matter what choice you make, you're betraying yourself or an important value. The husband who has to spend time taking care of his sick wife might feel guilty about not being able to give his children the attention they are accustomed to receiving from him. On the other hand, if he doesn't help his wife and spends time with the children instead, he might feel guilty for not assisting his spouse in her time of need and neglecting his children's mother.

The woman who is alone in the office with a co-worker who has just collapsed on the floor and is having trouble breathing can feel guilty for leaving her co-worker to search for help. On the other hand, if she had stayed with the co-worker and been unable to help him, she could feel guilty for not trying to obtain medical care. The abused wife who leaves her husband can feel guilty for depriving her children of a father and of a comfortable standard of living. On the other hand, if she chooses to stay, she can feel guilty for exposing her children to violence and to a chaotic lifestyle. The combat veteran who shoots a grenade-laden toddler can feel guilty about killing a child. But if he hadn't killed the child and the grenade went off and killed his squad, then he would feel guilty about not preventing the deaths of his comrades.

Kubany calls this type of guilt *catch-22 guilt* because no matter what choice is made, there is an undesirable outcome. In these situations, the least bad choice is the best choice, but people who have undergone severe stress or a major trauma rarely view matters in this way. They tend to evaluate their choice against a wished-for, magical, or unrealistic ideal choice that was not available at the time (Kubany 1996). Until they have the benefit of examining their behavior, feelings, or thoughts in a rational light, their suffering from guilt can be enormous. Indeed, this type of guilt is often at the root of substance abuse problems, eating disorders, and suicidal depressions.

## Superman/Superwoman Guilt

Some people feel guilty about being helpless or powerless during a threatening or dangerous time, yet being relatively—or totally—helpless and powerless in a situation of great danger is the very definition of trauma. Since people prefer to think that they are able to control their lives, it is easier to blame themselves for negative events than to acknowledge that sometimes life is unfair or arbitrary and innocent people can be victimized for no reason.

## *The Mind-Body Connection: Guilt over Fight/Flight/Freeze and Other Emotional and Physical Reactions*

Your emotions, thoughts, and physical sensations are inseparable. The way you feel affects how you think, and the way you think affects how you feel. The state of your body affects the state of your mind, as well as your emotional state. Nowhere is this more true than in the case of extreme stress or trauma.

Like the rest of your body, your central nervous system is vulnerable. Given enough physical or emotional stress, it too can bend or even break. When you experienced your extreme stress or trauma, your central nervous system received a series of shocks. The fewer the social supports and comforters you had during and after the trauma and the greater the intensity and the longer the duration of the trauma, the greater the possibility that the delicate biochemical balances of your body might have been disrupted.

Despite an increase in research on the biochemistry of trauma and extreme stress in recent years, there is no single definitive theory as to how severe stress affects the body. One theory is that trauma destabilizes the autonomic nervous system; another is that trauma changes body chemistry so that the individual is more prone to anxiety. Yet another hypothesis is that trauma disrupts certain specific biochemical balances, for example, serotonin or catecholamine levels (Murburg 1994, 1995; van der Kolk et al. 1996).

Another theory is that under conditions of danger, the organism coordinates a mental, physical, and emotional effort to respond in a self-preserving manner. After the emergency is over, then the organism returns to the thinking, feeling, and physiological states appropriate for daily (non-traumatic) living. However, when stress is extreme, such as in trauma, or when stress is prolonged, all systems do not return to previous levels of daily functioning. They may remain in a state of emergency (Giller 1994). Evidence for this theory are studies that show that some twenty years after trauma, some survivors live in an altered state of arousal.

No single biological explanation is satisfactory in that no one theory can explain the wide range of symptoms in trauma survivors. Nevertheless, certain general trends emerge: mainly that people who have been severely or chronically traumatized tended to either overreact or underreact during the trauma, as would be expected and as would be necessary for survival, and tended to either overreact or underreact to present-day situations, creating anxiety and shame within themselves and creating chaos in their relationships. If you have been traumatized, it's critical for you to understand the possible immediate and long-term biological consequences of the stress you have endured. If you got hyper during the trauma and still get hyper today when reminded of the trauma, or if you felt dead inside during the trauma and still, at times, do today when reminded of the trauma, it may help you to know that these extreme reactions are not signs of moral or emotional deficiency. Rather, these extreme reactions, which create so much pain in yourself and so much havoc in your relationships, are, to a great extent, the result of survival-based physiological processes out of your control.

## Acute Stress Reactions: Fight/Flight/Freeze Reactions

Emotional trauma gives rise to at least four overwhelming emotions: fear, grief, rage, and anxiety. These feelings are so powerful that to experience them in full force at the time of the trauma would be personally disorganizing and might endanger survival. Therefore, these emotions tend to be suppressed, to one degree or another.

When emotions are not suppressed during the traumatic event, at least in part, individuals can become nonfunctional. For example, they may not be able to move or think clearly due to uncontrolled bouts of weeping or screaming or due to hallucinations or any one of a number of psychotic breaks from reality. When overwhelmed by emotion during the trauma, some individuals have committed suicide, homicide, or acts of self-mutilation (such as cutting, burning, head banging) that hamper their coping abilities and endanger the safety of others.

The life-threatening nature of trauma also gives rise to certain physical emergency responses that are designed to help people survive the trauma. Included among these are the "three *F*s"—fight, flight, freeze. Under conditions of danger, the adrenal glands release either adrenaline or noradrenaline. Adrenaline strengthens functions essential to survival, enabling people to move quickly and powerfully, whether to fight with renewed strength or to run (flight) with increased speed. Some rape victims, for example, have become so empowered with adrenaline that they have fought off attackers three times their strength. In other cases, rape victims have found themselves "frozen"—literally unable to move—or otherwise unable to act on their own behalf due to the release of noradrenaline. This numbing reaction is similar to the way some animals play dead when threatened.

Some mugging victims have reported being surprised by how they reacted to being attacked. One woman explains, "I always thought that if I was mugged, I'd totally comply with the mugger. I'd hand him my purse, write him a check, or do whatever he wanted in hopes that he wouldn't cause me bodily harm. But when I actually was mugged, I fought back. I punched the mugger, pulled his hair, and tried to tear the clothes off of him. The mugger was one foot taller than me and double my weight. It wasn't a matter of logic. Something came over me—a surge of energy—and I just lunged at him like a wild woman. Looking back I can't believe it was me, timid me, who to this day is afraid to squash a fly."

When this woman was mugged, she was with her four-year-old child. When she tried to attack the mugger, she completely forgot about the child. "What if my child had run into the street and was hit by a car or taken by a stranger while I was pulling off my Amazon act?" she now wonders and feels guilty over what might have happened due to her adrenaline surge. She also feels guilty because her child told her that he became frightened when he saw her fight back. "You were like a witch, Mom," the child said. "Are you going to be like that with me when I do something wrong?" The types of guilt this woman feels are forms of content survivor guilt.

This "timid" woman had been struck by a surge of adrenaline that made her feel as physically powerful and daring as a professional boxer. On the other hand, professional boxers and those trained in the martial arts have found themselves "frozen" by noradrenaline when in danger. For example, Sam, a former boxer and an ex-marine, was held up in his home. When he was asked to open the safe, much to his amazement he couldn't remember the combination, even though, until that moment, he knew the numbers by heart.

"My mind froze," Sam says. Then, to Sam's further amazement, when he put his hand in his pocket where his gun was hidden, his hand "froze" too. He couldn't grab the gun. Sam was used to violence and physical aggression, but in this instance, the numbing response flooded his central nervous system, temporarily paralyzing his mind and his limbs. Because his wife was assaulted during this robbery, Sam not only feels ashamed of freezing, but also suffers from survivor guilt over going numb. For more information on responses to trauma, read my books, *I Can't Get Over It: A Handbook for Trauma Survivors* (1996) and *Trust After Trauma: A Guide to Relationships for Trauma Survivors and Those Who Love Them* (1998).

## Why Fight and Flight and Not Freeze?

It has yet to be determined why some people have fight-or-flight as opposed to freeze reactions. One theory is that the more severe the trauma, the more likely that a "freeze" reaction will occur. This theory holds that at the first sign of danger the body pumps adrenaline that energizes the organism to respond. However, after a certain threshold of stress is reached (that is, if the stress is too severe or too long), the adrenaline flow ceases and a numbing reaction begins.

Perhaps an analogy can be made to putting your foot on the gas pedal in order to increase the speed of your car. You press down to go faster, but if you press down too fast or too many times, you might flood the engine and it stops. This is similar to what can happen when adrenaline is pumped too fast or too long: eventually the energizing adrenaline response ceases and the numbing response takes over.

Experiments show that when laboratory animals are subjected to shock or some other form of punishment, they first secrete massive amounts of adrenaline, epinephrine, and other activating hormones. The animals then scamper all around the cage trying to find a way out. Or they "fight" the bars of the cage by biting them or pushing against them. However, if the electric shock persists and the animals see that no matter how much they try to fight or escape, they are still being shocked, the adrenaline surge ceases. In its place comes the SIA (stress-induced analgesia) response. The animals become "numb" or "passive." They stop trying to escape and show little interest in food, play, or sex. (These experiments are the basis of Seligman's theory of learned helplessness, described in my 1996 book *I Can't Get Over It: A Handbook for Trauma Survivors*.)

However, not all of the animals react the same way at the same pace. Some become numb and passive right away, others only after repeated shocks. Are the ones who become numb early on "weaker" for not continuing to fight, or are they "smarter" in that they can foresee that putting up a fight is hopeless?

Passing moral judgment on these animals makes as much sense as passing moral judgment on traumatized people, some of whom become numb faster than others for reasons that no one has yet adequately explained. In Western culture, action is valued over inaction, hence trauma survivors who "put up a fight" or try to beat the odds by trying to escape tend to be valued more highly than those who "freeze." However, an individual's response may have more to do with the severity and the duration of the traumatic stressor or that person's biologically determined threshold of stress than any character trait. Indeed, the numbing response needs to be seen as the body's attempt to preserve the organism from unbearable pain and stress, as well as a way to conserve energy to deal with future stress (Glover 1992). According to Glover, "numbing represents an effort to diminish the psychophysiological experience of stress" (644).

So while some trauma survivors may feel guilty about having intense fight/flight/freeze reactions, all of these reactions are involuntary. The combat medic whose hands begin to tremble as the result of extreme combat trauma isn't choosing to develop these tremors. The rescue worker who becomes overwhelmed with fear isn't choosing to be afraid. The rape victim who "freezes" and can't defend herself doesn't chose to "freeze." On the other hand, the rape victim who fights back and is beaten for it by the rapist doesn't choose to become filled with an adrenaline surge, attack her attacker, and be punished further for it.

## *Atrocity or Moral/Spiritual Guilt*

In some types of trauma, people participate in or witness morally questionable activities. In war, soldiers are exposed to or engage in atrocities; in abusive homes, family members may be exposed to or participate in cruel and sadistic forms of torture of people or pets. As a result of being exposed to the "monster" or "beast" in yourself or in others, you can come to feel that you are tainted and come to view all other aspects of your personality as being evil or despicable. There may also be a feeling of being cut off forever from society because of what you did or what you saw. The kind of guilt involved in having witnessed or participated in atrocities has been called moral pain, moral guilt, or *atrocity guilt*.

The agony of this guilt is much worse if you have actually committed an act with "real and terrible consequences" than if you merely witnessed it (Marin 1981). However, even people who harmed no one but simply observed an atrocity or immoral act can feel contaminated by what they saw or heard. It's as if they absorbed the evil they witnessed into themselves, even though they did not conceive of or participate in the act. On some level, they feel responsible for the event simply because they were physically present.

For example, some Holocaust survivors report feeling like subhuman beings, not only because of how they were treated but also because they saw so many acts where others were treated inhumanely. Even though they didn't commit any acts of cruelty and even though it was impossible for them to stop the slaughter, some survivors suffer from atrocity guilt because they feel contaminated simply by having observed the inhuman acts of others (Niederland 1964). In a parallel manner, survivors of ritual or cult abuse can feel morally "dirtied" by having been present during cult rituals, even if they did not participate in the torture or killing of animals or in the abuse or murder of human beings.

Soldiers are profoundly affected by this type of guilt. Grossman writes, "The combat soldier appears to feel a deep sense of responsibility and accountability for what he sees around him. It is as though every enemy dead is a human being he has killed, and every friendly dead is a comrade for whom he was responsible. With every effort to reconcile these two responsibilities, more guilt is added to the horror that surrounds the soldier" (1996, 75). Survivors of other kinds of traumas, for example, domestic violence, sexual abuse, cult abuse, or political torture, can probably identify with the feelings of soldiers. For instance, someone growing up in a violent home can feel responsible for all the abuse he or she sees, not just any abuse that he or she might have perpetrated under coercion.

Another part of this type of survivor guilt stems from being unable to protest the atrocity or make it stop. Yet there are circumstances in which stopping an atrocity may be virtually impossible without endangering your own life or the lives of others. In some circumstances, even sacrificing your life to try to avert the atrocity would be ineffective. For example, cult abuse survivors who refuse to participate in the mutilation and abuse of others might be abused or tortured as a punishment for noncompliance and still be unable to stop the horror around them. In fact, their noncompliance could spur the abusers to become even more abusive of others. Under these circumstances, the choice with the fewest negative consequences is compliance, as morally unacceptable as that might be.

After World War II, people wondered how law-abiding, decent German citizens could have become involved in maintaining the Nazi death camps. A psychologist named Stanley Milgram designed a set of experiments showing that a majority of people would agree to torture another person if told to do so by an authority figure (1963, 1965). In these experiments, Milgram used Yale college students as subjects. The college students were taken into a booth and told to administer an electric shock to subjects who were in another room strapped to a chair. The students were told that the shocks were harmless and would cause no pain.

In reality, no electric shock was being administered, but the students didn't know that. When they administered the shock, the subjects in the chairs moaned in pain. The experimenter, who functioned as the authority figure in this situation, then asked the students to increase the voltage. Approximately 65 percent of the students complied, even though the subjects in the chairs seemed to be in considerable agony and pain. The experimenters kept telling the students to increase the voltage, even when some of the strapped subjects seemed to faint from the voltage. These experiments showed that even "good" people would harm other human beings if told to by an authority figure.

Since the Milgram experiments were first completed in the 1960s, they have been replicated over thirty times with subjects of different ages, races, and ethnic backgrounds and in different countries. The results are always the same: people tend to do what they are told to do by an authority figure, even when it involves harming or killing others. Additional experiments have shown that the power of the demands of authority increase with proximity to and respect for authority (Grossman 1996).

Another factor that counteracts the inhibitions against harming or killing others is the pressure to conform. In a famous series of experiments, Solomon Asch (1955) showed how group pressure could make people say that long lines were short and short lines long. In other words, under the pressure of the group, people would distort their own senses and make statements that contradicted what they could plainly see for themselves.

Understanding the power of authority figures and group pressure can help some survivors lighten their burden of guilt. Nevertheless, the sense of guilt experienced by people who, as part of their trauma, harmed or killed animals or other people can come to ruin their lives. It is a major underlying cause of suicide among soldiers and abuse survivors who were forced into harming or killing others by their abuser.

For example, Rachel recalls being made to kill her dog and to sexually abuse a four-year-old child by members of a cult to which her parents belonged. The shame and guilt she feels about these acts has caused her to feel worthless and undeserving of any happiness. Her survivor guilt has been so intense she has become suicidal at times, even though therapy has made her aware that there was no escape from the cult when she was a child. Had she not followed the cult's orders, she might have been harmed, or even more pets and children might have been abused or killed as a means of punishing her disobedience.

Prior to the Vietnam conflict, soldiers generally received absolution for their killing and maiming in the form of societal validation and appreciation for their military actions. Warriors of the Vietnam conflict tended not to receive this societal validation, and hence many

of them bore alone the weight of having killed, without societal absolution (Grossman 1996). Cult abuse survivors, family violence survivors, and other kinds of trauma survivors who are coerced into illegal
activities or actions they find immoral hardly ever receive societal
understanding or absolution, which only heightens their sense of
moral guilt.

One of the difficulties in writing about atrocity guilt is that killing is a taboo subject. As Grossman (1998) explains, even in the military there is no discussion about the experience of killing other
human beings. While soldiers are prepared for seeing friends die or
become wounded, or for their own death or injury, there is no preparation for what it feels like to take a human life, at close range. In fact
in recent years, in some military circles, the subject has been skirted
by avoiding the very word "killing." Instead of being told that soldiers are going to kill the enemy, now we are told they're going to
"service the target" (Grossman 1998).

Another difficulty in discussing atrocity guilt is the notion that
therapists are supposed to be morally neutral; they're not supposed
to pass judgments about "right" and "wrong." In the therapy session,
most mental health professionals have been trained to either avoid
the subject of moral pain or treat it like a symptom that can perhaps
be analyzed away.

However, treating moral pain as a "neurosis, or a pathological
symptom, something to escape from rather than something to learn
from, a disease rather than . . . an appropriate if painful response to
the past" is a woefully inadequate way to deal with it, writes Marin
(1981, 71). This type of perspective on atrocity guilt trivializes the
pain and anger felt by people who have been in situations in which
they were propelled into acting against their conscience and who
must face the fact that they caused another person's death or injury.

Not only is psychotherapy limited in being able to alleviate and
respond to atrocity guilt, but it can also exacerbate the frustration of
people who suffer from moral pain by promoting the myth that "the
past can be avoided, that happiness is always possible, and that insight
inevitably leads to joy" (Marin 1981, 75). In the case of moral pain,
more insight into the experiences involved can sometimes bring more
pain, more despair, and a greater feeling of alienation from others.

This section on moral pain is not intended to indict or chastise
people who have injured, killed, or tortured living beings as part of
their trauma. These deeds, like other acts committed under conditions
of extreme stress such as war or family violence, must be seen in the
context of the pressures of the situation and the relative unavailability
of alternative courses of action. In my experience, people suffering

from atrocity guilt tend to forget that they were operating in life-or-death situations or were living in circumstances that would have hardened the heart or brutalized almost anyone. They also tend to forget that they did not create these barbaric circumstances and that had they not been in a particular situation, they probably would not have generated a plan to commit an atrocity or to kill or injure others. Instead they tend to take on the guilt for the entire situation, including the guilt belonging to the original instigators of the violence.

Some survivors of war, cult abuse, or other situations in which they were coerced into committing acts that they judge immoral feel guilt not only about committing the act but also about feeling numb or emotionless while doing so. If you feel guilty about how you were feeling while engaged in an act about which you feel ashamed, reread the sections in this chapter on fight/flight/freeze reactions. Keep in mind that emotional numbing usually reflects extreme terror or a deep loyalty or compassion toward the victims.

For example, in the ancient story of the Trojan War, the Greek king, Agamemnon, is told that he must kill his daughter, Iphigenia, if he is to be granted favorable winds so that the ships carrying his troops can sail to Troy. For quite some time, Agamemnon doesn't know what to do: sacrifice his daughter and ensure passage to Troy, or let his daughter live and let down his troops. Finally he decides that he cannot forsake his role as military leader; therefore, his daughter must die.

Upon making this decision, he begins to weep uncontrollably. However, by the time he actually slays his daughter, he is numb. He feels nothing and he kills his daughter as easily and unemotionally as if she'd been a fly on the wall. Agamemnon had become so hardened by what he had to do that he basically stopped having any kinds of feelings other than anger or lust. He was so hardened he didn't even feel guilty about killing his daughter. But he was criticized by others, not so much for killing his daughter, because it was understood that he had little choice but to follow the dictates of the gods, but for doing so emotionlessly. Yet he had as little choice over going numb as he did over the gods' decree. In fact, the degree of his numbness was a reflection of the degree of his love for his daughter and his horror at having to kill her.

## ✍ Self-Assessment for Content Survivor Guilt

Do you feel guilty for exhibiting or engaging in any of the following during or after your trauma or stressful event? Answer yes, no, or sometimes as honestly as possible.

1. Going "numb," "freezing," or the opposite, "overreacting" _____

2. "Tuning out," "spacing out," "forgetting," or "feeling inhuman or unreal" _____

3. Witnessing or participating in immoral or unethical actions _____

4. Thinking certain thoughts or feeling certain feelings that you judge to be selfish, uncaring, or otherwise inappropriate or inhumane _____

5. Not foreseeing the negative outcome of your actions _____

6. Making certain choices that you now feel proved disastrous _____

7. Making mistakes _____

8. Refusing requests for help from others when to have done so would have endangered your life or safety _____

9. Making the preservation of your life and sanity a priority over the welfare of others _____

10. Neglecting certain duties _____

11. Not becoming physically or mentally ill _____

12. Developing an addiction, such as an alcohol or drug addiction, an eating disorder, a gambling problem, or an overindulgence in sex

    _____

13. Trying to escape the situation by overworking or engaging in other escapist activities, such as dangerous activities, vacations, or watching too much TV _____

14. Being or feeling powerless to save the lives of others or spare them from injury _____

15. Minimizing or denying the true extent of the dangerousness or cruelty of the events you were observing or involved with _____

16. Not remembering parts of the traumatic or stressful events, or not being able to see as sharply, hear as accurately, or move as quickly as you wanted to during that stressful time _____

17. Wishing that someone might be injured or punished harshly ____

   If you have answered "yes" or "sometimes" to more than two of the questions, you may be suffering from content survivor guilt. If this is the case, the next step is assessing the degree to which your content survivor guilt affects your self-esteem, your relationships, and your ability to love, work, and play.

# 4

# Causes and Circumstances

Survivor guilt is usually associated with traumatic circumstances, such as natural or man-made catastrophes. However, it can also occur in normal life situations that are not traumatic by definition, but that involve significant loss or stress. These include the expected death of a loved one, a chronic illness and miscarriage, and the presence of emotional abuse or addiction in your family. Survivor guilt in normal life circumstances is not limited to the home. You can develop both existential and content guilt from a work environment where there is harassment and discrimination.

Ironically, survivor guilt can also be the result of positive life experiences or achievements, such as financial, social, or psychological success. In these cases, the survivor guilt stems from separating from or leaving behind members of your social, religious, political, or emotional group combined with the feeling that your advancement will harm those left behind. However, in order to be considered survivor guilt, as opposed to the normal strains of a life transition, the feeling of guilt must result in some type of disability or impairment, such as low self-esteem, social withdrawal, angry outbursts, or somatic symptoms such as headaches or backaches. Non-traumatic survivor guilt is more prevalent among minority groups and other historically oppressed groups. As stated in the introduction to this book, expanding the definition of survivor guilt to include such circumstances may be controversial. However, the fact that individuals are suffering from psychological or physical symptoms that impede their ability to function or to enjoy life, and that those symptoms stem from feelings of guilt from reduced contact with their original group, makes this extension consistent with the traditional definition of survivor guilt. This type of survivor guilt can also be found among members of therapy and recovery groups who make so much progress in their therapy that they "outgrow" their group or can no longer identify to the same degree with members of their group.

This chapter explores the various types of life situations that can lead to survivor guilt. The first part of the chapter concerns trauma-related circumstances; the second focuses on normal life circumstances.

# Trauma-Related Survivor Guilt

In life, we all face crises, large and small, ranging from the loss of a wallet to the death of a loved one. Yet these events, although stressful and often called traumatic, are not considered true trauma. *Trauma*, in the technical sense of the word, refers to dangerous situations in which you are rendered powerless. It's important for you to understand what trauma is before you learn about trauma-related survivor guilt.

## What Is Trauma?

Man-made events such as war, family violence, crime, technological disasters, and vehicular accidents and natural catastrophes such as fires, floods, earthquakes, and hurricanes are usually considered traumatic. Traumatic events usually involve death or injury, or the threat of death or injury. However, it is not just the events themselves but how the events are experienced that makes them traumatic.

In this sense, trauma involves three elements: being afraid, feeling overwhelmed, and being or feeling helpless. If you are afraid but don't feel overwhelmed and can take decisive action on your behalf, this may be stressful, but it doesn't necessarily constitute trauma. Similarly, you may be in a situation where you are overwhelmed and feeling helpless, but if you are not also afraid of possible loss of life or injury to yourself or others, this is not technically trauma (James 1994).

Research indicates high incidences of survivor guilt not only among combat veterans but also among survivors of natural catastrophes, vehicular and other accidents, political terrorism, concentration camps and genocides, and childhood or adult physical or sexual abuse.

## Man-Made vs. Natural Catastrophes

It has been argued that survivors of man-made catastrophes suffer from longer and more intense traumatic reactions, including survivor guilt, than survivors of natural catastrophes. Because, it is assumed, natural catastrophes can be explained away as bad luck or acts of God, natural catastrophe survivors are less likely to blame themselves for negative outcomes, including the death or injury or others.

However, in many cases, the suffering caused by natural disasters involves one or more significant human errors, either by individuals or institutions. For example, individuals responsible for operating tornado warning systems can feel guilty if their equipment fails to warn local residents in sufficient time to save lives. Similarly, manufacturers of construction materials and local developers who built homes that were destroyed by floods or hurricanes can experience survivor guilt if they believe that their materials or construction plans may have contributed to the loss of life or property.

Furthermore, natural catastrophes usually involve rescue operations and other services, where human error can have disastrous results, leading to survivor guilt on the part of the service providers. Just like man-made trauma survivors, natural catastrophe survivors may be suffering existential survivor guilt when they wonder why they were saved or were relatively unharmed compared with others. They can also suffer from content survivor guilt if they refused to help a neighbor in order to tend to their own families or property or if they felt glad that someone they harbored hostile or jealous feelings toward was injured more than they were or lost more property than they did during the natural catastrophe. Consequently, natural catastrophe survivors may be more likely than is often thought, to develop survivor guilt just as intensely as survivors of man-made catastrophes.

In addition, it is common for natural catastrophes to increase the rates of man-made disasters, such as family violence, rape, and crime. Hence some natural catastrophe survivors will be subject to situations that give rise to survivor guilt from man-made traumas.

However, survivors of natural disasters do differ from other types of survivors, especially abuse survivors, in that they tend to be less stigmatized by society. Natural catastrophe survivors are generally spared the "blame the victim" attitudes that frequently afflict survivors of man-made catastrophes and can exacerbate and deepen survivor guilt. For example, victims of rape, incest, and other types of abuse are often blamed for either provoking the abuse or for accepting it—as if it had been their choice. They are also likely to be seen as lacking in strength, caution, intelligence, or moral integrity. The message they are given is, What happened to you is your own fault. If you had been more careful, less stupid, more righteous, it wouldn't have happened to you.

If they are already feeling guilty for some of the coping mechanisms they used, such as denial, dissociation, or developing an addiction, these "blame the victim" attitudes heighten their content survivor guilt. If they are already feeling guilty because, as part of their trauma, someone else died or was less injured than themselves, then the "blame the victim" attitudes increase their existential survivor guilt.

These and other nonsupportive messages are part of a process called secondary wounding, which you can read about in chapter 4 of my book *I Can't Get Over It—A Handbook for Trauma Survivors* (1996).

## Single- vs. Multiple-Trauma Survivors

People who have been traumatized often wonder, "Why me? Why did this terrible event have to happen to me?" If they were in a trauma where someone died or was injured and they feel as if that death or injury was partially or totally their fault, they may conclude that the second trauma they experienced is a punishment for the mistakes they made during the first trauma. For example, Smitty encouraged his friends to enlist in the military when he did. Two of his friends were killed in battle, but he was not. When his first friend died, Smitty asked, "Why me? Why did my friend have to die?" When the second friend died, Smitty didn't have to ask the question. He already had an answer. In his view, the second friend's death was his punishment for encouraging the first friend to join the army.

Another example is that of Ramona. Ramona and her younger sister were walking home from school when they were abducted and raped. Ramona suffered from survivor guilt because she could not prevent the rape of her younger sister. She felt that because she was older, she should have found some means of protecting her younger sibling even though they were both held captive by an armed rapist. Years later, Ramona's home caught fire. No one was injured, but there were major financial losses. In Ramona's mind, the fire was a punishment for failing to protect her sister from harm. Although there was no logical connection between the rape of her sister and the fire, Ramona's survivor guilt had a logic of its own that told her that the two incidents were closely related.

There is also a tendency for people who have been traumatized repeatedly to view one or more psychological symptoms or medical problems they've acquired as punishment for their traumas. Once again, it is the illogical logic of survivor guilt that leads to these conclusions. For example, Paul, who served three tours in Vietnam, killed women and children suspected of being enemy sympathizers. At times he was so brutalized by the war that he also engaged in random violence against civilians and civilian animals. Today he suffers from extreme survivor guilt based on participating in these killings and atrocities. He also suffers from recurrent nightmares about these experiences. The nightmares are expected symptoms of having been traumatized; however, Paul views the nightmares as punishment for his actions.

Odonna, an incest survivor, feels contaminated by her incestuous experiences and suffers from content survivor guilt in that she feels guilty for having enjoyed some of the favors and special status given to her by her abusive father. She also feels guilty for having talked against other relatives in order to please her father. Today she experiences job problems because of recurring bouts of depression, which are a common aftermath of years of incest. However, rather than view the depression as a normal reaction to having been exploited for many years, Odonna views the depression as a punishment for enjoying the few rewards she received as a result of being maltreated and for trying to pacify her father by agreeing with him when he ridiculed and criticized other family members whom she loved.

## Survivor Guilt in Abusive Homes

Survivor guilt has often been found among people from homes where there is physical or sexual abuse. Family members who witness or know about the mistreatment of another family member (or members) and *(a)* are not mistreated themselves or *(b)* receive less abuse than other family members can suffer from intense survivor guilt. This type of survivor guilt tends to be especially strong if, unlike themselves, family members who were being abused were severely injured, died, or were forced to leave home.

This type of survivor guilt can contribute to the development of an alcohol or drug addiction or an eating disorder. While such addictions are multicausal and can't be simply explained away as the results of survivor guilt, very often mental health practitioners and clients themselves tend to overlook the impact of guilt, including survivor guilt, in the genesis of an addiction or other psychological difficulty.

For the purposes of this book, *abuse* is a broad term that encompasses any kind of physical cruelty in a domestic situation. *Sexual abuse*, whether of an adult or child, means unwanted sexual contact of any kind, regardless of the victim's age, gender, or relationship with the abuser. Emotional abuse and manipulation play a role in both physical and sexual abuse.

Women and children are those most often victimized in these ways, but increasingly, cases of the abuse of elderly people and grown men are coming to light.

## Battering

Physical abuse of adults, or *battering*, is a multidimensional phenomenon. Physical assault must exist in order for the relationship to be considered a battering one; emotional abuse without the assault does not constitute battering. However, battering often includes not only emotional abuse, but economic, social, and sexual abuse as well. Economic battering refers to the abuser's use of money as a coercive tool. Social battering refers to the abuser's attempts to isolate the victim and severely limit or control the victim's public interactions.

The abuser may even attempt to isolate the victim from other family members, or to severely limit or control the victim's interactions with family members. The victim may also be used as a pawn to manipulate other family members without physically abusing them. For example, if you knew your child (or sibling or grandparent or aunt) would be harmed if you did not comply with what an aggressive family member wanted, you would probably comply with what the aggressive person wanted. It would not be necessary for the abusive person to attack you directly. He or she could coerce you into certain actions by threatening the victim.

Similarly, the victim can be controlled by any statements that indicate the intent to assault. In many states, the threat of violence is a crime and, on a psychological level, battering includes threats. But for a pattern of battering to be shown, there must have been at least two deliberate, severe physical attacks.

Police officers and judges tend to consider only black eyes, broken ribs, and burns as acceptable evidence of battering. Similarly, vaginal lacerations are often needed to prove marital rape. However, psychological humiliation and degradation are just as devastating as physical aggression. Surveys of abused women and studies of abused children show that psychological abuse goes hand in hand with physical attacks, and many battered women remember the psychological injuries they have endured more than the physical ones. Given the damage inflicted on the psyche as well as to the body, battering might best be defined as any violation of the physical or psychological space of another person within an intimate or bonded relationship.

Note, however, that a battering relationship is not one in which an individual simply feels unhappy due to lack of love, respect, or appreciation. Rather, the individual must have experienced at least one life-threatening situation and know that the abuser is capable of killing him or her. It is not necessary for the abuser to continually beat the victim. What is relevant is that the victim has been terrorized or humiliated into a submissive posture by the threat of injury or death. Even threats of violence, accompanied by minimal physical abuse, are sufficient to establish a pattern of domination by force.

Once victims know their partner or caretaker is capable of harming them, they come to live in fear of his or her anger. The behavior and threats of abusive people can also come to control family members other than the victim, because they are witness to the kinds of punishments the abuser is capable of and willing to inflict on those who become the objects of his or her wrath.

If you grew up in a violent home but were not physically abused yourself, you may have been emotionally abused or otherwise stunted in your development and controlled in your behavior by the abuser's behavior. You may feel that the emotional and other scars you bear are minor compared with the types of violence inflicted on other members of the family and hence discount your pain. However, you are entitled to acknowledge, and grieve, the pain that was inflicted upon you, even if you were not physically assaulted.

### Child Abuse

Child abuse, like battering, does not refer to a onetime assault, but to the repeated battering, neglect, or sexual molestation of a child by a parent, relative, or other caretaker. Just as a man or woman need not suffer repeated fractures and knife wounds to be considered battered, a child need not be covered with burns and scars to be classified as abused. The definition of child abuse used by the National Center on Child Abuse and Neglect (NCCAN 1983a, b) includes many forms of maltreatment not considered in the definition of battering. For example, emotional abuse by itself is an official category of child abuse. There need not be the violence or threat of violence that is necessary for an adult relationship to be considered abusive.

Officially, an abused child is a person under the age of eighteen whose physical or emotional health is harmed or threatened by parents or other people responsible for the child's welfare. The specifics of what legally constitutes child abuse vary from state to state. In general, however, four types of child abuse are recognized: physical abuse, neglect, emotional abuse, and sexual abuse (NCCAN 1983a, b).

## Witnessing Family Violence

Seeing a stranger being assaulted is traumatic; however, seeing someone in your own family being injured is even worse. The horror of witnessing family violence is that you see one member of your family being hurt by someone who is supposed to love and show concern for that person as well as others in the family. If you lived in a home where a child was being abused, you may be experiencing survivor guilt based on the natural helplessness of a child. If you were older than the child being abused, you may feel that, as an older person, you would've been better able to withstand the neglect or the emotional, physical, or sexual abuse. Hence you might have wished you could have taken the child's place. There are instances, however, when even offering to take the punishment for the victim could further enrage the abuser and create more difficulties for the victim. This is especially the case if the abuser is paranoid, or becomes paranoid, when violent. He or she may then think that you and the victim are conspiring against him or her and punish the victim even more. You are then in a terrible double bind: If you try to help the victim, even to the extent of offering to exchange places, you take the risk of the victim being victimized even further. On the other hand, if you don't try to help, you feel as if you are betraying the victim and acting in a cowardly manner. If you are experiencing survivor guilt because you were not physically victimized as another person in your family was, you need to consider your role in the family in light of the dynamics of abuse.

The emotional dynamics common to abusive families include denial, guilt, and shame.

Denial is a common phenomenon in violent homes. Both the abuser and the abused person (as well as other family members) tend to deny, discount, or trivialize the abuse. Take Sarah's account of her childhood, for example:

> You psychologists are all the same! You're all a bunch of softies. I don't feel betrayed, powerless, or any of those other things you say I feel. My father only whipped my sister to straighten her out. She was always acting up. He just used the belt to keep her in line.
>
> Yeah, he drew blood and left welts on her legs. But she appreciated it. She knew he was doing it for her own good. Personally, I don't think there's anything wrong with what he did. You're making a big deal out of nothing. These things happen in families. They're normal.

The key word here is *normal*. Sarah didn't validate the traumas her sister endured as a child because for Sarah they were normal. As an adult, however, Sarah has begun to look back on her denial of her sister's abuse with horror and feels guilt for her denial. Like others who live in violent homes, Sarah was aided in her denial by both the abuser and the abused. Both her father and sister called the violence "nothing" and dismissed major injuries as "scratches."

Some family members take it upon themselves to try to rescue the victim. But more often they share in the denial, numb themselves to the violence, or imitate the aggressor. If they come to identify with and copy the aggressor's behavior, they may also begin to abuse the victim, another family member, or people or property outside the home. They are then candidates not only for survivor guilt but also moral or atrocity guilt as described in chapter 3.

If you grew up in a violent home, the first step toward healing is acknowledging the abuse. Such an admission may be painful and difficult for you. It means relinquishing the illusion that your family was normal and that the abuser "really loved" you and the victim. Perhaps this person truly did love you both, but he or she was also abusive. You need to look that abuse square in the face, in all its gory details, before you can fully understand yourself.

In many cases, having witnessed physical or sexual abuse in the family is the missing piece in self-understanding. It is not unusual for individuals who have suffered stress as adults to undergo counseling for their adult difficulties, but still be plagued with survivor guilt and other symptoms. Sometimes they interpret the persistence of the symptoms as signs that they are hopeless cases. Their physicians and therapists, too, may view them as especially resistant cases. Instead, however, the problem may be that exposure to childhood abuse or family violence, with its attendant pain and guilt, has not been recognized. Or, if it has been recognized, it may have been discounted or minimized, as in Sarah's case. In other instances, adult trauma, such as a vehicular accident, brings childhood trauma to the fore.

Along with denial, guilt and shame are the hallmarks of those who endure, as well as those who witness, family violence. This guilt and shame is based on two myths: that you caused the abuse and that you should have been able to prevent it.

*Myth 1. "It must be my fault."* Consciously or unconsciously you may feel that some attribute of yours spared you from the kind of abuse inflicted or caused it to happen to someone in your family. The attribute may be positive or negative. For example, if you got better grades than the family member who was being abused, you might feel that your dedication to your schoolwork or your high intelligence level spared you. On the one hand, you may feel glad that something positive about you helped you. On the other hand, you may feel guilty that you have certain positive qualities that the victim lacked.

On the negative side, suppose you did something to anger the abuser and instead of harming you, the abuser harmed the victim in the family. In such cases, your guilt could be tremendous, especially if the abuser says, "See what I'm doing. You're making me do it." But even in this circumstance, you are not responsible for the abuse. It is the abuser, not you, who uses force. You are not shoving, kicking, hitting, or sexually abusing the victim. These are the actions of the abuser. All abusers are responsible for their own behavior.

In addition, it is not your personal inadequacies and failures, or even your positive traits, that cause the abuse. The abuse has more to do with the abuser's feelings of inadequacy and difficulties handling frustration and other feelings than anything you said, did, or thought. Violence in the family reflects the emotional temperament of the abuser, not the actions or personality of other nonviolent family members.

*Myth 2. "I let it happen."* Family members often feel guilty for having "allowed the abuse." Although the abuser betrayed the family unit by harming someone in the family, you may also feel as if you betrayed yourself—your dignity, your self-esteem, your worth as a person—by not having been able to stop the abuse.

"I should have at least run away from home to protest what was going on," the son of an abused woman states. In truth, many children who witness violence between their parents do run away from home, but not while they are very young. Financial and emotional dependence on the family may leave you no choice but to stay at home. Also, there are many traps that keep family members (including victims) in homes where there is violence.

## Traps

There are numerous complex and powerful forces that keep family members stuck in emotionally and physically destructive homes and unable to take action to stop the abuse or assist the victims. Due to these forces, adolescents and adults can be as paralyzed in taking action or as entrapped in homes where there is violence as a preschool child would be.

If you grew up in a home where there was abuse, you may have been stuck in it and unable to help those who were being harmed for reasons that had nothing to do with your alleged cowardice or insensitivity. The ways the abusive family member can trap you may be physical, financial, or psychological.

*Physical traps.* Abusers often threaten to harm or kill their victims, other people, pets, or even themselves if family members protest or report the abuse or try to leave home. In some cases, the abuser may actually lock family members in rooms. If a family member is disabled, the abuser may threaten to exploit the disability in order to prevent him or her from reporting the abuse or leaving home.

*Financial traps.* Abusers often financially imprison not only their victims but other family members, by taking control of or squandering the family's income or property or by threatening financial warfare or ruin should someone in the family decide to protest the abuse, leave home, or otherwise "make difficulties." It's part of the pattern of control in abusive situations for the abuser to come to hold all the financial power in the family, either by psychological manipulation or through other forms of coercion. Such financial control is as powerful, if not more powerful, than the weapon of physical abuse.

*Emotional traps.* Still other traps are virtually invisible. These are emotional traps. They can be even harder to overcome than the economic chains that the abuser can wrap around the family. Often these emotional traps revolve around love and need. Although you might be ashamed to tell your therapist, support group, or others, a part of you may still love the person who is abusing your family member.

If you grew up in a home where there was violence, there is a high probability that your legitimate needs for nurturing, emotional support, and love were not met. You might have been severely neglected. Given this background, your need for love and approval from the abuser may understandably be very high. Today, however, you might feel guilty for loving and needing the person who was hurting someone else you loved, and that guilt can be a part of your survivor guilt.

Your legitimate need for love from the abusive family member becomes especially confusing when the abuser does truly love you and may even love the victim. There are abusers who are genuinely bonded to and have real positive feelings for the victim and other family members, but nevertheless use the victim as a scapegoat for present or past frustrations.

Another force that keeps family members quiet about the abuse and prevents them from reporting it and helping the victim is the abuser's threat of suicide. Such threats may be sincere or they may be attempts at manipulation. But even manipulators sometimes commit suicide. For example, in one instance a fifteen-year-old girl threatened to report her father to the police if he did not stop molesting her sister. The father threatened to commit suicide if she did so. Other family members, including the victim, begged her not to involve the authorities. Undeterred, the young girl reported her father. Before he could be apprehended for questioning, the father threw himself in front of a train. In the suicide note, he blamed his suicide on being reported. Afterward, the family ostracized the girl for "killing" her father. She does not have survivor guilt about her sister's incest, but she does about her father's suicide.

The battering cycle is one of the most powerful emotional traps. Lenore Walker (1979), the first psychologist to systematically study violent relationships, found that battering is neither random nor constant, especially when abuse occurs in the context of marriage or a sexual relationship. Instead battering often occurs in a repeated pattern, a cycle with three distinct stages:

1. The tension-building stage

2. The acute battering incident

3. The phase of kindness and contrite, loving behavior (the "honeymoon" stage)

In stage one, the tension-building stage, tensions arise between the abuser and the victim that ultimately lead to stage two, the acute battering incident. The abuser's repentance is totally believable, and the family believes that there will be no more violence. Stage three is powerful. It is in this stage that the family's dream of having a stable, harmonious family life is renewed. This stage accounts for the violent family's enigmatic ability to quickly forget or minimize painful episodes, sometimes almost as soon as they occur.

## Survival Guilt Stemming from the Death of a Child

In an ancient Greek myth, Thetis, a sea goddess, wanted to be sure that nothing harmful would befall her newborn baby boy, Achilles. As a goddess, Thetis was immortal, but her baby was the child of her union with a human and could not live forever. So, to protect the baby from harm, she held him by his heel and dipped him in the magic waters of the River Styx.

The baby, touched by the magic waters, became physically invulnerable—save for the one part of his body his mother had held him by, his heel. When Achilles became a warrior, many arrows and swords assaulted his arms, legs, and torso, but he was never wounded. His mother's magical protection kept him invincible. Ultimately, though, an arrow did pierce the one small spot on his body that the magic river had not touched, and he died of that wound.

The myth of Thetis symbolizes the universal human desire of parents to provide their children with invisible shields of protection. Both men and women are biologically wired to be responsive to cries for help from young children, especially their own children. Hence the death of a child can be more devastating than the death of a parent or sibling. In Western society, where it is expected that children will outlive their parents, the death of a child is considered a form of trauma.

Like other traumas, the death of a child can activate intense feelings of helplessness and self-blame. Parents, siblings, and other relatives of the child may suffer from intense survivor guilt, even if the child's death was not the result of a traumatic incident, but of an illness or minor accident. If the parents or grandparents had bad habits or felt guilty about some aspect of their lives, they may erroneously conclude that their bad habits or some objectionable aspect of their lifestyle caused the death of the child. Kubany (1996) cites the case of a grandfather whose grandchild died of sudden infant death syndrome. This grandfather felt he had caused the death of the grandchild because he smoked. In some cases, parents who quarrel frequently or who divorce may feel that their conflicts caused, or at least contributed to, the death of the child.

Survivor guilt may be exacerbated in circumstances where the child was seriously ill and numerous medical expenses were incurred. The child's illness may have taxed the parents not only financially but emotionally and professionally as well. Given the tremendous burden that caring for a sick child can entail, even the most devoted parent might think, "I wish my child would die so this hell would be over with." Few parents would admit to such thoughts, but it would be abnormal for a parent, or anyone else, not to have some resentment about the interruption to their life and the anxiety and costs involved in taking care of a chronically or seriously ill child.

In other cases, the child may have been a problem child, for example, a drug addict, an alcoholic, or a juvenile delinquent. The child may have wreaked havoc in the parents' lives and made it difficult for the parents to tend to their other children or other responsibilities. There may have been a feeling of relief upon hearing that this problem child was dead. While the feeling of relief is entirely normal and the feeling of relief did not cause the death of the child, the parents may experience considerable guilt when they reflect on having such a feeling.

The same holds true for other relatives. Children who are destructive toward themselves or others disrupt the lives of not only their parents but also their siblings and other relatives. These other relatives may feel guilty for having been angry at the child and for any feelings of relief that someone who troubled them will trouble them no more.

In some cultures, children who die before they reach adolescence and have the opportunity to contribute to their families are seen as having failed in meeting their obligations to the family. For example, in some traditional Chinese peasant groups, children who die young are not given a soul card, which is a prerequisite for being honored in death (Henricks 1994). The feeling is that the child doesn't deserve to be honored since all he or she has done is consume the family's resources without having given back. Such feelings complicate any feelings of survivor guilt, since the family members must cope with two contradictory sets of feelings: on the one hand, a sense of loss and guilt and on the other hand, a sense of betrayal and anger at the child for having abandoned the family.

Nevertheless, the death of a child, even a problem child, is one of the most devastating losses a parent or close relative can experience. It was the loss of his son Tad that escalated President Abraham Lincoln's depression and pushed Mrs. Lincoln into seclusion and severe mental illness.

The story of the mythological figure of Aegeus, King of Athens, provides a classic example of parental grief over the loss of a child. When King Aegeus was subject to Minos, King of Crete, Minos inflicted on the Athenians the worst form of torture and punishment he could devise: he required the Athenians to send him twelve young women and twelve young men every year to be fed to the Minotaur, a monster whom he kept in a labyrinth.

Each year, the young men and women of Athens had to parade in front of Cretan officers who would pick out the healthiest and handsomest young people to be eaten alive. King Aegeus kept his son, Theseus, hidden for many years. But when his son grew up, he felt it wasn't fair that he should stay safe just because he was the son of the king, and he wanted to be part of the parade. Aegeus protested, but Theseus would not listen. As luck would have it, Theseus was chosen by the Cretans to be sent to die in the labyrinth. Aegeus begged Theseus to flee, but Theseus wanted to save Athens from future human sacrifice. He was confident that with the help of the gods, he could kill the Minotaur once and for all.

The ship that took the Athenian children to be eaten by the Minotaur had black sails, the color black being a symbol of mourning. As Theseus boarded the black-sailed boat, Aegeus gave him a set of white sails. "If you succeed in slaying the Minotaur, then put on the white sails. I will see the sails from a distance and rejoice. If I see black sails, I will die of a broken heart. Don't forget, my son," said Aegeus.

Theseus promised not to forget, but he did forget. When he succeeded in slaying the Minotaur in Crete, he was in such a hurry to get home and tell his father, that he forgot to take off the black sails and put on the white ones.

After Theseus left, every day Aegeus went to a cliff that overlooked the ocean and looked for the boat. While Aegeus waited, he agonized. He wondered why he hadn't offered Minos all his wealth in exchange for his son's life. He was so distraught he forgot that he had offered Minos all his wealth and that Minos had refused it. "Your child is your wealth," Minos had said. "If I take that from you, I take everything."

Aegeus then wondered why he hadn't hidden his son and gone in his son's place. He forgot that Theseus had adamantly refused to be hidden and that the captive Athenian boys were put on the ship half-clothed. Even if Theseus had been willing to hide, if Aegeus had tried to pretend to be his son, his aging body would have given him away. Obviously this was not a time for reason, but for feeling.

One day Aegeus saw a ship coming toward Athens. It had black sails. Aegeus was so struck with grief, and guilt, that he flung himself over the cliff. The Agean Sea is named after him.

## *Survival Guilt Stemming from Suicide or Homicide*

Every twenty seconds, someone in the United States commits suicide (Heckler 1994). It is the eighth leading cause of death in the United States.

People who commit suicide leave behind parents, family members, friends, neighbors, and others who are beset not only with grief but also with a multitude of agonizing, often unanswerable questions. Why did it happen? Did I miss some of the warning signs? Why didn't I pay attention to the warning signs I did see? What could I have done to prevent it? What could others have done? Who is really to blame? How much am I to blame?

Similarly, homicide victims leave behind parents, teachers, friends, and a host of others who wonder if they contributed to the homicide, and if so, how much, or if they could have done something to prevent it.

The suicide or homicide of a family member, friend, neighbor, or co-worker can generate tremendous survivor guilt, as well as other feelings. Survivor guilt over one suicide or homicide can also activate repressed survivor guilt from previous situations, both traumatic and non-traumatic. For example, the death of Joseph's friend by suicide activated his survivor guilt regarding the fact that his father was injured in a car accident many years ago.

Suicides and homicides can generate survivor guilt in nonfamily members who tried to help the victim, for example, friends, twelve-step sponsors, neighbors, and therapy group members, or who knew the victim in a professional capacity, such as co-workers, therapists, clergy persons, physicians, teachers, coaches, and personal trainers. Suicides and homicides can also generate survivor guilt in those who did not know the victim well, but whose vocational role includes the attempt to prevent such deaths. For example, a school principal may feel survivor guilt regarding the homicide or suicide of a student, even if he or she didn't know the student well, because a principal's role includes trying to foresee and prevent such events.

Survivor guilt over a homicide or suicide is compounded when the homicide or suicide victim is a child, or if there are other conflicts in the family. When a child of divorce commits suicide, parents will usually wonder if their divorce contributed to the suicide. It's easy for any guilt regarding the divorce to become mixed in with survivor guilt over the suicide of the child. In some cases, one parent will not experience the survivor guilt, but will project the guilt onto the other parent.

For example, Esther and Jeff divorced when their daughter Erica was thirteen. They had two children younger than Erica and two older than Erica, but Erica seemed to be the most affected. When she stayed with Jeff, she cooked and cleaned and tried to comfort her father emotionally. When she stayed with Esther, she also cooked and cleaned and tried to soothe her mother. She listened to her father talk angrily about her mother and her mother talk angrily about her father. She was always patient and calm, never taking sides, but always showing love to each parent.

One night Jeff and Esther fought bitterly over Esther taking on an evening job. Jeff called Esther a whore and denigrated her in other ways. Esther claimed she had to take the job because Jeff wasn't paying enough child support. Erica went from one parent to the other, trying to calm them down.

That night, Erica swallowed a bottle of lethal medication. The next morning her mother found her dead in the bathroom with a suicide note asking both parents to please stop fighting so much.

Each parent blamed the other. To this day, the parents deny having any guilt feelings, or any grief. Neither parent mentions Erica's name, and both of them act as if Erica never existed. They do not allow her name to be spoken in their homes.

Yet their survivor guilt expresses itself in other ways. They stopped fighting immediately and go out of their way to support their remaining children. Now Erica's father calls his other children every night to make sure they're safe. If there's any kind of storm, he calls two or three times a night. He's bought them expensive security systems and takes their cars to be serviced on a regular basis. Erica's mother lavishes large sums of money, expensive clothing, and whatever she can afford on her surviving children. She even married a man she didn't love because he was wealthy and she knew that he would take good care of her children.

## Intergenerational Aspects of Trauma-Related Survivor Guilt

Parents, children, and other relatives of trauma survivors (including siblings) may absorb some of the trauma survivor's pain, anger—and survivor guilt. There is considerable evidence that trauma, including survivor guilt, can be transmitted from one generation to the next. As Carmella's story illustrates, the lives of family members may well be shaped or significantly affected by the survivor guilt they inherited from a traumatized family member. Carmella, the granddaughter of an atrocity survivor, carries with her the traumas her grandmother endured.

When my grandmother Amelia was seven years old, civil war broke out in her country. Her family fled, but within a year her parents died of starvation in a refugee camp. She felt responsible for her parents' deaths because they used to give her and their other children most of their food. She feels, and justifiably so, that if her parents had had more to eat, they wouldn't have died. The fact that in the camps it was usually the children who died before the adults made her feel even guiltier.

When her youngest brother died of typhoid, she felt guilty about that, too. Lots of times she'd grab some of his food for herself. When he protested, she'd pull his ear and tell him to stop complaining. "You're smaller. You don't need as much food as I do, and if you tell that I took your food, I'll hit you," she told him. Until the day she died, she said she wished she had died in his place.

You're probably wondering how I know all these details. The truth is I know my grandmother's story inside out. When I was little, I used to pray with her. She'd cry a lot and ask God to forgive her for taking the food from her brother and wishing that he would die so that she could have more food for herself. I was the one who had to sit with her when she had her heart attacks. They weren't real heart attacks. They were panic attacks. But some of the symptoms are similar.

Every time there were pictures of a war on the TV, my grandma would start hyperventilating and almost pass out. She'd ask us to call the priest because she thought she was having a heart attack and going to die. My dad would put her in bed, and then I had to sit by her and listen to her mutter: "The people are dying . . . Mother, father, brother . . . I took their food. God forgive me. God forgive me."

If I tried to give her some juice or food, she'd become hysterical. "I don't need food. I don't deserve food," she would say and sob even harder. Then she'd start muttering about all the atrocities she had seen and start praying for all the people who died and for forgiveness for all her sins.

Grandma stayed in the camp until she was fourteen, when she was able to return to her village. I know she had survivor guilt because after she got to the village she took on a martyr role. She wouldn't let any of the relatives help her and tried to be mother and father to her brothers. She sent them to school, but wouldn't go herself. Instead she worked in the fields and took care of the home. Her brothers had the best meals and the best clothes. She ate leftovers and wore the same old clothes all the time. Even before she died, she refused to buy nice clothes for herself, always saying the money was needed for her brothers or some other relatives from the village.

My grandma was a beautiful young woman, but she would have died an old maid if an American soldier hadn't fallen in love with her and offered to take her to the United States. She didn't love him, but she married him anyway because she figured that in America she could work and send money to her brothers and other survivors of the civil war.

In the United States, she worked all the time. Her husband made a good living, but she slaved in a bakery ten to twelve hours a day to send money to her brothers. She put them through graduate school and helped finance their homes. She denied herself all the time, but it made her happy to give to others. She used to tell me God gave her a chance to atone for her guilt by letting her work hard and help her brothers and others in the village. One of her crowning achievements was building a small medical clinic in her village. She named it after her brother who died.

I'm an adult now. Grandma Amelia died over twenty years ago, but she, and her sorrow and guilt, is alive and well in me. Her lamentations are permanently embedded in my mind, and I can visualize every atrocity she described as if I were there. If I close my eyes, I can see my great-grandparents giving food to their children, my grandmother grabbing food from her brother, and my great-uncle dying of typhoid. I also see the corpses of people who died in that civil war. And inside, I feel guilty.

It's crazy, but even though I wasn't even born yet, I feel responsible for what my grandmother saw. I feel guilty being happy and having so much when my people suffered so. Why was I so lucky to have been born in the United States?

Because of my grandmother, I feel a moral obligation to help people who suffer, and, like my grandmother, I feel guilty when I eat good food or buy nice clothes. Because of

our family's history, my brothers and sisters feel an obligation to help the needy too, but my grandmother's guilt
doesn't run their lives like it does mine. Sometimes I think
of changing jobs and doing something that doesn't involve
helping people in need. But whenever I contemplate the
idea, the images of my great-grandparents and great-uncle
and all the others who died as a result of that civil war flash
in front of me. It's amazing to me that I'm having flashbacks
about a trauma I was never in but that is, nevertheless, very
much a part of me.

It's as if the trauma sets off a shock wave that reverberates
through the next generation, and sometimes though the generation
after that, as in Carmella's case. There are several ways that survivor
guilt can be passed down from one generation to the next. One of the
chief ways is through identification with the parent, where the child
identifies with the parent's emotional pain, including the parent's
survivor guilt. However, in families where the traumatized parent is
severely depressed and guilt-ridden, children, especially adolescents,
may reject the parent and try not to identify with the parent because
they don't want to be as depressed and unhappy as their mother or
father (or both). However, not identifying with this parent can lead to
guilt, since the child may feel he or she is abandoning a parent who
has had more than his or her fair share of pain in life (Dimsdale
1964). The child can feel so guilty about having a better life than his
or her parent that, in some cases, the child wishes he or she had
borne the trauma instead of the parent. When the child wishes he or
she could exchange places with the adult, then this is a case of intergenerational transmission of survivor guilt. Sometimes children have
fantasies or daydreams about going through the parent's trauma and
coming out victorious or rescuing the parent. Or perhaps they wish
they could carry the parent's load of anger, pain, or guilt so the parent would be happy and free to love them and be a nurturing parent.
This is also a case of intergenerational transmission of survivor guilt.

There are other ways survivor guilt can be passed from one generation to the next. These include the effects of the emotional distancing of the traumatized parent; the possibility that one child becomes
the traumatized family member's helper and emotional support system; and secondary traumatization.

### Effects of Emotional Distancing

Many traumatized parents with survivor guilt are extremely
capable and involved parents. Some, however, have difficulty with

intimate relationships, especially with their spouses and children. As a result they may either withdraw, become overinvolved, or use their family members as scapegoats for the unresolved pain, anger, and other feelings left over from their trauma. When a parent emotionally withdraws from a child, the child usually sees the parent's alienation as a rejection, even though it may not be.

Young children, between the ages of four and seven, may blame themselves for the parent's withdrawal. Between these ages, children's understanding of the world is egocentric. In their view, the world revolves around their needs, and they believe their thoughts and wishes can actually cause external events. Hence they often blame themselves for their parent's alienation, anger, or depression. Even if the child were to be given some education about the parent's traumatic experiences, that child would have difficulty digesting and comprehending such information. Furthermore, under stress adolescents, like young adults and even adults, can regress into egocentric ways of thinking (Suhr 1986).

By the time children have reached the ages of seven or eight, their capacity for concrete reasoning has increased. Now they are able to see cause and effect more clearly. Yet, since they are usually not told about the impact of the trauma on their parent, they may still personalize the parent's alienation. They may feel that the parent doesn't like them or is rejecting them because they did something wrong. Hence, the parent's survivor guilt is passed on in the form of guilt of being or guilt of doing in the child. (See chapter 1 for the definitions of guilt of being and guilt of doing.)

## When Children Repress Anger

If children sense that the traumatized parent is depressed or sad or if they fear that the parent will be irritable or have a rage reaction, they may learn to be quiet. Among children of Nazi holocaust survivors, an inhibition of angry feelings has been found. These children often keep their angry feelings to themselves because they do not want to cause additional suffering to their obviously already suffering parents. Also, they do not want the parents to feel guilty about doing something that resulted in their children's becoming angry and rejecting them; they know or sense that their parents already feel guilty enough for having survived. If they do say or do something to upset the traumatized parent, they may experience deep guilt feelings at having further burdened an already emotionally burdened parent.

Children also tend to repress because they have a hard time being angry at those on whom they are emotionally or financially dependent. If the anger is expressed, there is a high risk of alienating the person whose love, attention, and support is so desperately needed. Children's repressed anger can eventually emerge in the form of self-mutilation, suicidal thoughts, and sudden outbursts of aggression.

When the traumatized parent sees the child being self-destructive or violent toward others, that parent's guilt feelings may increase. The parent may now feel guiltier than ever because his or her child is acting in a violent manner. If the parent can't differentiate survivor guilt from the other types of guilt, the survivor guilt may increase or the parent may see the child's negative behavior as a form of punishment for his or her actions or inactions, thoughts, or feelings during the traumatic event.

## Mother's Helper

In homes where one parent is exceptionally stressed, as well as lonely, that parent may, in desperation, turn to one of the children for excessive emotional or other forms of support. The parent may be stressed either because he or she has an untreated trauma history or because the other parent does and is therefore not sufficiently emotionally available as a partner or a parent.

In Marsha's home, for example, the birth of a fourth child set off a panic attack in her father, Robert, who suffered from survivor guilt as the result of being an army surgeon during a mass casualty. As a result, her mother, Lena, began to depend on eight-year-old Marsha for a lot. Robert had saved many lives, but he couldn't forget the many people who died in his operating room. "Birth reminds me of death," Robert wrote in his diary. "When I first saw the shriveled mass that was my newborn daughter, I felt pangs of guilt, thinking about how all the people who died were once little babies like that. Some of them died like that—as shriveled masses.

"As much as I hate to admit it, right there, in the delivery room, I decided not to love my daughter. Why should she be alive when those guys died? As a matter of fact, why should I be alive and entitled to have yet another child when a lot of the guys who died under my knife didn't even have the chance to get married? It makes me wonder what it's all about, why we struggle so hard in life, only to die in the end. Sometimes I wonder why I bother to live at all. Maybe a man like me, who saw so many people die and who can't even love his newborn daughter, shouldn't be alive at all."

As Robert's last statement reveals, he was depressed and suffered from severe survivor guilt as well. Yet Robert found it difficult to admit that he suffered any psychological effects from the war. During his medical training he, like most medical professionals, was taught to "develop a high degree of clinical detachment" (Shovar 1987). Such emotional detachment, he learned, was absolutely necessary in order to make the right medical decisions, but it also served to harden him to many of his own emotional reactions to the war. But he could not detach himself from his guilt. In addition, Robert was reluctant to admit to having survivor guilt, or any other kind of emotional problem, because he feared losing his professional standing and position.

Despite his wife's insistence, Robert refused to seek help. Even when his depression affected his ability to stay focused on intellectual tasks and Lena had to help him with his report writing, he refused to see a therapist or doctor. When he withdrew from her and the children, Lena had to shoulder the burden of parenting alone. She felt like a "married single parent."

"It started when I found Mom crying in the kitchen, saying 'God help me. I can't do it all. I just can't do it all,'" says Marsha.

"'I'll help you, Mommy,' I said, and from that day on I helped with all the dishwashing and dinner preparations and cleanup. I felt proud to be able to help my mom, and when the new baby got old enough for me to hold, I took over being Mom to him, too.

"I didn't mind not being able to watch TV after school, but I did mind having to give up Girl Scouts. But Mom needed me more and more, and I had to help her so she could help Daddy so our family wouldn't be poor and have to move."

It wasn't Lena's turning to her daughter for household help that was destructive, but rather Lena's sharing her marital secrets and emotional pain with her daughter. As Lena instructed her daughter in certain chores, or as they did them together, Lena would often graphically describe to Marsha how Robert verbally denigrated her and how disappointed she was in her marriage.

At the age of eight, Marsha was unprepared to hear her mother's secrets about her father, yet she also felt privileged that her mother would turn to her. Since her father was usually emotionally distant from her and had often disappointed her, Marsha quickly sided with her mother. Yet, as a child, she still wanted and needed to believe that her father was a good man.

Surely her Daddy wasn't that bad, she thought. And if he was so horrible, didn't that make her, as his daughter, horrible too? Also, Marsha felt disloyal listening to her mother talk against her father. But how, at age eight, could she tell her poor overworked Mommy to stop?

As a child, Marsha had few defenses against her mother's feelings. She was easily overpowered by them and they became a part of her personality. Instead of developing along her own lines and having her own feelings, Marsha took on her mother's personality and emotions.

Like her mother, she felt guilty for not being able to alleviate Robert's depression. She also felt guilty for not being able to "save" her mother from emotional pain, overwork, and feelings of futility. She felt guilty for being happy when her mother was so unhappy and hence, via an indirect circuit, was suffering from survivor guilt that stemmed from her father's survivor guilt. Just as her father felt guilty for not having been able to save dying soldiers and for still being alive while they were dead, Marsha felt guilty for not having been able to "save" her mother and for being joyful about life when her mother was so disappointed with her own life.

There are many Marshas in the world. As they mature into young women, they may keep their "good girl" role of mother's helper or caring daughter, or they may become "bad girls" and abuse alcohol, drugs, and sex, all as a means of showing disregard for parental needs and rules.

In some cases adolescent sexual, addictive, and other forms of destructive behavior can be a defiant act against one or both parents or against being forced into a parental role in the family. The same interpretation may also hold for reckless behavior in that it may be a means of expressing anger toward the parent (or parents) to whom the child was formerly tightly bonded in a helper capacity. All these behaviors may be attempts to, as one child stated, "get my parent's stupid trauma out of my head."

The impact of the child's acting-out behavior on the parent with survivor guilt is generally that of increasing that parent's survivor guilt. Not only does the parent feel guilty for what occurred in the past, but the parent can also feel guilty for having failed his or her child. Even though in today's world, children are subject to many influences other than their parents, a parent with untreated survivor guilt may well take on all the responsibility and guilt for a child's misbehavior, just as he or she did for the traumatic or stressful incident that caused his or her survivor guilt.

## Secondary Traumatization

Marsha and her mother illustrate a case of mother-daughter enmeshment stemming from the father's unresolved survivor guilt and other untreated traumatic reactions. Such enmeshment can also occur when one of the children becomes traumatized by the parent's trauma. This process, called *secondary traumatization*, involves the child, in some manner, reliving the parent's or other close relative's trauma or becoming obsessed with the trauma-related issues that trouble and concern the relative. The child may even manifest symptoms similar to the relative's, such as having nightmares about the trauma or worrying a great deal about death and injury.

I have observed several children and young adults evidencing secondary traumatization. Many displayed symptoms of post-traumatic stress disorder, such as an obsession with power and violence, difficulties concentrating, irritability, and rage reactions. Some children who suffer from secondary traumatization may assume a "rescuer" role in relation to the traumatized family member; some do not. In other cases, the rescuer role may be assumed by another child in the family who takes it upon himself or herself to make the traumatized relative happy (Rosenheck 1985, 1986). These children often spend an inordinate amount of time with the traumatized family member and may make that family member their best, if not only, friend.

For example, the daughter of a rape victim can visualize the rape as if it were part of a movie she were watching. Not only does she visualize the rape, detail by detail, but she feels her mother's feelings, thinks her mother's thoughts, as well as the thoughts and feelings of the rapist. She spends most of her free time with her mother, trying to protect her mother from overwork and others' criticisms, and in any way possible tries to save her mother from her pain. She feels guilty when her mother expresses any anguish over the rape and wishes she could have been raped instead of her mother or that she could have rescued her mother from the rapist. Her wish to save her mother and guilt about not having done so are even expressed in her dreams.

Problems arise when, due to the natural changes of adolescence and adulthood, the growing child or young adult wants to separate from the traumatized relative. At this point, the child may feel guilty about experiencing the normal adolescent process of separating and becoming an individual, as if in growing up he or she is abandoning the traumatized family member. If the traumatized family member becomes more depressed, withdrawn, or angry as a result of the child's growing independence, then the child may feel as if his or her leaving is harming the relative, which in turn contributes to survivor guilt.

# Normal-Life Survivor Guilt

Normal life circumstances can also create survivor guilt. Survivor guilt is common following the death of a loved one due to normal causes or following a miscarriage. Both content and existential survivor guilt can develop in families where there is emotional favoritism or emotional abuse; where there is chronic or severe illness; or where there is alcohol- or other forms or addiction. Witnessing a co-worker being harassed is another possible cause of survivor guilt. If you are a member of a minority or historically oppressed group, being more successful than others in your group may also give rise to feelings of survivor guilt.

## Normal Bereavement

The death of a grandparent, parent, spouse, sibling or friend can give rise to survivor guilt marked by questions such as: "Why did she have to die?" "Why couldn't I have died in his place?" This type of survivor guilt can be viewed as part of the bargaining phase of the grieving process, as described by Dr. Elizabeth Kubler-Ross (1981). It is commonly experienced as part of normal bereavement. Anniversary reactions to such losses can also contain elements of survivor guilt.

## Survivor Guilt Related to Severe or Chronic Illness or Miscarriage

Severe or chronic illnesses are potentially life-threatening and can lead to loss of bodily integrity. Technically, having cancer, MS, leukemia, or some other severe or chronic condition can not be classified as trauma; nevertheless, survivor guilt can occur when a family member, friend, or co-worker is stricken with a severe illness, such as cancer or diabetes, or a chronic disability.

Women who miscarry can also experience survivor guilt. They may feel guilty that they lived and the baby died, especially if a choice had to be made between the mother's life and the life of the child. Siblings may feel survivor guilt regarding a sibling lost to miscarriage or early death.

## Survivor Guilt Related to Alcoholism or Addiction

One response to having an alcoholic, drug-addicted, or eating-disordered family member or friend is to feel somehow responsible for that individual's addiction. This is a kind of global guilt where you feel you've caused or contributed to the family member's addiction. This type of guilt, however, is not survivor guilt. In situations where there is addiction in the family, survivor guilt refers to *(a)* the feeling that you should suffer the addiction in place of the addicted family member or *(b)* guilt over not being similarly addicted.

In Western society the term *co-dependence* has been used to describe situations where one person becomes so enmeshed in another person's life that he or she is willing to sacrifice his or her own needs and development in hopes of helping the other person. The notion of co-dependence could only arise in a society that values the individual over the community and the family. What Western society calls co-dependence would be expected loyal behavior in societies that value community and family over the self.

It's a misnomer to call a person who would like to take on the affliction of a family member co-dependent. Rather, the individual who wishes to suffer in place of another is someone who loves the other person dearly and feels powerless to help that other person stop the self-destruction of his or her addiction. The only possible solution is the primitive one of substitution: the superstitious idea that you take someone else's place in suffering.

For example, Renna's mother suffered from bulimia nervosa. When Renna was thirteen, she, too, developed an eating disorder. There are many possible interpretations for Renna's eating disorder. For example, she could have simply been imitating her mother, or perhaps the same family pressures that made her mother subject to an eating disorder affected Renna in a similar way. However, when Renna was asked what sparked her eating disorder, she replied, "If I do it, then Mommy won't have to. If someone in the family has to do it, I better do it because Mommy's doctor said she would have a heart attack if she kept on doing it." With this type of motivation, Renna's eating disorder can be seen as being rooted in survivor guilt.

## Survivor Guilt Related to Emotional Abuse or Favoritism

Even though emotional abuse or favoritism in a family is not necessarily traumatic, it can create survivor guilt among those spared abuse or those who receive the favors of the parents or other empowered individuals in the family. Beth explains:

> I was the prettiest girl in the family. My father doted on me, and my mom bought me the best clothes. My sisters were jealous, and justifiably so. But all I wanted was to be a part of them, to feel like I belonged to the family. That never

happened. The jealousy was too strong. Not only did my sisters push me away, but my aunts and female cousins did too. None of them wanted me around their husbands or boyfriends. Even though my looks were superior, I felt inferior inside, and guilty.

So to punish myself, I acted the part of the vain, selfish beauty. I used my looks to seduce supervisors, get good jobs, and special favors. Then I could hate myself for doing what good-looking women have been accused of doing for centuries.

When my sister's husband left her for a younger, prettier woman, I felt guilty, as if I caused it. I made big scratches on my face to punish myself. I wanted to go comfort my sister, but I knew she wouldn't want my help. So I sent her a big check instead.

When I got into my thirties, I wanted people to pay attention to more than my appearance, but all they saw was my looks. I entered a master's program in education, but no one took me seriously. When I got rejected for jobs because I was too good-looking for the men and the women, I saw it as punishment for having hurt my brothers and sisters by getting my parent's special attentions and love.

## Survivor Guilt Related to Work-Related Harassment

Workers who witness their co-workers being harassed or verbally abused may acquire survivor guilt, especially if the targeted co-worker is suspended, fired, or denied privileges accorded to most other employees. (See Arnie's story in the section on minimizing in chapter 3 for an example of this.)

## Survivor Guilt among Minority Groups and Historically Oppressed Groups

Denise, the divorced mother of two preschool children, came from a middle-class African American home that provided her with comfortable surroundings, good medical care, and a college education. Denise earns enough to pay her bills, but not much more.

When Latisha, one of Denise's co-workers, was evicted from her apartment, she asked Denise if she could stay with her until she found a new place. Denise hesitated. She felt a bond with Latisha as a fellow African American woman, but she feared, and justifiably so, that Latisha and her three children, in combination with her own two children, would make life in her two-bedroom apartment unbearably cramped. Denise also wondered how long she could afford to feed Latisha and her family, as Latisha had made it clear that she had no funds. Furthermore, Denise did not particularly like Latisha. Several times, Latisha had been sarcastic with her at work.

Nevertheless, Denise let Latisha and her children move in. When Denise's therapist asked her why she had made this decision, Denise explained that she felt guilty because her life had been so much easier than Latisha's. Latisha had been raised in poverty and had never had the economic and other advantages that Denise and other middle-class African American women had enjoyed. Denise wondered why she had been fortunate enough to have escaped the hardships that Latisha and other impoverished African American women had to face and felt guilty for not wanting to share what she had.

Even when Latisha's children began to quarrel with her children and Denise had to borrow money to help feed Latisha and her family, Denise did not ask Latisha to move out. Denise developed severe headaches and anxiety attacks due to the stress of coping with Latisha and her family, but she still could not bring herself to ask them to leave.

As Denise's story illustrates, members of minority groups may experience survivor guilt when they overcome certain societal and personal obstacles and achieve more economic security, social acceptance, and other rewards that have been historically denied to their minority group. The survivor guilt arises from having succeeded where others in their social, economic, ethnic, or religious group have not succeeded or have succeeded to a lesser degree.

Another aspect of this form of survivor guilt arises from no longer identifying with your original group to the same extent or in the same ways. The survivor guilt can also stem from not needing members of your original group as much as prior to the success or from feeling separate or alienated from your family of origin or original group.

For example, a young woman who obtains a medical degree may feel survivor guilt with respect to her mother (or other female relatives or friends) who were discouraged from pursuing medical careers due to gender discrimination or the dominant sex role stereotypes of their time. Lesbians and gay men who have not experienced significant job discrimination because of their sexual orientation may experience survivor guilt toward those who've been demoted, lost promotions, or been fired because of their sexual preference.

For example, Karl, twenty-six, owned a gym. Hearing snide remarks about his being gay had prompted him to leave his previous job and open his own business, where he wouldn't have to take orders from people who were prejudiced against gays. At Karl's gym, clients could purchase personal training. Half of the personal training fee went to the trainer; the other half, to Karl. Trainers were not allowed to use the gym facilities to train clients without giving half of their fee to Karl. Once, a trainer had tried to train a few gym members on the sly, pocketing the entire fee for himself. When Karl found out, he fired him.

In his place, Karl hired Bennie, fifty, who was also gay. Bennie had been the victim of two violent hate crimes, and discrimination against gays had cost him several jobs in his lifetime. Because he grew up prior to the gay rights movement, Bennie had been subjected to more prejudice than Karl had ever encountered or expected to encounter. Karl knew about Bennie's experiences with discrimination and was extremely sympathetic. He felt glad that he could give Bennie a second chance at a career and provide him with a comfortable work environment.

Bennie worked hard for Karl, but like the trainer who had been fired, Bennie began to train some clients on the sly. When Karl confronted Bennie, Bennie asked Karl to "give him a break." After all, he had endured persecution for being gay long before Karl had ever been born.

"I'm still paying off the lawyers who defended me when I was booted out of my last job because I was gay," Bennie argued. "But what would you know about all that? You young ones have it easy compared with us older guys. And don't forget, it's us older guys who organized and fought for legislation that makes it possible for you younger guys to breathe easier."

"But Bennie. I fired the last guy for doing what you're doing. If the other trainers see you get away with this, they'll pull the same stunt and that will hurt me financially," replied Karl.

"I'll look out for you. If I see anyone else doing this, I'll turn them into you on the spot. And, if you insist, I'll play by the rules, but wait and see, one day the rules may be used against you and then who will you come to for advice? Me. And who will you turn to when someone punctures one of your ribs for being 'queer'? Me, who spent six months flat on his back recovering from the last gay bashing.

"I've been through it all, but okay, we'll do it your way. I guess I can't expect someone as young and lucky as you to cut any slack for an old man like me. An old man like me should be grateful to even have a job, right?"

Karl felt so guilty that he hadn't endured persecutions, he immediately changed his mind. He just looked the other way when Bennie trained clients unofficially. Karl rationalized that he wasn't really losing money because the club membership fees weren't affected. He was only losing the percentage he could have made from Bennie's training contracts, and he chalked that up as a contribution to the cause of gay rights. If he could help Bennie pay legal fees incurred due to discrimination against being gay, then that was his way of helping the gay movement.

Karl was comfortable with this arrangement until other trainers learned of Bennie's unofficial sessions. They told Karl that Bennie was cheating him and expected Karl to take a stand. Karl was now in a quandary: on the one hand, he wanted to be fair to all his employees; on the other hand, his survivor guilt made it difficult for him to discipline Bennie.

## *Survivor Guilt Related to Therapy and Recovery Groups*

Survivor guilt can also be found among individuals in recovery from addiction or in treatment for mental disorders. In twelve-step programs and therapy groups, it is not uncommon for individuals who are making noticeable strides in mastering their problem to feel survivor guilt toward fellow members of their group who are either not progressing at all, progressing less rapidly than themselves, or regressing. Guilt may arise from feeling tired or bored with the issues that trouble other group members, even though those are the same issues that troubled them in the past. Survivor guilt may also be experienced when the individuals develop new interests and relationships.

Consider the following dialogue between Lucas and his therapist:

Lucas:     The group bores me now. I used to get a lot out of it, but I'm past a lot of the issues the others are talking about. I don't want to seem overconfident, because I know I could fall back into depression in a moment's notice. But I feel coming to group these days is a waste of time. Yet when I think about leaving, I feel sad. I know I'll miss the others, and they need me. Some of them are attached to me. They call me when they're down and I help them out. But there's a course I want to take that meets when group meets, and it isn't offered any other time.

Therapist:  It's normal to outgrow a group, but if you, or anyone else, needed to stay for a long time, that would be perfectly normal too. There's no timetable on personal growth. You could leave the group now, but at a later point in time come back if you needed to.

Lucas:  I know all that. But whenever I think of leaving the group, I think that would really hurt some of the other members.

Therapist:  I'm sure they'll miss you. You've made a lot of valuable contributions in group. But loss is a part of life. If some group members have a particularly hard time adjusting to your absence, I and the other group members will be there to help them.

Lucas:  You don't understand. And don't talk to me about "adjusting to loss." I hate psychobabble words like that. There's no such thing as "adjusting to loss." There's only hurting, and the hurt never stops.

Therapist:  Can you tell me more about that?

Lucas:  Leaving the group is wrong. Just wrong. You don't leave people once they've started caring about you. You have to stay, no matter what. It's your duty.

Therapist:  Duty?

Lucas:  Yeah, duty. Like if you leave, someone will suffer. So it's your duty to stay.

Therapist:  Did that ever happen to you in the past? What happened when you left home to get married?

Lucas:  My father had a heart attack and my mother went on antidepressants. They told me my leaving them was going to kill them. They still say it today, twenty years later. If I hadn't left home, they'd be healthy and happy.

Therapist:  And do you believe that? Do you believe your leaving caused your dad's heart attack and your mother's depression?

Lucas:  Sure I do. I know that doesn't make sense, but I believe it's true. If I could've stayed with them forever, they'd be happy.

Therapist:    And how do you relate what happened between you and your parents when you left to what you think will happen if you leave the group?

Lucas:    I never thought of it, but I guess I'm afraid someone will get sick or get more depressed, like my parents did.

Therapist:    Do you think that will really happen?

Lucas:    I know Marianne is going to miss me. She and I are really tight.

Therapist:    I'm sure she will, but can you keep in touch with her if you leave group?

Lucas:    Sure I can, but it won't be the same. It's never the same once you leave. And she stayed on the phone with me all night once when I was close to suicide. I owe my life to her, and the group. How can I leave them? I can't. But I don't want to stay stuck in that group for the rest of my life either.

Lucas is typical of people who have trouble leaving therapy or recovery groups due to guilt for outgrowing the group or developing new interests. In many cases, this guilt is related to guilt associated with leaving their family of origin or with a trauma. For persons who grew up in violent homes (even if they were not physically or sexually abused themselves), leaving a group may trigger memories associated with leaving a dysfunctional home environment and leaving other family members at the mercy of an aggressive person.

Leaving a therapy or recovery group does entail loss and change. Even if you remain in contact with members of the group or the group leader, your relationship with these persons will be changed. The kind of close bonding that can occur when you attend regular meetings may be hard to reestablish once you have left the group or program. Your feelings of guilt about leaving may be a defense against the sense of loss involved, but may also be a defense against the pain and sense of powerlessness you may feel regarding other group members who are still suffering and who are struggling to make progress. Your guilt and grief may also hearken back to previous traumatic or stressful experiences where your departure was associated with the death or injury of someone else.

# 5

# Psychological Consequences of Survivor Guilt

Survivor guilt is torturous. Part of the torture is that the burden of guilt feels unending because there is no way to undo the past. If you could simply raise the dead, restore to health and vitality those who were injured, or bestow emotional stability and joy on those who were psychologically injured, you could probably free yourself of survivor guilt. Instead you may feel chained to it, the way the mythological figure Sisyphus was to his unending labor. Sisyphus was condemned by the gods to push a heavy stone up a hill, let it roll back down from the top, then start all over again pushing the stone up the hill. For people with survivor guilt, life can feel as punishing and frustrating a fate as that of Sisyhpus.

Survivor guilt can also contribute to the development of substance abuse problems, eating disorders, clinical depression, certain medical problems, and many types of relationship problems. People with survivor guilt may find it difficult to move ahead in or enjoy friendships and love relationships, advance in their careers, or develop a spiritual dimension to their lives (Kubany 1994, 1997; Kubany and Manke 1995; Opp and Samson 1989).

During certain periods of time, people with survivor guilt can feel extremely alienated and acutely different from others and may withdraw from family and social events. They may experience difficulties setting boundaries in relationships; overworking; feeling tainted and unworthy of love, success, happiness or pleasure; and even feeling suicidal or violent.

# How Survivor Guilt Affects You

## Self-Abuse

Survivor guilt, like any other form of guilt, can be a terrible drain on your psychic energy. Guilt demands punishment, and people with survival guilt can engage in many forms of self-abuse, including alcoholism, drug abuse, eating disorders, self-mutilation, or suicide.

### Alcohol or Drug Addiction and Eating Disorders

There is never one single cause for alcoholism, drug-abuse, and eating disorders. However, the anxiety and physiological arousal (adrenaline reactions) created by feelings of survivor guilt can play a major role in the origin and perpetuation of any form of addiction. Substance abuse can provide solace from the pain of survivor guilt by creating a state of psychic numbing. Overeating can also serve as a way to dull the anger, pain, shame, and other uncomfortable tensions associated with survivor guilt.

Research has established a relationship between family violence and obesity. A layer of fat is, quite literally, an excellent defense against intra-family violence and other forms of abuse (Garner and Garfinkel 1985; Matsakis 1989). This defense may be used by the actual victims of violence, but also by other family members who observed the violence and suffer survivor guilt.

On the other hand, anorexia nervosa so starves the person physiologically that he or she is almost incapable of feeling any strong emotion. By remaining emaciated, the anorectic avoids many uncomfortable feelings, including survivor guilt. In addition, the anorectic is so preoccupied with food and body image concerns that he or she cannot focus on other life issues, such as the incidents that gave rise to survivor guilt and the significance of these events in his or her life.

Similarly the bulimic expends so much time and energy on the binge-purge cycle that his or her attention is deflected away from whatever life events and emotions are troublesome and their impact on his or her life. Bulimia can be seen as a symbolic means of taking in, or acknowledging, the guilt (or other unpleasant feelings) followed by a symbolic rejection of the unpleasant memories or feelings.

Phyllis, for example, would binge in response to feelings that reminded her of her sister's abuse. Once she consumed three dozen doughnuts after watching her son participate in a spelling bee at school. "The spelling bee reminded me of when I was in elementary school with my sister. She was very smart and very good at spelling. Years ago she was a final contestant for a spelling bee and probably could have won. But Mom beat her the night before, so she couldn't go to school. I was the one who had to tell the teacher that my sister was 'sick.'

"I felt guilty lying to the teacher, but the real guilt was about my sister. I felt I should have been beaten too—like I didn't have the right to be walking around when my sister was all bruised. The memories of my sister being hit and me being spared were so horrible I ate to forget them. It was the only way to stop the pain."

Anorexia, bulimia, and obesity can create a host of medical problems. For example, obesity can contribute to the development of diabetes, heart disease, and arthritis. Similarly alcohol and drug abuse can contribute to a host of medical problems including liver disease, hepatitis, and heart problems. To the extent that substance abuse and eating disorders create medical problems, survivor guilt can be injurious to your health. It can even lead to premature death.

## Self-Mutilation

"There, that's for Rusty," said Jack, as he pulled out a toenail with a pair of pliers.

Jack and Rusty had been working on a construction site when Rusty slipped and fell to his death off a high beam. Jack had seen the beam begin to shake, but was unable to warn Rusty in time. Even if he had warned Rusty in time, he wouldn't have been able to prevent Rusty's death.

When Jack leaned over Rusty's body, he stood in Rusty's blood. Later on, when he got home and saw his shoes spotted with blood, he cried out, "It should have been me. It should have been me!"

One way Jack expresses his guilt is to pull out his toenails. That way his feet bleed and he symbolically recreates the scene of Rusty's death. Also, mutilating himself serves two functions: that of punishing himself for Rusty's death and that of managing the anxiety that thinking about the accident creates in him.

Rusty's death made him question many things about his life. He began to wonder about his vocational choice, his marriage, and the meaning of his existence. For example, he realized he wasn't as happy with his wife as he pretended to be, yet he wasn't so unhappy that he wanted to leave her. When he has more questions than answers, one solution is to harm himself. Then he can focus on causing himself pain and dealing with the aftereffects of the self-mutilation, such as managing the pain and the difficulties walking.

Self-mutilation takes many forms and has many functions. Some of the most common forms include cutting; burning; head banging; fingernail or toenail mutilation; excessive scratching, using harsh abrasives on skin or scalp; poking sharp objects into flesh; pulling out hair or eyebrows for noncosmetic purposes; inserting objects into the body's orifices; refusing to drink, eat, or take necessary medication; and various forms of self-surgery.

Self-mutilation usually occurs among child abuse survivors or people who have experienced repeated or severe trauma. However, individuals without a history of childhood abuse can engage in self-mutilation, especially if they've had experiences that have led to survivor guilt. For example, police officers, rescue workers, and combat vets without histories of child abuse have reported banging their heads, cutting themselves, or burning themselves to "stop the memories" and "erase the guilt."

Self-mutilation does not mean the same thing for every person. For some trauma survivors, self-mutilation is a way of talking, of telling the world, "I was hurt" or "I hurt." Consequently, self-mutilation is especially prevalent among people who were told not to tell by the perpetrator of the trauma, who were abused at the preverbal level, or who simply do not have the language with which to tell their story or express their feelings about it.

Self-mutilating behavior also serves to contain the emotions, memories, and other psychological effects generated by the trauma. If people under stress wring their hands, bite their fingernails, or pull their hair to alleviate tension, imagine what trauma survivors fraught with survivor guilt might need to do to lessen the stress. Self-mutilation can also be a way to moderate the hyperarousal and numbing, or the fight/flight/freeze reactions, discussed in chapter 3.

Self-mutilation can calm people who feel so full of adrenaline that they might burst, or it can bring a feeling of life to people so numb they feel like vegetables. "The pain lets me know I'm still alive," states one survivor.

Self-mutilation can also be a form of self-punishment for survivor guilt or other forms of guilt. Usually this type of self-mutilation is kept a secret, and there is as much guilt and shame about the self-mutilation as the incidents that caused it. A full discussion of self-mutilation is beyond the scope of this book. However, it is a serious symptom that can lead to infection and perhaps permanent or serious medical complications.

## ✍ Self-Assessment: Self-Mutilation and Survivor Guilt

On a fresh piece of paper in your journal write the heading "Self-Mutilation and Survivor Guilt" and answer the following questions:

Do you cut or burn yourself; pull at or remove your eyelashes, eyebrows, pubic hair, or other hair; scratch yourself excessively, or injure your fingernails or toenails so that you feel pain? Do you ever use harsh substances on your skin or scalp or put sharp objects into your body? Have you ever refused to seek medical treatment, or not taken necessary food, drink, or medication? Are there other ways you harm your body or health?

These are all means of self-mutilation. If you are mutilating yourself, it is imperative that you seek the assistance of both a physician and a mental health professional.

### Suicide and Parasuicidal Acts

People commit suicide for a variety reasons, including survivor guilt. Suicide can be an expression of self-hate stemming from survivor guilt as well as other feelings, for example, anger at whomever or whatever was responsible for the incident that gave rise to the survivor guilt. A major motive for suicide lies in the hope of killing the physical or emotional pain. Some people kill themselves in order to be reunited with people whom they loved who are dead: a child, parent, war buddy, favorite sibling. Suicidal people have exhausted their capacity to cope with stress and are afraid all they can look forward to is a life of feeling guilty.

Survivor guilt has been linked not only to suicidal feelings and acts but also to parasuicidal, or high-risk, behaviors, which means that they put themselves in situations where they are likely to be killed. Examples of high-risk behavior are unsafe driving practices, provoking police officers or violent people into an attack mode, volunteering for high-risk tasks or choosing high-risk occupations, not following medical advice (such as to take necessary medications for medical or psychiatric problems), or not seeking medical attention when necessary. I have counseled dozens of people, both male and female, of all ages and races, who have purposely walked through dangerous neighborhoods, insulted known murderers, or frequented bars or drug dens known for their violence in hopes of attacks. Others have devised ingenius strategies for provoking police officers into shooting them while making sure that others, including the officers, would not be harmed. In almost every case, survivor guilt was an important motivation for this parasuicidal behavior.

If you are suffering from suicidal thoughts and feelings as the result of survivor guilt (or any other reason), you might expect to have more suicidal thoughts around the anniversary of the death of your loved one or when someone or something reminds you of the person you lost or the circumstances surrounding the loss. Suicidal thoughts and high-risk behaviors that could lead to death need to be taken seriously. If you have suicidal thoughts or feelings or find yourself trying to indirectly cause your death, you need to talk to a qualified counselor immediately.

## *Obsessive-Compulsive Disorders*

Like substance abuse, obsessive-compulsive disorders are multicausal. However, survivor guilt has been seen as a common underlying cause, especially when the obsession or compulsion involves washing, checking, and being scrupulous about religious practices (Tournier 1977). These types of obsessions or compulsions may serve as forms of atonement for wrongdoings, including real or perceived errors in thinking, feeling, or acting during a stressful event or trauma where someone died or was injured. They may also be symbolic means of reliving the stressful event or trauma and performing actions that might have helped avert the injury or deaths of others.

According to the *DSM-IV*, an obsessive-compulsive disorder involves the following:

An obsession is defined in this way: "(1) recurrent and persistent thoughts, impulses, or images that are experienced, at some time . . . as intrusive and inappropriate and that cause marked anxiety or distress; (2) the thoughts, impulses, or images are not simply excessive worries about real-life problems; (3) the person attempts to ignore or suppress such thoughts, impulses, or images or to neutralize them with some other thought or action; (4) the person recognizes that the obsessional thoughts, impulses, or images are a product of his or her own mind (not imposed from without as in thought insertion)" (APA 1994, 422–423).

The *DSM-IV* defines a compulsion as "repetitive behaviors (e.g., hand washing, ordering, checking) or mental acts (e.g., praying, counting, repeating words silently) that the person feels driven to perform in response to an obsession, or according to rules that must be applied rigidly." It states that "the behaviors or mental acts are aimed at preventing or reducing distress or preventing some dreaded event or situation; however, these behaviors or mental acts either are not connected in a realistic way with what they are designed to neutralize or prevent or are clearly excessive."

Not all persons who suffer from obsessive-compulsive disorder have survivor guilt, but some people manage their survivor guilt through obsessions and compulsions. For example, an emergency room nurse who worked in an understaffed and undersupplied hospital saved many lives. Yet she has considerable guilt about the lives she *didn't* save, even though the deaths had more to do with the severity of the injuries and the insufficient medication, bandages, sterilization equipment, and other medical supplies than her competency or the competency of the other medical staff. Nevertheless, she feels she should have died instead of some of the young people who died prematurely in car accidents or as the result of crime.

Her home is full of old newspapers, magazines, and junk mail. She can't bring herself to throw away even a scrap of paper. She is obsessed with stacking and organizing these papers, as if doing so would save someone's life. The obsession became so strong she could not bring herself to stop organizing the papers so that she could tend to her other duties.

In therapy she realized that the hoarding and arranging of these papers was a symbolic way of obtaining and organizing medical supplies to be used in an emergency. The papers were a substitute for the supplies she lacked while on duty. Although her obsession with the papers was greatly interfering with her life, as well as angering her husband, she felt if she stopped her ritual, someone would die. When she did try to stop her ritual with the papers, she'd be flooded with anxiety and guilt, as well as suicidal thoughts.

"Organizing the papers was safer than facing the truth of what happened, the fact that so often I couldn't help because the hospital administration refused to get us what we needed. Part of it was that they didn't have the funds; the other part was that they used some of the funds for their own perks. If I gave up my survivor guilt, I'd be stuck with two feelings I don't know if I could handle: rage and grief. If I got into my rage at the administrators, I'm afraid of what I'd do. If I got into my grief at all the lost people, I'm afraid I'd never stop crying. No wonder I organize papers. It's a lot safer than hating myself, wanting to blow away administrators, or crying for forever."

## ✍ Self-Assessment: Obsessions, Compulsions, and Survivor Guilt

On a fresh piece of paper in your journal, write the heading "Obsessions, Compulsions, and Survivor Guilt" and answer the following questions:

Do you find yourself doing something over and over again, knowing full well you don't need to be doing it? Do you wish you could stop yourself from repeating this behavior but find that you can't? What are some of these behaviors? Do you feel that any of them are related to your survivor guilt?

Do you find yourself thinking about something repeatedly, although you realize that thinking about it repeatedly serves no purpose and is only standing in the way of going ahead with what you need to do or think about that day? What are some of these thoughts? Is there any relationship between these repetitive thoughts and your feelings of survivor guilt.

## Overfunctioning: Workaholism

Another way to manage survivor guilt, and the anxiety, pain, and anger that go with it, is to channel energies toward work. An overfunctioning person, or a workaholic, is not a person with abundant energy who likes to be creative or to make a contribution. Neither is he or she simply someone who works even when work becomes demanding or uncomfortable. Such a definition would include many working people because few jobs are almost always personally pleasurable. Furthermore, some people are in economic situations where they must remain in jobs that are exceptionally stressful for them. It's not fair to label these unlucky people as "workaholics" or "overfunctioning" people when they are simply trying to survive under difficult circumstances.

Rather the terms *workaholic* and *overfunctioning* should be saved for persons (*a*) who work hard or long hours in order to compensate for feelings of failure or feelings of guilt in other areas of life and *(b)* who continue to work hard even when working hard is not necessary for economic survival and is destructive to physical or emotional health, spiritual life, or relationships.

Being overly responsible, overfunctioning, or working excessively can lead a person away from his or her innermost thoughts and feelings toward an external goal or toward the thoughts and feelings of some other person. Being a workaholic is a legal, often much-applauded means of avoiding emotional pain and of avoiding intimate relationships that would involve the disclosure of deep feelings (such as survivor guilt). At the same time it can be a means of atoning for perceived misdeeds. According to Kolb (1983), working can block thinking about guilt experiences and provide a way to avoid close relationships.

## ✍ Self-Assessment: Workaholism and Survivor Guilt

On a fresh piece of paper in your journal, write the heading "Workaholism and Survivor Guilt" and answer the following questions:

Do you feel you are a workaholic? If so, why? Remember that just because you work hard or have long hours doesn't mean you are a workaholic. You are only a workaholic if working is a way of avoiding deep feelings or close relationships. One way to find out is to ask yourself how you feel during times that you aren't working. Are you troubled by uncomfortable emotions or thoughts? Are any of these emotions or thoughts related to your survivor guilt?

## Clinical Depression

What happens to a car that is driven cross-country many times without a tune-up, oil change, or tire rotation? What happens to a car that is well maintained but is driven coast to coast a thousand times? Would some parts start to wear out? Might the car eventually cease to function altogether?

People aren't cars. However, what happens to a car due to overuse or inadequate care is similar to what happens to people when they live under conditions of chronic stress or repeated trauma, or when they fail to take care of themselves as a form of self-punishment for their survivor guilt. Perhaps the incidents that led to the survivor guilt leave people without the time, money, or ability to take care of themselves. Under such conditions, their emotional and physical reserves become taxed to the point where they easily develop a clinical depression.

The term *depression* as used here does not refer to the normal down periods experienced by almost everyone, that is, temporary feelings of sadness, more commonly known as "the blues." Rather, depression refers to biologically based clinical depression, which usually needs to be treated with psychiatric medication as well as psychotherapy.

Symptoms of depression include feelings of worthlessness, hopelessness, and fatigue; irritability and anxiety; problems falling or staying asleep; and loss of the ability to experience pleasure. While depression can be caused by many factors, both psychological and physical, in many cases, survivor guilt plays a role. Neiderland (1964) cites the example of a nursing mother in a concentration camp whose child was taken from her breast and killed. For years she criticized herself for not having saved her child and for not having died in the child's place. When she sought psychiatric care, she was diagnosed with clinical depression. She indeed had the symptoms of depression; the trauma of being in the camps and her survivor guilt were determined to be the cause. If you suspect you suffer from clinical depression, you may want to complete the self-assessment for clinical depression in appendix D.

## Perfectionism

If you feel that someone died or was injured because you made a mistake, you may try to compensate for that mistake by trying to be perfect in the present. Also, if you were involved in any kind of trauma (such as combat, fires, floods, or family violence) or in certain occupations that involve injury and death (nursing, rescue work, firefighting, police work), mistakes are intolerable. Even the tiniest error can result in death or injury. If you've been in such a situation, you've likely seen how the mistakes of others caused needless deaths, injuries, and other losses. As a result, you may have developed a mind-set of "no mistakes allowed."

People living in abusive households, whether they are being abused or not, usually try to avoid "mistakes" at all costs, because making a mistake, even a small one, can be an excuse for a beating or some other form of torture if not for oneself, for another family member. Persons trapped in domestic violence situations often develop the hope that if they are perfect, they can stop their abuse or the abuse of another family member. The abuse, however, is more a function of the abuser's internal state than the victim's behavior or the behavior of other family members.

Perfectionism creates problems for many people, including yourself. When you judge yourself with perfectionistic standards, you'll always fall short and your self-esteem will suffer. Perfectionistic standards impose a heavy weight on you, and they can affect your relationships. You may impose the same perfectionistic standards you place on yourself onto others, thus making others feel incompetent or inadequate or angering or alienating them by your high standards. Your need to be perfect may also stand in the way of developing relationships. For example, you may be spending so much time trying to meet your perfectionistic standards that you don't have time for others.

You may have such high standards for how you behave in a relationship that the minute you don't live up to your perfectionist standards, you conclude you are a failure and withdraw from the relationship (either permanently or temporarily). Similarly, when someone else fails to meet one of your perfectionistic standards, you reject that person.

## ✍ Self-Assessments: The Shoulds

The following "shoulds" impose burdens on many people (McKay and Fanning 1987). Do you subscribe to any of the following?

I should be the epitome of generosity and unselfishness.

I should be the perfect lover, friend, parent, teacher, student, spouse, and so on.

I should be able to find a quick solution to every problem.

I should never feel hurt. I should always feel happy and serene.

I should be completely competent.

I should know, understand, and foresee everything

## Shame

Shame and guilt are closely related; however, shame refers to negative feelings about your entire self, whereas guilt refers to negative feelings about specific actions or parts of yourself. The shame-ridden person thinks, "If only I weren't . . ."; the guilt-ridden person thinks, "If only I hadn't . . ." (Niedenthal, Tangney, and Gavanski 1994). Shame and guilt also differ in that shame involves public exposure, some kind of disapproval in front of others. In contrast, guilt is a "more private affair—between one's self and one's . . . conscience . . . when confronting a breach of personal moral standards" (Robertson 1994, 16).

## Physical or Somatic Symptoms

The following discussion on the relationship between severe stress, survivor guilt, and medical problems is not intended to suggest that illness is a punishment for "sin" or misbehavior. Neither is it intended to suggest that people bring their illnesses upon themselves by their feelings or their psychological makeup. Rather the notion is that strong, uncomfortable emotions, like all emotions, whether they be anger, guilt, or grief, have physiological components, such as hyperarousal and numbing, that affect the body. As explained in the section on fight/flight/freeze reactions in chapter 3, when the body is subjected to severe stress or repeated trauma, the body's functioning is affected.

The interrelationship of the immune system and the brain is well documented. Physicians, psychiatrists, psychologists, social workers, and other therapists have found survivor guilt to be a factor in the development of medical problems, from relatively minor symptoms, such as sties, to more serious medical symptoms such as ulcerative colitis, coronary disease, and clinical depression. Even under non-traumatic circumstances, the loss of loved ones has been found to suppress the immune system, making the bereaved more susceptible to many illnesses, such as viral infections (Hales, Yudofsky, and Talbott 1994). When survivor and other forms of guilt are involved in the loss, the emotional stress is even greater, further weakening the immune system.

## Somatization

Closely associated with the development of physical symptoms and medical problems is the process called somatization. *Somatization* occurs when the body expresses the pain, anger, guilt, or other feelings associated with the trauma in the form of physical pain or impairment (Chapman 1993). As Herman (1992) points out, somatization tends to occur more commonly in situations where speaking up is dangerous and may be punished or be cause for ostracism.

Somatization does not mean that the sufferer is mentally deficient or a manipulator who is trying to pull a fast one. Somatization also does not mean that the pain isn't real or that it is "all in the head." The pain is true bodily pain. The illness is genuine. But the body is also expressing the feelings and the memories that cannot be easily or sufficiently put into words because, if expressed, they will put the individual in jeopardy. For example, Holocaust survivors who were punished for complaining while in concentration camps and who often kept silent after they were freed have been found to "describe their troubles . . . in somatic terms (headaches, fatigue, dizziness, sleep disturbance)" (Neiderland 1964, 471). Survivor guilt is the cause of many of these symptoms.

In trauma survivors, somatization can take the form of physical pain or an increase in the pain of injuries experienced during the trauma. For example, Gregory's son lost his arm in a car accident on October 5. Since the incident, each year around October, Gregory has pains in his shoulder. "I think I'm punishing myself for my son being hurt in that accident. Whenever I think about him, I start getting pains in my arm—pains that have no medical basis. Maybe I'm trying to bear the pain for him, hoping that if I hurt some, he'll hurt less."

## ✍ Self-Assessment: Physical Pain and Survivor Guilt

On a fresh piece of paper in your journal, write the heading "Physical Pain and Survivor Guilt" and answer the following questions:

Do you have any chronic or frequent physical pain? If the pain could speak, what would the pain say? Do you think there is any relationship between the pain and your survivor guilt? It bears repeating that these questions are not meant to imply that that pain is not real or that it exists "only in your head." Your pain is real, however your survivor guilt or other strong emotions or the meanings you ascribe to that pain might contribute, to one degree or another, to its intensity.

## Anniversary Reactions

If you are suffering from survivor guilt due to the death or severe injury of another person, you may experience anniversary reactions. An anniversary reaction refers to having psychological or physical symptoms (or both) around a time that's connected with the loss or injury. For example, if you are suffering survivor guilt regarding the death of your father, who died on June 30th, you may experience certain psychological or physical symptoms every year around the end of June. Alternatively, you may experience these symptoms when you or other family members reach the age your father was when he died or when one of your children reaches the age you were when your father died.

Anniversary reactions are closely associated with separation and loss and are seen as having two meanings: first, they are a form of identifying with the dead or injured person, and second, they may be part of a delayed mourning response. Survivor guilt plays a role as part of the grieving response. Adriana explains:

> My grandmother died when I was seven. After she died, my mother developed a severe depression from which she only partly recovered. My mother blamed me in part for my grandmother's death because I was in the same room with her when she died. My mother thought that I should have heard that Grandma stopped breathing, but I didn't. Subconsciously, I felt guilty about Grandma dying and started having nightmares about her coming to get me and take me with her to the land of the dead. Whenever we'd get a big package in the mail, I was afraid the ghost of my grandmother would come out and kill me.
>
> Since my mother was never as happy as before my grandmother died, I feel I should have died in her place. Everyone told me I had to help my mother now that her mother was gone, and I felt like a failure because I couldn't make my depressed mother happy.
>
> My grandmother died on January 19th. Every year at that time I get something—an infection, an allergic reaction, cysts, or a bout of depression. It happens like clockwork. Right after the winter holidays, I hold my breath and wait to see what new anniversary symptom will come up next.
>
> Therapy has helped reduce the symptoms, but they still occur. I did my therapeutic homework—I talked to family members about what happened. My mother says she didn't blame me for her mother's death, although she did ask me a lot of questions over the dead body, which, I guess, made me feel responsible. I know in my heart that my mother loved her mother more than she loved me. The adult in me is angry that I was put in that position as a little girl, but the little girl in me still wishes I had died in Grandma's place so Mom would be happy.

## ✍ Self-Assessment: Anniversary Dates and Survivor Guilt

On a fresh piece of paper in your journal, write the heading "Anniversary Dates and Survivor Guilt" and answer the following questions:

What is the anniversary date of your trauma or loss? Looking back over the years since the trauma or loss, have you felt or acted differently around the anniversary date? Do you tend to have more medical problems or other forms of distress around this date? Do you see any relationship between your anniversary date and your mental or emotional health?

## Paranoia and Projection

Survivor guilt can lead to paranoia and the projection of guilt onto others. It's natural to disown your undesirable feelings and put them onto another person or group of people. As discussed in the section on shadow guilt in chapter 1, people generally want to disclaim thoughts and feelings they consider socially unacceptable. If you are suffering from survivor guilt and you project your guilt onto others, you are denying that you feel guilty.

Projection can lead to paranoia, or the feeling that others are secretly plotting to harm you. If you are projecting your guilt onto others, then you have decided that others are thinking, feeling, or acting in unethical or illegal ways. It's only one step further to then assume that these others are planning to harm you. You become suspicious of others, even when the suspicion is not warranted. This extreme form of suspiciousness, which may stem in part from your survivor guilt, can make you feel threatened and vulnerable. If sufficiently threatened, you may lash out in rage as a form of self-protection.

## ✍ Self-Assessment: Paranoia, Suspiciousness, and Survivor Guilt

On a fresh piece of paper in your journal, write the heading "Paranoia, Suspiciousness, and Survivor Guilt" and answer the following questions:

Do you find yourself becoming suspicious of others, even when you are fairly certain that your suspicions cannot be substantiated?

Do you feel that your guilt plays any role, even a small role, in your becoming distrustful of others?

## Anger and Aggressiveness

The ancient Greek warrior Achilles suffered from survivor guilt when his friend Patroclus died in battle. In the story, Achilles sent Patroclus to fight in his place, and when Patroclus died, Achilles was consumed with guilt. If only he had gone to battle, his friend would still be alive. In a flash, Achilles' survivor guilt turned to rage. He began killing everything in sight, except for his fellow comrades. He killed so many enemy soldiers and animals that the rivers ran red with blood and corpses and the river gods complained to Zeus, King of Gods, to stop Achilles before he destroyed them entirely.

Research shows a high correlation between survivor guilt and aggressiveness (Glover 1985; Shay 1994). Tournier writes that guilt of any kind can lead to anger. "Irritation . . . aggressiveness: this is the law of unconscious and repressed guilt (1977, 150). The anger associated with survivor guilt has two sources: first, unresolved grief and second, frustration at not being able to get rid of the sense of guilt. The person who feels condemned to a life of guilt may be understandably irritable and at times, explode in anger or rage. The effect of this guilt-related anger on relationships is discussed in the next section.

# How Survivor Guilt Affects Relationships

Your survivor guilt can be so strong that it can affect your relationships. You may feel that you don't deserve to be loved or cared for. There may be people in your life who care for you a great deal, or who are beginning to show signs of caring for you and who could possibly come to care about you even more (if you let them). Yet you might find yourself rejecting these people or keeping them at a distance. Behaviors that are caused by your survivor guilt may serve to help you destroy your relationships.

## Alienating Others

There are many ways to kill a person's affections for you, whether that affection is familial, platonic, or romantic, and you may find yourself so afflicted with survivor guilt that you do things to alienate others without conscious intention. You may even be surprised at your behavior. For example, you may find yourself not returning phone calls, showing up late or not showing up at all for a planned date, or disregarding a previously agreed upon agenda. Or you may find yourself disregarding the known needs of another person. If you are burdened with survivor guilt, the roots of such behavior may be much deeper and more complex than simple self-centeredness, sheer insensitivity, or outright cruelty. The roots lie in the need to create emotional distance and in having ambivalent feelings about being close.

So you build an emotional wall around yourself. You may want to be close, but you may be afraid to trust or be unsure how much to trust the other person. Or, when you begin to get close, your survivor guilt may surface and tell you that you don't deserve to be close or that it's dangerous to be close because you might reveal aspects of yourself about which you have great shame or guilt. Then the person may reject or leave you. You don't trust that you can get close and not, inadvertently, mention something about the trauma that frightens or repulses the other person. As a result, you wall other people out, or are very guarded about how close you let them come to you.

Another way to create distance is to start a disagreement over a trivial or meaningless matter. Instead of saying, "I need space or quiet time," you hurl an insult or say or do something you know will trigger a negative response. Although unpleasantries result, the goal of emotional distance is achieved. Your reasons for pushing away others may have very painful origins. Nevertheless, your actions only communicate that you don't care much about the other person's time or feelings.

It would be more effective to simply say, "Look, I need a little time to myself right now. I'm not rejecting you, nor am I angry at you. I simply don't have the energy to relate to you right now." But if, deep down, you are feeling guilty or ashamed of something, then you may not feel you deserve to ask to have your need for personal space and quiet respected.

It's much easier to start a disagreement and blame the disagreement on something the other person did wrong, even if you later realize that you started the conflict. You might then feel guilty about your behavior and realize that you were taking out your frustrations with yourself on the other person. What you may not realize, however, is that your guilt about hurting or distancing someone who wanted to be close to you is a way of punishing yourself for whatever survivor guilt you still carry deep within your heart. In essence, your survivor guilt forces you to punish yourself, and you become involved in situations in your relationships that create more guilt. It becomes an endless cycle.

## ✍ Self-Assessment: Alienating Others and Survivor Guilt

On a fresh piece of paper in your journal, write the heading "Alienating Others and Survivor Guilt" and answer the following questions:

Think back on your interactions with others over the past month. Do you think you started a disagreement with someone as a means of getting some space for yourself or as a means of pushing the person away when you felt yourself becoming close to him or her? Do you think your survivor guilt may be affecting your ability to trust and be close to others? Write four or five sentences about how your survivor guilt affects your ability to share and be close with others and keeps you from participating as fully as you might like in relationships with others at home or at work.

### Death Taint

Survivor guilt can not only make you feel you don't deserve the support and love of others, but also that you should not get close to people—for their own good. Some survivors of war or other traumas involving death feel as if they have a "death taint." If you were in a trauma where many people died and, to one extent or another, you feel guilty about some aspect of those deaths, you may fear that if you become close to someone, that person may be affected by your death taint. The thinking goes like this: "If I love you and get close to you, then you may die. So if I love you, to save you, I stay away."

Some people are convinced or sincerely fear that, as punishment for their incompetence or some other personal characteristic about which they feel guilty, their loved ones will be injured or die. When Joe's wife developed cancer, for example, he was certain that his having affairs during their marriage caused his wife's illness. After his wife died, he never remarried, or even dated, because he was certain that the next woman he loved would also be punished for his sins. He even stayed away from his children for fear that being near them might cause them to come to harm.

Pointing out to Joe that many men cheated on their wives and that not all of these men's wives developed cancer or died could not convince him that he wasn't responsible for his wife's death. Joe could have benefited from more counseling, but he quit therapy abruptly, saying that he didn't even deserve to get help.

If someone in your family becomes ill, dies, has a major mishap, or even a minor disappointment, you may instantly feel that you are the cause of it because of your survivor guilt. Despite evidence to the contrary, you may feel convinced that you are responsible for your niece being raped, your son flunking math, your partner developing a chronic illness, or your cousin being in a flood. People who feel guilty expect to be punished and often see their loved ones' misfortune as punishment for their own actions. Therefore, you may conclude that it's best not to get close to others, for when they are hurt, you don't want to feel the pain of feeling responsible.

Alternatively, when someone close to you does get hurt, you may be surprised to find that you have no emotion, that you feel shut-down and unempathic. You feel less than human because you don't feel concern. This only convinces you that you are "damaged goods," an inferior person who is fated to suffer and to cause suffering to others. Such an understanding can propel you into a deep depression or a rage reaction, either of which renders you emotionally unavailable to the person who is hurt or to others in the situation who may be counting on you for assistance during the crisis at hand.

Your inability to respond as you would like during the current crisis might remind you of the stressful events or traumas you endured, especially if you were unable to respond as you would like or felt helpless and powerless to save yourself or others. Even though the current situation may not be a hopeless one and you could contribute and be helpful, your past guilt has paralyzed you, which you find humiliating and infuriating. The present becomes a repeat of the past, and once again, you aren't acting, feeling, or thinking in an adequate way.

If you are fortunate, the people around you are understanding. But if they don't understand your reaction and are angry with you or critical of you for not doing things or showing certain emotions, you are made to feel more guilty, which either causes you to further tune out emotionally, actually leave the situation (which causes more anger and hurt in the others), or explode. Or, you may be tempted to turn to alcohol, drugs, food, or gambling to numb your pain.

## Lack of Assertiveness

Your survivor guilt may prevent you from being assertive or standing up for your rights in a relationship. If you have trouble expressing your opinions or desires or stopping others when they hurt or take advantage of you, you may choose to not be involved with others and stay to yourself.

While lack of assertiveness might have many origins, survivor guilt can be the cause if you feel you deserve pain and suffering and that you don't deserve to have choices in a relationship because of the guilt you bear due to the trauma. As a result of survivor guilt some survivors allow themselves to be financially misused, or even exploited, by a wide range of persons, from employers and friends to family members, intimates, or members of their therapy or support groups.

Anthony, a police officer, has considerable guilt about the death of one of his fellow police officers and about having wounded and killed certain people while on the job.

As a result, when others don't repay him the money he has lent them, he says nothing. Joanne, the mother of a teenager who committed suicide is the same way. She lets people borrow her belongings and money and says nothing when these items are not returned. She also allows her other children to verbally abuse her and her employer to harass her. On some level, Joanne feels she doesn't deserve to be respected, because, in her distorted view, the reason her son killed himself was because she was a failure as a mother.

## Overgiving

Overgiving might reflect not only a generous spirit but also an attempt to atone for survivor guilt. Standards of what is an appropriate amount of time, love, money, or service to give to another human being, or group, is a highly individual matter. However, overgiving can be defined as giving to the point where there are serious financial, emotional, physical, or other consequences as the result of the giving. For example, if a woman gives away so much money that her own family suffers or that she does not have enough money to provide for her own medical care, then that might be overgiving. If a man spends so much time helping others that he neglects himself or others to whom he has a commitment, this situation could also be viewed as overgiving.

It's not uncommon for people with survivor guilt to be found overgiving in an intimate relationship from a sense of guilt. Giving in a relationship is good. It is healthy. But when the emotional or physical price tag for the giving includes harm to others or yourself or puts you at physical, mental, or financial risk, then survivor guilt might be playing a role.

## ✍ Self-Assessment: Overgiving and Survivor Guilt

On a fresh piece of paper in your journal, write the heading "Overgiving and Survivor Guilt" and answer the following questions:

Do you find yourself overgiving at home or at work or in your friendships or other relationships? What do you overgive: your time, money, affection, possessions, or professional expertise? Do you think your survivor guilt might play a role in your overgiving? Write four or five sentences about the relationship between survivor guilt and your overgiving.

## Difficulties with Separation

Separations are difficult for most people, but they can become painful for people if the separation triggers survivor guilt. During the stressful events or traumas you experienced, leaving others may have meant their death or leaving these others in the hands of individuals who you felt were not as qualified, or caring, as you. For example, Lily, an incest survivor, ran away from home when she was fourteen, leaving behind two younger sisters. To this day Lily feels guilty for leaving home, because while she was there she tried to protect her sisters from incestuous attacks. Even while Lily was at home, her sisters were being abused, yet, to this day, Lily feels as if her leaving caused her sisters to be abused, or at least to be abused more often.

This survivor guilt is so strong in Lily that she has trouble breaking off friendships with both men and women whom, for one reason or another, she doesn't desire to spend time with anymore. She also had great difficulty saying good-bye to her original church family. She had found another church that she felt better met her spiritual needs, but she felt that she was putting the people in her original church in jeopardy by leaving. A logical examination of the situation revealed that the only harm Lily would cause by changing churches was the loss of revenue to the first church and the loss of her contributions to some committees she had worked on. But nobody would become ill, die, or be abused because she left, as she unconsciously had thought.

For Lily, every separation hearkens back to the separation from her sisters. Almost every time Lily has to say good-bye, even to her pets as she leaves for work, she feels the pain of the past and has to carefully examine her decision to leave to be certain she is not causing harm.

For many people with survivor guilt, as with Lily, saying good-bye even to casual acquaintances is not an easy matter. It can be so agonizing that they decide to stay in an unrewarding relationship rather than go through the guilt of initiating a separation. Guilt is often a part of most separations, but for people with survivor guilt the guilt involved in separation may be quite intense. The decision to terminate, or lessen the degree of involvement in, a relationship, is even more conflictual and problematic if the relationship is a significant one, such as with a partner.

Survivor guilt can affect employment decisions and work relationships as well. For example, Peter, a nurse, had the opportunity to leave his nursing position and become a medical administrator. The decision involved many factors, but he couldn't be totally rational about it because of a trauma he had suffered as a teenager. He had just received his driver's license and, to celebrate, had taken his mother and grandmother out for a ride. His car ran out of gas, and he left his mother and grandmother in the car while he walked to a nearby gas station. During his absence, his mother and grandmother were raped, beaten, and robbed. He felt responsible for these crimes because it was his fault his car ran out of gas. For Peter, leaving a nursing job where he took care of adults and the elderly reminded him of leaving his mother and grandmother vulnerable to attack. He had to work through his guilt feelings about the attacks on his relatives before he could accurately assess whether or not he wanted to make a career change.

Therapists with histories of survivor guilt may have difficulty separating from their clients when the client moves on to another therapist or decides to leave therapy. In such situations, the therapist's sense of loss is compounded by a sense of guilt for not having done enough for the client or not having succeeded in helping the client with all of his or her problems. Some of these feelings are normal; however, the intensity of the guilt and loss may stem back to survivor guilt issues.

## ✍ *Self-Assessment: Separations and Survivor Guilt*

On a fresh piece of paper in your journal, write the heading "Separations and Survivor Guilt" and answer the following questions:

Have there been any separations that have been particularly difficult for you? Pick three or four of them and briefly describe them in your journal. Did survivor guilt play a role in the conflict or pain you experienced during any of these separations? Write three or four sentences about the role of survivor guilt in each separation where survivor guilt was present.

## Overprotectiveness

People with survivor guilt often relate to others with a sense of protectiveness or urgency. While some guilt-ridden people tend to withdraw from others and perhaps even distance themselves from partners, children, other family members, and friends, others tend to be extremely protective toward those whom they consider to be in their inner circle. They don't ever want to experience such loss again, so they are motivated to do everything possible to make the world safe, not only for themselves, but for those they care about.

If you engage in protective behavior, some of your loved ones may call you "overprotective," but whether you are being protective or overprotective is a matter of judgment. The truth is that there is danger in the world. Some of your overprotectiveness may not be overprotectiveness at all, but a healthy caution about potential danger. You learned something during your trauma—you acquired valuable information about all the ways things can go wrong: about human error, human frailty, human corruptibility, and about the breakdown of machinery, bureaucracies, and other man-made objects and systems that are designed to protect but often do not function as intended.

You and your loved ones are just as vulnerable to traffic accidents, criminal victimization, medical or bureaucratic malpractice, natural catastrophes, or technological disasters as anyone else. But given your experiences with death or injury, you expect the worst might happen and are determined to be prepared for it. "Never again" is the motto of many trauma survivors; deep in their hearts they have vowed to never again be unprepared or vulnerable to human or man-made disaster. Therefore you may be overly cautious about everything, from the seatbelt to the fanbelt in your car to the kind of restaurant you will go to. A part of you trusts no one and nothing, so you check out people, places, and objects for possible danger. You don't want any more mistakes, but your family members and friends may not appreciate your overprotective attitudes and behaviors.

# You and the Dead

The ties that can form between people during stressful times or traumatic incidents are intense, long lasting, and irreplaceable. The bonding that occurs among people who are engaged in a common struggle for survival can equal, and sometimes surpass, the bonding that can occur in a family. Many combat veterans consider their war buddies closer to them than their siblings. Many rescue workers, police officers, and firefighters feel the same way about their co-workers. Parents who lose a child to suicide or homicide or in a vehicular accident can become closer as a couple, if the loss doesn't drive them part.

During stressful times, the people involved become a family and if they are already family, they can become an even tighter family. A car accident survivor explains:

> My entire family was in the car when it was hit by an eighteen-wheeler. As I saw the truck plow into the car, I felt my life was over. I prayed not for myself, but that my kids would make it. My wife and I had only minor injuries, but my son was in the hospital for a year and my daughter needed four surgeries.
>
> After the accident, sometimes my wife and I would just look at each other and start crying. We'd just cry and cry. We were stressed, caring for the kids in the hospital and at home. Medical insurance didn't cover everything and money was tight. We were emotionally wrung out and financially almost bankrupt, but we were never closer.
>
> That was years ago. Everyone's all better now, but sometimes I miss those times, how close we were, how much we appreciated one another, how we cooperated for the sake of the common good. When we argue now, about small things, I think back to the accident times, when we were all willing to put aside our individual desires and preferences and made helping one another our number one priority. We all rose above our selfishness and came together to save money and find ways to make things work. We didn't argue about little things then. In *A Tale of Two Cities*, Charles Dickens wrote, 'It was the best of times, it was the worst of times.' That's how I feel about the time after the accident. It was terrible because we didn't know if the kids were going to make it, but it was wonderful because we were really a family.

The kind of closeness between people that stressful events can create and the kind of closeness between two people who love each other, such as spouses, can extend beyond the grave. No matter how you lost someone, whether through a trauma or an illness, although that person is lost to you physically, you still have a relationship with that person. You think about and may even talk to the person; the person may influence your thoughts, actions, and feelings. There is nothing psychologically unhealthy about this. Throughout the ages people have maintained contact with dead relatives and loved ones; remembering the dead is part of being human and truly loving.

Your survivor guilt may lead you to unconsciously give up a part of your life as a tribute to your dead friend or loved one. For example, you may give up an activity that gives you joy as a way to honor the deceased, or you may feel you aren't entitled to have children, an intimate love relationship, or good friends because it would be disrespectful to those who are dead.

For example, Nick, a combat vet, feels he shouldn't go dancing because his best friend, Tom, who loved to dance, lost his legs in battle. "Giving up dancing is my way of honoring Tom's sacrifice," Nick explains.

## ✍ Exercise: The Dead and the Living

In this exercise, you'll do some work on understanding another obstacle toward developing relationships in the present: your relationships with those who died or were injured.

1. Make a list of people you lost during or because of trauma.

2. How does the memory of these people affect your life today?

3. How do your feelings about the dead have an impact on your relationships today?

4. To what extent does the death of those people influence your choice of friends or relationships or the degree to which you can become close to certain others? Do you find yourself holding back in certain relationships because of your memory of the dead?

5. Do you ever have mental conversations with the dead? Do you feel closer to the dead than to the living? When you're having conflicts with people in your present-day life, do you seek out the dead to converse with? Do you feel those who died understand you better and appreciate you more than

those around you today? Are there times you feel the dead are sitting next to you or walking with you? Do you take them with you sometimes?

## ✍ Exercise: Honoring the Dead

On a fresh piece of paper in your journal, write the head "Honoring the Dead" and answer the following questions. Write at least two or three sentences in response to each question.

1. Do you feel the need to honor the person or persons who were injured or died in the incident which helped cause your survivor guilt? If so, why?

2. Are there others who might feel similarly to you whom you could approach for ideas and support? List three or four of these people.

3. Are there organizations which might feel similarly, for example, organizations which the deceased or injured was emotionally invested in or had contributed to, which could offer you support and ideas? If so, list three or four of these organizations or institutions.

4. What ways can you think of to honor the dead? You can seek to honor the dead in traditional ways, such as through formal religious services or the construction of some sort of monument, but you can also be creative, such as writing a poem about or to the individual or some other literary effort. If you have talent in the arts, such as drawing, painting, or writing, an expression along these lines might suit you. Or you could make an audio-tape or video-tape in commemoration, along the lines described above in the case of Valerie.

Do these means of honoring the dead sound too complicated and expensive for you? There are simple ways of honoring the dead that require no special talents and little money. For example, you could place a picture of the deceased in your wallet or in your room or office. You could light a candle for that person on their birthday, death date, or some other anniversary. You could say a short prayer for that person or visit their grave more often.

If there is no grave site, you may want to do something about changing the situation and creating a space dedicated to the memory of that person. It needs to be a gravesite. It could be a section of a home or a garden.

Some people honor the dead by carrying something that reminds them of the dead on their person. For example, George carries a pen that belonged to his father. "I never cried for my dad and I don't feel the need to make a display about my grief. But I carry his pen with me all the time and every day, when I see that pen, I think of him and how much I loved him. To me, that's honoring him."

Other ways include planting a special flower or plant or simply allowing yourself to think about and reminisce about him or her without feeling you are wasting time or dwelling in the past or otherwise not being constructive or productive. Yet another method is service: making a commitment to donate time or money to help others in honor of the deceased. Your commitment need not be great. For example, you could commit to five or six hours of some type of volunteer work or community service. For some people, this type of initial commitment has grown to be a source of considerable personal pleasure and satisfaction.

5. Can you make a commitment to yourself to act on your ideas? In two or three sentences, explain why it is important to you to keep your commitment to honor the dead in the ways you have identified as possible and meaningful to you. Now write an additional two or three sentences about what obstacles you expect to encounter, within yourself or outside yourself, in attempting to make your plan a reality and how you plan to cope with these obstacles.

Don't be afraid to answer "yes" to any of the questions in number 5. If you have an active relationship with some of those who died during the trauma, don't think that you're "crazy" or a "lunatic." It's quite normal for some trauma survivors to have an ongoing and significant relationship with someone who died during the trauma. To help you better understand this relationship, you may want to do some writing about your relationship with each person you identified. Sometimes writing that person a letter is helpful.

## *Replacement Children*

Some children are replacement children in that they are conceived or perceived as substitutes for a child or person who was lost during the trauma. If a child is lost to suicide or homicide or lost in an accident or natural catastrophe, another child may be conceived to replace the lost child, or an existing child may be looked to to take the place of the child who has been lost. A child may be named after a dead friend or relative who died during the trauma, giving the child an important symbolic identity.

That child may be highly valued and, in some cases, may become the survivor's only real reason for living. As the child grows, he or she may feel highly valued and special, but may also feel the burden of being a replacement and the frustration of not being valued for himself or herself.

## ✍ Exercise: Replacement Children

Are there any replacement children in your life? If not children of your own, perhaps nieces, nephews, grandchildren, or other children? If so, do some writing about the importance of that child in your life. What losses is that child being expected to fill? In what ways does the child's status as a replacement child help the child? In what ways does this status impede the child's growth? Looking ahead, how are you going to handle the child's growth and eventual separation from the family? What kinds of supports do you need to help you bear not only the original loss, but also the slow loss of the replacement child to the maturation process? Do you feel as though you were a replacement child? Is your replacement child in any way a replacement for yourself as you might have liked your life to be?

## Replacement Others

Not only children, but friends, lovers, partners, and others can serve as replacements for someone who was lost during the trauma. Elvis Presley's mother died of natural causes; and his wife-to be, Priscilla, had lost her father to natural causes. According to Priscilla Presley, "When Elvis and I met, he was still grieving for his mother. . . . That's how we became real close. . . . I guess I brought out the father in Elvis, and he brought out the mother in me" (Rader 1996).

If you went through a trauma with a group of people and only two of you survived, the other person may symbolize, to you, all the others who were lost. People can also serve as replacements for qualities you feel you may have lost during the trauma. Children are often turned to because they are naturally innocent and trusting, and innocence and trust are two of the first qualities to go when a person is traumatized. Hence a trauma survivor may cherish a particular child because that child represents certain virtues the trauma survivor feels he or she has lost.

Trauma survivors who abandon their religious faith or spiritual beliefs because of the trauma may find themselves enamored with or needing the company of people who are deeply religious or unwavering about their spiritual beliefs. By being close to these people, they can be close to who they were prior to the trauma.

For example, Nancy fell in love with David. Unlike Nancy, who had known much abuse and whose body and health were disfigured by years of alcohol abuse and bulimia, David was the picture of health. David had been adored by his parents and experienced few discouragements in life. No one in his family had died, and he had never had any alcohol, drug, or food addictions. He had a strong religious faith, which had never been tested by adversity. Nancy had lost much of her religious faith due to years of mistreatment.

David didn't understand Nancy, but Nancy adored him. "When I'm close to him, I feel close to the girl I was before the traumas. I feel young again and full of faith in life and in God. I have hope for the future, too," she explained. When David left Nancy, she was shattered beyond her expectations. Not only did she lose a love relationship, but she also lost her connection to qualities that David had represented, qualities she had cherished in herself but that were maimed by her traumas.

## ✍ *Exercise: Replacement Others*

Is there a replacement "other" in your life, whose qualities or attributes you value not only for who he or she is but also because he or she represents qualities you lost or feel you lost during the trauma? Is it possible that this person can really carry these qualities for you, or restore these qualities in you? It may be possible that you can rebuild some of these qualities in yourself, but it may also be true that some of these qualities or attributes are permanently lost or scarred. If this person has qualities that you cannot possibly recapture, such as youth or certain physical skills you lost due to the trauma, your sense of loss must be enormous. Can you enjoy these qualities in the other person without burdening the other person with the expectation that he or she must fulfill these qualities to help make up for what you lost? When and if this person goes, or grows, away from you, do you expect to see it as a normal part of life, or will you experience it as a deep personal rejection?

## ✍ Self-Assessment for Psychological Consequences of Survivor Guilt

### Part One

The following questions are designed to help you assess the impact of survivor guilt on various aspects of your life: your feelings about yourself, your ability to relate to others, your ability to experience pleasure, and your ability to work toward your personal and vocational goals. Before answering the following questions in your journal, however, take some time to think about what your life was like and who you were prior to the incident or series of incidents that gave rise to your survivor guilt. It may be helpful to look at a photograph of yourself prior to having experienced survivor guilt and to compare it to a present-day photograph of yourself.

1. Visualize what you looked like, where you were, who you were relating to, and how and what you were doing about a week prior to the incident. Now write a brief description of the person you were then. Be specific about the kind of personality you had, the kinds of social activities you engaged in, and the kinds of interests you had prior to the incident. Include two or three sentences about how you felt about yourself. Can you identify three qualities you liked about yourself and three qualities you did not like about yourself? Overall, did you like yourself or not?

2. Visualize yourself today: what you look like, where you are, who you relate to, and how and what you do on a daily basis. Now write a brief description of the kind of person you are today, the kinds of social activities you engage in, and the kinds of interests you currently hold. Include two or three sentences about how you feel about yourself today. Can you list three qualities you admire about yourself and three qualities you do not value in yourself?

3. Consider the time prior to the incident and your present-day life. Are there any differences in who you were, what you were interested in, or in your relationships? Make a list of these differences. In your opinion, which of these changes in your lifestyle, self-esteem, and relationships can be attributed in whole or in part to your survivor guilt?

### Part Two

Keeping in mind the picture of who you were prior to the incident and who you are now, answer the following questions to the best of your ability. Answer as honestly as possible. Remember, no one will be reading your responses unless you choose to share them.

Do not be ashamed to admit the degree to which you might be destructive to yourself or others. The first step toward any positive change is recognition of where you are right now.

Write at least one or two sentences for each question. Use a separate page for each question, since you will be asked to return to that page later and do some more writing about that topic. On the top of each page, write the name of the topic you are writing about. For example, you would label one page "Self-Esteem"; another, "Alcohol and Drug Usage," and so on.

### 1. Writing Task One: Current Self-Assessment

Briefly describe the following as they pertain to your life in the present:

- Your self-esteem

- Your alcohol or drug usage

- Your eating habits

- Your physical health

- The degree of perfection you expect in yourself and others

- Your tolerance of mistakes in others or yourself

- Your desire to live

- Your intimate relationships

- Your family relationships

- Your friendships

- Your socializing

- Your work relationships

- Your work performance

- Your irritability and anger levels

- Your fear of others

- Your judgment of others

- Your generosity to others

- Your protectiveness toward others

- The care of your body

- Feelings of depression

- Assertiveness

- Feelings of belonging in your family, community, or church

- Feelings of guilt about present-day matters

- Ability to separate from others and handle changes in relationships

- Ability to focus on the present instead of the past

- Thoughts of people who are dead

- Ability to complete tasks or assume responsibility

### 2. Writing Task Two: What If?

In this exercise you will be asked to describe how you think different aspects of your life might be if the incident or trauma that caused you to feel guilty had never taken place or if no one had died or been injured during that time.

Return to the pages you've just written for Writing Task One and write one or two sentences describing what you'd be like or feel like for each of the various aspects of your life if the stressor had never happened or if no one had died or been injured.

### 3. Writing Task Three: Determining the Impact

In this exercise you will be asked to assess the impact of the incident and the survivor guilt that came with it on various aspects of your life. Return to what you have written in Writing Tasks One and Two, and by comparing what you have written about how you are today and how you might have been if you did not suffer from survivor guilt, you will be able to identify some of the ways survivor guilt has had an impact on your life. For each topic, write a brief summary of how survivor guilt has affected that aspect of your life.

For example, Barbara's survivor guilt stemmed from her childhood, when she witnessed her younger brother have serious asthma attacks. Her parents were too busy drinking and quarreling to attend to him. She tried to draw her parents' attention to her almost-dying brother, with limited success. As a child, she felt she should have had the asthma since she was older and stronger and could have probably borne it better. She wrote the following about her self-esteem:

1. Today my self-esteem is low. Every time someone gets sick or upset, I feel so guilty that I feel I have to help them get well or help to calm them down. Since I hardly ever succeed, I have many feelings of failure.

2. If my brother didn't have those attacks, I wouldn't feel guilty when people around me get sick, and I wouldn't run myself ragged trying to do things for people so they don't get sick. The problem is that I get sick from overwork, but if I don't work hard and do everything that's expected of me, and more, I feel guilty.

3. My survivor guilt has made me take unnecessary responsibility for other people's well-being and caused me to work too hard and play too little. I used to feel guilty playing when my brother was sick, and that feeling of guilt about enjoying life carries over to this day. One way I compensate for not enjoying life is by buying things I don't need. I have so many clothes and CDs I don't have anywhere to put them. My survivor guilt has contributed to my being a workaholic and a compulsive shopper.

# Part Two

# The Healing Process

# 6

# Healing from Survivor Guilt

Healing from survivor guilt does not mean forgetting what happened or forgetting the person who died or was harmed. Neither does healing mean you will never again feel guilt or regret. Healing means that your guilt and regrets will be founded on realistic assessments of your role in what happened. Healing also means that the destructive impact of your survivor guilt on your life will lessen and that some of the energy currently bound up with your guilt can become the source of a new, more vital, and more meaningful life.

Survivor guilt has two parts: the *emotional* part, which includes the grief you feel over the person or people who were lost or injured, and the *cognitive*, or mental, part, which includes your assessment of what happened and why. Grieving for someone who mattered to you can last a lifetime. No amount of reasoning or rethinking of a trauma or stressful incident can change that! However, the cognitive part of survivor guilt is amenable to change. A realistic appraisal of what your options were during the trauma or stressful incident can help you tell the difference between what you can legitimately feel guilty about (rational guilt) and what you unrealistically blame yourself for (irrational guilt). Modifying how you view what happened according to the realities of the situation can help diminish some of your feelings of self-blame or self-loathing.

It isn't fair to judge what you did, felt, or thought by some fantasy or ideal that was not available to you. For example, if you feel someone in your family committed suicide partially because your family did not have the funds to provide good mental health care, then judging what you did or did not do for the deceased according to an ideal situation, where you had unlimited funds or unlimited time off work to take care of that person, is not a fair or logical standard.

This chapter and those that follow will outline steps you can take to help rid yourself of unnecessary pain by helping you obtain a more rational and balanced view of your role in the situation that led to the death or injury of another person. The suggestions made in these chapters are based on my work with trauma survivors and others who suffer from intense self-blame and guilt as well as the work of a number of theorists and specialists in the area of stress, trauma, guilt, and grief. As part of the healing process, you will be asked to describe the life-changing situation with which you were involved and to carefully evaluate your actions, thoughts, and feelings. You will be asked to differentiate your survivor guilt from other types of guilt, such as guilt about failure to meet societal expectations, and also to examine your survivor guilt in light of common thinking errors identified by Kubany (1994), Resick (1994), and Beck (1976). Once you become familiar with these thinking errors, you will be able to challenge the way you perceive other situations in the present and any future difficult situations. Your familiarity with these thinking errors will be invaluable in coping with your survivor guilt.

Not all guilt is bad, and there may be aspects of your trauma for which you think you deserve to feel guilty. A part of your healing may involve making amends to or establishing some type of memorial for those who were injured or killed. Most likely, however, there are many parts of your trauma for which you deserve to feel *less* guilt, or *no* guilt at all.

Examining your survivor guilt is an important part of any type of therapy. The exercises that follow can be used in conjunction with your individual or group therapy or recovery program to help you examine the different ways you feel guilty about how you acted (or didn't act), how you felt (or didn't feel), or what you thought (or didn't think) during the trauma. If you have survived more than one traumatic or stressful incident, then the guilt involved in each incident may need to be examined.

While you may still feel guilty after reading this book and completing the written exercises, you will probably not feel *as* guilty about *as many* aspects of your trauma or stressful life incident. Most people tend to exaggerate the kinds of power and choices they had in certain situations and tend to minimize the obstacles and pressures with which they had to cope.

Healing also involves addressing questions pertaining to the meaning of life, specifically *your* life. If you sincerely feel that someone died or was injured in your place, then you need to confront the difficult question of why you were spared and your purpose for having the health and life that you do when someone else was not so fortunate. There are as many answers to those questions as there are people. However, there are two answers that are not acceptable: self-destruction or harming others. First, you were not spared so that you could squander your talents and life's possibilities for you on self-defeating and self-destructive behaviors, such as an addiction, or on negative emotions such as self-loathing. Second, you were not spared so that you could vent your guilt and anger on others.

If there is an answer to the question of why you were spared, that answer certainly involves living as meaningfully, safely, and enjoyably as possible. It also involves enhancing your capacity for love—to give love and receive it, to work—in endeavors that contribute to the world and that are creative, and pleasure—to relax and find enjoyment in recreational activities.

## How to Use These Chapters

Generally speaking, you will want to work through the chapters in part 2 in the order they appear. However, if you begin to experience some of the warning signs listed in the "Cautions" section of the introduction, you should stop reading this book or working on any of the exercises and follow the suggestions in the "Cautions" section.

This book is not a complete trauma-processing book. It deals with one aspect of stress and trauma—survivor guilt—but not the other strong feelings that having gone through a major stressful event or trauma can arouse, for example, anger. Ideally you are working with an individual or are in group therapy or a recovery program. (For suggestions in finding a trained therapist, see appendix A; for a listing of trauma-processing books and other resources, see appendix B.) Reading this book and completing some of these exercises will most likely increase your emotions. This is to be expected and is desirable in that part of the healing process involves feeling some of the feelings associated with your trauma or difficult life events. In fact, if you read this book and work on these exercises and experience little or no emotion, this may be a sign that you are in a state of emotional numbing or denial or have a medical problem (in which case you should seek medical attention). Having little or no emotional reaction to this book could also be a sign that you have resolved many of the emotional issues associated with the incidents that caused your survivor guilt.

However, if your emotions are intensified to the point that you begin to experience symptoms or feel overwhelmed, you will need to seek professional medical or mental health assistance before reading more of this book or working on any additional exercises.

The irony of the healing process is that you must delve into the past, in order to help put it behind you. You must also become more self-preoccupied as you attempt the healing process so that ultimately you will be less self-preoccupied and more interested in others. While you are going through the healing process, others may see you as selfish for spending so much time reading this or other books, working on these or other exercises, going to therapy or participating in a recovery or healing group or program. However, one of the ultimate goals of spending so much time working on yourself regarding your survivor guilt is that, down the road, as you make strides in the healing process, you will be more open and giving toward others and more involved with people in the present rather than the people who have died.

Another contradiction is that the healing process involves retreating from present-day life in order to deal with the past so that eventually the present becomes more and more important to you in relation to the past. (Notice I didn't say that you forget the past: only that the present becomes increasingly important.) The short-term objective of any healing or recovery endeavor is to analyze and process the past. However, the long-term purpose of this process of examining the past is to help you develop a new perspective on the past so that you can more fully engage in present-day life.

## On the Path to Positive Growth

Carl Jung, a student of Freud and a famous psychologist in his own right, used the metaphor of a growing tree to describe the client in therapy. The client, he said, is like a tree, naturally growing taller and fuller while its roots spread out wider and deeper into the ground. When the roots of a tree hit a large stone or other obstacle, do they try to shove the stone away or crack it? No. The roots just grow around the obstacle and then keep going. The stone may have interrupted or slowed the tree's growth for a while, but no stone, no matter how large, can stop the tree from growing.

In Jung's view, the stones in the way of tree roots symbolize obstacles to personal growth. These obstacles can include an internal emotional conflict (such as survivor guilt) or an external stressor (such as a trauma). Jung theorized that certain emotional conflicts are never totally eliminated; they are simply outgrown. They stay a permanent part of the psyche, just as the stones surrounded by tree roots become part of the tree. In the same way that roots can move far past the stones in their path into new territory, you can work through and grow beyond your survivor guilt.

Perhaps today your guilt feelings and the incidents that caused them feel far away from the rest of you. However, once you have confronted and assessed your guilt feelings, you can use some of the powerful energy in that guilt to benefit you, to use in pursuing goals of your own choosing. Your survivor guilt can become a source of positive change—just as the stones support and strengthen the root structure of the tree and give it character.

The path to positive growth can sometimes be a rocky one. Healing is never easy. It'll help you to understand some general information about the healing process before you begin on your journey.

## Guilt and Positive Change

As paradoxical as it may sound, the very guilt that is strangling you today may provide you with energy for positive change. For many people, coping with survivor guilt can be the starting point of taking their lives and their self-care more seriously. This process is probably familiar to you if you've participated in a twelve-step program such as Alcoholics Anonymous, Narcotics Anonymous, Overeater's Anonymous, or Al-Anon. These programs encourage members to take a good hard look at past behaviors that trouble them, discuss them with others, and then, based on a realistic assessment of those behaviors, take actions to make amends for any real (not imaginary) wrongdoings in a manner that does not harm themselves or their loved ones.

Twelve-step members are also encouraged to look at how they have harmed themselves and make amends to themselves, just as they would to others. The theory behind the twelve steps, that looking at past guilts and making efforts to deal with these guilts constructively rather than destructively through addiction or some other harmful method, is a valid one. It helps free people from the weight of the past and releases energy to be used for living more fully in the present.

## Don't Do It Alone

The twelve-step programs emphasize that no one can go through the process of recovery alone. Each step of the way, members are encouraged to share their thoughts and feelings with others, who can often provide emotional support, objective feedback, and a broader perspective on the issue at hand. In the twelve-step model of recovery, involving others is both necessary and productive.

I highly recommend that if you wish to embark on the process of healing from your survivor guilt, you involve others in the process. These others could include a trained professional therapist, a trusted and knowledgeable religious or spiritual advisor, or a close friend. (Suggestions on finding a qualified therapist are provided in appendix A.) Left on your own, you might look at your past and blame yourself entirely or distort events so that you make yourself the sole or major cause of someone else's injury or death. You may also avoid acknowledging and dealing with certain aspects of what occurred, which others may be able to point out to you.

While the feedback of others is helpful, in the end, you are the main judge. Only you know what you thought, felt, and did and what it was like to go through what you went through, and only you can come to some understanding of the complex mix of pressures, thoughts, and emotions that were present during your traumatic or difficult event.

There are also dangers in asking for help. Some persons, even therapists and twelve-step program members, may present you with overly simplistic or otherwise unhelpful feedback, or feedback that isn't based on the unique reality of who you are and what you experienced. Generally speaking, nobody knows you as well as you know yourself. Beware of feedback that consists of simple slogans, moralisms, or clichés, or of other types of feedback that may only add to your self-blame, grief, or anger without increasing your understanding.

## Growth vs. Deficit Model of Therapy

One of your healing goals should be to rid yourself of the idea that because of what happened to you, you are diseased or deficient. Such thinking hearkens to a deficit model of therapy, which assumes that you, the client, are "sick," "wrong," or "inadequate" in some way. The role of the therapist in this model of therapy is to help you discover your deficiencies and purge you of them.

In contrast, in a growth model of therapy, which is used in this book, the therapist's role is to help you discover and develop your strengths. A growth model assumes that you are not deficient or abnormal; instead it deems the events you experienced as highly abnormal. And as a result of those events, you may have developed coping mechanisms that served you well for a while, but do not do so now.

As you grow and heal, many of these negative patterns will naturally fall by the wayside, because you won't need them anymore. In addition, the more you are able to look at your guilt directly, the less need you will have for defenses that limit your life.

Healing, as explored in the following chapters, means confronting what you haven't yet confronted and examining it in light of the totality of what was occurring at the time. Many therapists feel that symptoms such as anxiety, depression, and nightmares are due in part to, or made worse by, avoidance of painful and problematic emotions, including guilt. Just by facing your guilt you are taking a major step toward your own healing; it is a courageous step that many people avoid at all costs. The notion that the "truth shall set you free" applies to guilt as well as other matters. You will never be able to examine your guilt and see if it is realistic or not if you don't first acknowledge that you have guilt.

You don't need to be "fixed"; you simply need help in rethinking and reevaluating the tragic events that have caused you so much pain and guilt. The following sections give several guidelines for the healing process.

## *Healing Is a Nonlinear Process*

Healing does not run a straight path; it inevitably involves setbacks. Consider this: In recovering from the flu you may have several days of improved health, followed by a temporary relapse. This setback doesn't mean you won't recover from the flu. All it signifies is that the human body is not an inanimate object. It can't simply be repaired and then be expected to stay that way once and for all. Rather it is delicate and complex; yet it has a great ability to withstand stress.

Like the body, the human psyche is also not inanimate. You may find yourself taking three steps forward in the healing process and then two steps back. That's fine; you're still making progress.

Sometimes you go backward because you need to go backward—if, for example, you've taken on more emotional material than you can handle at a particular time. At that point you may have to retreat so that you can absorb the emotional shock and otherwise make sense of the material.

## Healing Takes Time

Healing from survivor guilt is a lifelong process. Depending on the intensity and duration of your particular experiences, it may take months or even years to fully remember or gain perspective on the events that trouble you now. Similarly, it may take a long time for much of the guilt and the feelings that are usually associated with that guilt, such as anger and grief, to diminish.

If you've been extremely traumatized, healing may take five, ten, or even twenty years. But that's okay; the main point is that you have begun. Your healing process will take its own course and unfold in its own time, not according to some formula.

You may be in a great hurry to get it over with. If so, you can accelerate your recovery by working harder in therapy and using other aids, such as support groups and books. However, in general, it's better to deal with painful memories in doses. This way, you run less risk of becoming overwhelmed. Just as you get more out of a meal if you eat slowly and chew each bite, it's important to take the healing one step at a time, slowly, rather than to attempt to do too much and understand yourself only superficially.

## Restorative Experiences

Your healing process will be heavily influenced by what has happened to you since the events that caused your survivor guilt. If you were besieged with more stresses or traumas or with misunderstanding or hurtful remarks by others, your healing process will be longer and more painful than if you had affirming, restorative experiences.

For example, if you suffered from survivor guilt due to the suicide of a loved one and your church, mosque, or synagogue has had discussions about the illness of clinical depression and the possibility of suicide among those who have this illness, you may have experienced support and caring from your religious community. The discussions about depression educated you and others that suicide is the result of a psychological and medical condition called depression, which can cause people to feel they have no reason to keep on living. As a result, others will tend to be less blaming of you, and this could lessen your survivor guilt. In contrast, if your religious or other community openly or subtly blamed you for the suicide, your survivor guilt would probably be increased.

Restorative experiences can be economic, vocational, political, and interpersonal. If you were given a financial reward or political recognition for your positive contributions to a stressful situation, then any survivor guilt you had about what happened might have been somewhat alleviated by the awareness of what you did do to benefit others.

For example, for soldiers who did not have the benefit of extensive therapy, their existential survivor guilt over having lived while others died is often compounded by content survivor guilt over the actions they took to stay alive during war. When society acknowledges the soldiers as heroes and applauds their killing as a form of patriotic duties, soldiers tend to suffer from less content survivor guilt than soldiers whose society denigrates them or considers them immoral for having killed during war.

The classic example of this difference is the difference between soldiers who fought in World War II and those who fought in Vietnam. After World War II, soldiers, many of whom had killed civilians along with enemy soldiers, were seen by society as heroic patriots. They were not called "babykillers" or portrayed in the media as brutes, as were soldiers from the Vietnam war. In a sense, the societal approval of World War II functioned as a form of absolution for the killing. Many returning warriors from the Vietnam war did not receive this kind of warm reception and hence were denied the symbolic societal absolution for the killing. Their survivor guilt tends to be greater than those of soldiers from World War II.

If you have been retraumatized since the original traumatic event, your healing will be longer and more complicated than the healing of someone who was fortunate enough to have escaped subsequent stresses or disaster.

## Medication

If you are in an extreme state of depression, anxiety, or hyperalertness, you may need medication to help reduce your symptoms so that you can concentrate on healing. For example, if you can't sleep at night and start dozing off at work or during therapy sessions, you may need to consider medication to help you sleep. Similarly, if you are having so many flashbacks and intrusive thoughts that you can't concentrate on your job, you may need medication so that you can function. For such medication, you will need to consult a psychiatrist with expertise in stress or trauma.

## The Prerequisite of Safety

In order to begin the healing process, you need to feel and be safe. You cannot begin to heal from your wounds, psychological or physical, if you are still being abused or injured in some manner. If you are being exploited at work or mistreated in a love relationship or if you are in an abusive living environment or otherwise in danger, you will need to take steps to create a safer existence. Indeed, creating a safe living environment for yourself is part of the healing process.

Your sense of safety will also be internal. You need to feel safe with your thoughts, feelings, and behaviors before you can begin to deal with your survivor guilt. This doesn't mean you won't sometimes have troublesome thoughts or feelings, but rather that you feel you can manage them. It is not wise to begin the unsettling process of remembering what happened without feeling you can exert at least some control over the symptoms that are creating havoc in your life. In some cases medication may be needed.

## The Stages of Healing for Survivor Guilt

The healing process can be divided into seven stages:

1. **Remembering what happened.** This involves putting together the story of the trauma or stressful incident in as much detail as you can remember, including significant events that happened before or after. In order to assess your role in the trauma or stressful incident, you need to know what you thought, felt, and did at various points in time. You also need to have an awareness of whatever else was going on before, during, or after the events that caused the survivor guilt.

2. **Separating survivor guilt from other guilt feelings.** This involves identifying your guilt feelings and separating your guilt feelings from other emotions and issues.

3. **Reconstructing your role in the trauma or stressful incidents mentally.** This step involves looking at the bigger picture or reevaluating your behavior in light of the total context of what was occurring before, during, and after the death or

injury of the person about whom you carry survivor guilt. It also involves examining your view of what happened in light of common thinking errors in order to help you separate rational from irrational survivor guilt.

4. **Countering self-blame and irrational guilt.** This involves developing positive but realistic ways of viewing what happened so that you can challenge your self-blaming attitudes with power. This process also involves identifying the strengths you exhibited during your difficult time and appreciating those, in addition to identifying those acts for which you still feel guilty.

5. **Accepting guilt.** No matter how much you examine your guilt feelings from a logical perspective, some guilt may remain. Part of the healing process is accepting guilt that you feel is "irrational" and guilt that you feel you deserve. This section will also explore ways of resolving certain guilt-related issues and trying to make your remaining guilt work for you.

6. **Examining personal consequences.** How has the survivor guilt affected your self-esteem, self-care, physical and emotional health, work performance, and ability to enjoy and contribute to life?

7. **A commitment to honesty.** This involves making a commitment to be honest with yourself about your survivor guilt and to take positive action toward understanding that guilt and putting it to constructive use.

Another component that may be important to you involves recognizing any spiritual or moral concerns you have. Not everyone has such concerns, but if you do, you may want to consider talking to a clergyperson, priest, rabbi, or other spiritual advisor. Keep in mind though, that with these individuals, as with any others, you need to be on guard against any subtle or overt blaming attitudes. If you are seeking help to sort out your self-blaming attitudes, the last thing you need is for someone to add to your burden of guilt. Rather you need someone to help you put your guilt into a spiritual perspective and help you sort out rational and irrational guilt. Whether you decide to take a closer look at any spiritual or moral concerns with a religious or spiritual professional, with a trusted friend or family member, or within yourself, it is important that you recognize, rather than deny or minimize, any such concerns.

The stages of healing will be progressive. For example, examining your guilt feelings will be more intense and meaningful if you actually remember some or most of what occurred during the traumatic event or stressful time than if your memory is hazy. On the other hand, you may have guilt and other feelings about the event without any recollection whatsoever about what happened. This is commonly the case with individuals who were abused as young children.

It's important to remember that the healing stages do not necessarily flow in a neat progression. You may find some resolution, for instance, without recalling much of what happened. Similarly, you may already be resolving your guilt when suddenly you remember a highly significant aspect of what happened that changes almost everything you previously thought about it. Much to your surprise, the new revelation puts you back into a state of overwhelming survivor guilt.

# Cautions: When the Healing Process Is Not Advisable

If you've been severely or repeatedly traumatized or are currently coping with a great deal of stress, the healing process described in this book may not be advisable. In some cases, counseling is helpful; however, in others, it has been shown to increase symptoms and depression. For example, some Nazi concentration camp survivors have fared much better by keeping their memories in repression and denial than others have by remembering the horror. Similarly, preliminary studies of torture survivors from Cambodia and other Southeast Asian countries indicate that counseling focused on the trauma made many of these people feel worse, not better.

If you fall into one of these categories or feel that you, too, are better off not remembering what happened to you, then you need to focus on improving your ability to cope with your feelings, rather than on gaining insight. Most beneficial to you would be working on anger management, coping with grief and loss, and finding constructive outlets for your energies with the help of a qualified counselor or a self-help book such as those listed in appendix B. You may also want to discuss medication with your therapist or counselor.

Although it is natural and normal for you to experience distress upon trying to follow some of the healing suggestions in this book, keep in mind the warning signs listed in the "Cautions" section of the introduction. If you experience any of these signs, seek professional help immediately.

If one of the following statements applies to you, it's probably best that you discontinue reading this book until you receive the approval of a physician or trained mental health counselor. Instead you can learn means of stress reduction, such as relaxation techniques and deep breathing. (These techniques are briefly discussed in appendix C. Many therapists can also train you in these methods.)

- *I should not attempt to remember the past at this point in time because this is the advice given to me by a trained mental health professional or because when I remember, I begin experiencing some of the symptoms outlined in the "Cautions" section in the introduction to this book. I'm afraid that remembering would endanger my mental or emotional stability to the point that I would need to be hospitalized in a psychiatric ward.*

- *I have so much stress in the present that looking at the past is best saved for another point in my life.*

- *I need some other form of counseling, such as substance abuse rehabilitation or medication for depression, before I can tackle my survivor guilt.*

- *I'm afraid that if I start thinking about the past, especially my guilt, I'll kill or harm myself, another person, or another living being, or I'll be unable to maintain my sanity.*

- *I need to be in a safe, controlled environment, for example, an inpatient ward devoted to trauma survivors, in order to begin the healing process.*

For example, Priscilla came to therapy wanting to deal with her survivor guilt regarding her sister's breast cancer. However, Priscilla, had just separated from her husband, was in the middle of a job change, and had recently discovered that she had diabetes. At the same time, her eldest child was having a severe negative reaction to her parents' separation. Although her sister's cancer was an important issue, it was therapeutically inadvisable for her to delve into her survivor guilt issues until some of the other areas of her life had stabilized. Dealing with her survivor guilt issues would have increased her sense of being overwhelmed and made her less effective in coping with the shock of single parenthood, her separation, job change, and medical problems. We waited until she had begun to adjust to her illness, new work environment, and the single-parent lifestyle to commence in-depth work on her survivor guilt.

# How Will I Know When I Am Healed?

As I stated before, just simply being able to acknowledge, talk about, and write about your guilt is a major step toward healing because you are free of the shackles of secrecy. However, healing from survivor guilt does not mean you will never again think about the circumstances surrounding the guilt or that you will never feel guilty again. If you must measure your progress, try not to think in terms of outcome, but in terms of having made your best effort. Also, think less about eliminating your symptoms and more about the evidence that you are increasing your involvement in the present and your willingness and ability to take better care of yourself. To help you assess your progress, a self-care questionnaire is provided in chapter 9.

# Difficulties Getting Started

You may want to experience some relief from your survivor guilt, yet there may be many obstacles to getting started on the healing process. As Opp and Samson (1989) point out, guilt can serve one of several psychological purposes, any of which might lead you to resist working through it. For example, guilt can produce sufficient anxiety and pain so as to prevent you from violating social or personal rules. Guilt can protect you from experiencing feelings of helplessness and grief. For some people, guilt is a defense against psychoses or murderous rages. (If you fear becoming psychotic or homicidal as the result of feeling less guilty, then you need to stop working through this book; read the "Cautions" section in the introduction and follow the suggestions given there for calming yourself and seeking help immediately.)

Along with resistance, there are other obstacles toward healing from survivor guilt. Here are a few of the main ones:

## *Survivor Guilt*

The first and foremost obstacle is your survivor guilt itself. You may feel you need to keep your survivor guilt as a memorial to the dead, as a way of punishing yourself for something you did or did not do, or for something of which you feel ashamed. Your survivor guilt itself may be a means of coping with your survivor guilt, which can lead to your pursuing healing halfheartedly or not pursuing it at all.

## Unresolved Grief and Insufficient Commemoration of the Dead

If your survivor guilt is a type of memorial to the dead, you may feel that if you reduce your guilt you'll be betraying those who have died. This is especially the case if the people did not receive a proper burial or were not sufficiently recognized and memorialized. You may fear that if you start to feel better about life, you will be guilty of abandoning the memory of those who died or were injured. Being sad, miserable, and guilty can be a way of grieving, showing respect for the dead, or staying close to them.

While our culture tends to lack rituals and other formalized means of honoring the dead, there may be other ways for you to express your grief and show your respect toward the dead and to preserve their memory than draining your psychic energy with constant survivor guilt. For example, you could memorialize the dead through a religious or some other type of ritual. This could be a formal ritual or one that you created for yourself. You could pay tribute in the form of a work of art or literature, or a contribution of time or money to a charitable organization or cause. Concrete expression of your feelings toward the dead is preferable to making emotional pain the memorial for the dead.

For example, Marianne's father and sister committed suicide, and another one of her sisters was murdered. "My father and sisters were not important people. Their deaths didn't make the headlines, and there's hardly anyone left in the family to remember them since after all those deaths, the family basically fell apart. But they were important to me and I remember them all the time. I can't build a monument to them, but I can take a day off work and visit their graves. I can light a candle in my living room in their memory. I can talk to a friend about them. It can't be a casual friend. It has to be a compassionate friend, who won't tell me to 'get over it' but who'll just listen quietly and show me a little love."

One of Marianne's surviving sisters volunteers one day a month at a nursing home, and another sister volunteers one day a month at a local Parents of Murdered Children's group as a way of honoring their dead relatives.

If you are artistically inclined or are interested in writing, a literary or other type of artistic monument to the dead is an excellent way to channel grief, love, and guilt. For example, Thomas Toivi Blatt whose many family members were killed during the Holocaust, wrote a book describing his life and how his relatives were slaughtered. Without this book, his family members might have been just another statistic among the many nameless and largely unrecognized dead in his country. His book, *From the Ashes of Sobibor*, serves as a form of monument. Individuals who feel they can't write or create a work of art have sometimes paid tribute to the dead, and immortalized them, by making audio- or videotapes on which they describe the dead and recount the story of their lives, and their deaths.

## Fear of Criticism, Fear of the Dead

You may fear that if you start being less depressed and more creative or productive, others will view you as disloyal to the dead. You may also fear that the dead will punish you or your loved ones if you begin to feel better. This notion hearkens back to the idea that the ghosts of the dead sometimes seek revenge on the living.

This primitive idea was held by many early peoples who offered sacrifices to the ghosts of dead animals in hopes of appeasing their anger at having been murdered. A similar idea was held about the ghosts of humans: the ghost of a person may be angry about having been wronged or not properly buried. In Shakespeare's *Hamlet*, the ghost of Hamlet's father, who was murdered by his brother, comes to Hamlet and urges him to avenge his death. In the dreams of some people with survivor guilt, ghosts of the dead demand sacrifice, retribution, or proper recognition of their deaths and deeds (Campbell 1988).

You may feel that the idea of ghosts is an antiquated one and that it would be embarrassing to admit that you fear or have any kind of relationship with a ghost. However, in my clinical experience I have seen many highly intelligent and educated people feel terrorized by ghosts. While seeing or hearing things that aren't there is usually considered having hallucinations and as being part of a psychotic disorder, many trauma survivors have visual or auditory flashbacks of their trauma that are not signs of schizophrenia or other psychotic disorders, because the voices and visions are directly related to their traumas.

In some cases traumatized clients have brought the ghosts with them to session. For example, a combat vet revealed to me that he never came to sessions alone: he brought the ghosts of his two dead buddies with him. He did this to protect them. After they died in battle, he promised them he would never leave them and that he would protect them for the rest of his life. He was now keeping his promise. Everywhere he went, the ghosts went with him, and he took care of them. In this case, there was no fear of the ghosts: rather love and protectiveness.

In another instance, the mother of a boy killed in a car accident revealed that she talked to the ghost of her son every night. They had long conversations about what happened and why. She stated that she actually felt the presence of the ghost and was comforted by it. Like the combat veteran, she promised the ghost she would take good care of him and never let him be hurt again. The ghost, in turn, warned her of possible future circumstances where someone in the family could be injured and instructed her in protective measures.

These poignant cases may seem extreme—and they are. But what they illustrate—the feeling that there are ghosts and that these ghosts can be feared, loved, or protected—is not uncommon. Survivor guilt, grief, and other feelings pertaining to the loss of a loved one can be so strong that they take on the embodiment of a ghost. In the dramas of Shakespeare and other writers and artists, the ghosts assume a visual form. Among most of the traumatized people I've worked with, the ghosts are more of an idea or a presence rather than a concrete entity.

The ghosts can also take the form of voices that are closely associated with a traumatic incident. For example, a young man whose father was lost in a boating accident suffers from survivor guilt because when the boat was overturned, he was able to stay afloat but his father drowned. Part of his survivor guilt includes hearing his father's voice call for help, just as his father did as he was drowning. In another instance, a young woman who managed to escape a fire that killed her sister hears her sister call out her name. The sister's voice is not accusatory or condemning, but when the young woman hears it, she is consumed with survivor guilt. The voice tends to surface around the anniversary of the death date of her sister, on her sister's birthday, and at other times when she is reminded of her sister.

These voices are a type of auditory flashback, rather than a symptom of a psychiatric disorder such as schizophrenia or paranoia. Although they are not common or "normal" in the general population, it is perfectly normal for trauma survivors to have such experiences, especially under three conditions: if they were repeatedly traumatized or revictimized after the original trauma; if they did not receive help with the trauma soon after it occurred; or if their major coping mechanism for the trauma was repression or denial. If you meet any of these conditions, and hear voices, you need to see the voices as a type of reexperiencing symptom, a sign of unfinished work in dealing with the trauma, rather than as a sign of insanity.

In other auditory flashbacks, you may hear sounds associated with trauma. Such sounds include human voices, such as screaming or sobbing, or other sounds, such as banging or explosions. These auditory flashbacks differ from the voices associated with schizophrenia and other psychoses in that the sounds are almost direct replicas of those heard during the traumatic event.

For example, when Gregg walks by ditches, sometimes he hears the screams and sobs of the soldiers he saw die in ditches during World War II. He also hears these soldiers ask him for help or to join them in death. Sometimes flashbacks include only one of the senses, sometimes more. For example, some flashbacks are only auditory; others are visual and auditory.

## Feelings of Worthlessness and Hopelessness

Feelings of worthlessness and hopelessness can also get in the way of healing. If you were traumatized, these feelings may stem from the trauma, where you undoubtedly felt hopeless and may have been made to feel worthless. These feelings could also simply be the result of survivor guilt. Because you cannot redo the past to bring about a happier ending to the situation that plagues you, you may have generalized your feelings of hopelessness about changing the past to present-day situations. Fortunately, most present-day situations, regardless of how oppressive they might be, are probably not as hopeless as attempting to bring back the dead or reverse physical and psychological injuries such as those sustained during a trauma or stressful event. Most situations today are amenable to some form of improvement or change, unless they are traumatic in themselves.

If you are feeling worthless, ask yourself if you believe in the value of human life. If your answer is "yes," then you need to believe you are worth something too. If your answer is "no," then that means you consider those who died or were injured to be worthless also. If this is the case, then there is no cause for survivor guilt because those who died or were injured didn't matter much anyway.

If you have survivor guilt, you obviously must think that those who died or injured mattered a great deal. If they were worth something, then so are you. You need to operate on the assumption that every human life matters, even your own, regardless of the fact that when you feel sad or guilty, you don't feel that this is the case.

## Untreated Clinical Depression, Post-Traumatic Stress Disorder, or Substance Abuse

If you suffer from clinical depression, post-traumatic stress disorder (or some other trauma-related anxiety disorder), or a substance abuse problem and are not receiving adequate medical and psychological help, you may feel too mentally disorganized, fatigued, unmotivated, hopeless, or worthless to begin the healing process. Your efforts in healing from survivor guilt need to be in conjunction with sufficient qualified help for your depression, substance abuse, or post-traumatic stress disorder.

If you have an addiction, you need to seek help to gain some control over your symptoms before you can profit from this book. While it is not necessary to be totally free of an addiction, it is necessary to be in a recovery program and have the symptoms under some control; otherwise, realistically, you will not have the time or energy to deal with your survivor guilt.

Similarly, the exercises in this book are not suitable for people who have never dealt with their past or who have a form of mental illness that is controlling their lives, such as multiple personality disorder, paranoid schizophrenia, or some other significant psychiatric disorder. If this is the case, you should only use the exercises in this book under the guidance of a qualified mental health professional.

## Fear of Change

You may find it difficult to continue reading this book and complete the remaining written exercises because you fear change. This does not mean you are a masochist who enjoys suffering. Nor does it mean that you are insincere in expressing a desire to deal with your survivor guilt as honestly as possible. Rather your fear of change reflects the well-known fact that all change, even positive change, can create anxiety and fear. It's human nature to become bored with the same old routine and tired of feeling unhappy. Yet to try something new and let go of guilt and grief can feel threatening, because it opens up an unknown emotional world. You may fear that if you change, more will be expected of you at work or in your relationships.

## *Ambivalence about Dealing with the Past*

The hallmark of having been through a trauma or an extremely stressful situation involving significant loss is ambivalence. You may want to remember what happened, but you can't stand to remember. You want to deal with your survivor guilt, but you don't want to have to think about it and feel the pain, fear, anxiety, shame, and exhaustion involved with it ever again. You want healing for your survivor guilt, yet you fear being overwhelmed if you start to read, write, think, or talk about it.

These contradictory feelings are normal and expected. It's only human to wish to forget a painful situation. If you could actually forget about it, however, there would be no need for you to read this or any other book having to do with pain and loss. The problem is you can't forget about it, and even though the event happened long ago, your feelings about it are shaping your behavior and influencing your life today. Some of the impact of the past may be positive: for example, having survivor guilt may be making you a sensitive, caring person who is protective of others and who is committed to promoting life and well-being in those around you. Or perhaps you are in a human services occupation, such as education, medical work, police work, rescue work, or a mental health field, and help to save lives on a daily basis.

Positive consequences like these are to be applauded. However, they are not what is motivating you to read this book, and they are not the cause of your ambivalence. To ease some of the negative consequences of your survivor guilt, such as depression, addiction, shame, low self-esteem, and other consequences described in chapter 5, you must begin the healing process and come to a more complete understanding of your survivor guilt. This will inevitably involve taking a carefully detailed look at the sad and tragic events in your past and your role in them.

It should be clear by now that by working on your survivor guilt, you can obtain a more rational picture of the tragic events in your past. You may also begin to forgive yourself for behavior, thoughts, and feelings associated with these events about which you felt guilt or shame. It is also acceptable, and in many cases extremely advisable, to remain in counseling or otherwise work on your trauma and survivor guilt issues for as long as is needed.

# 7

# Remembering

If you were traumatized, you face a dilemma. Remembering the trauma is painful and at first can even give rise to more psychological distress. But if you don't make an effort to remember what happened consciously, you'll continue to relive the trauma and remember it indirectly, through symptoms such as addiction or anxiety attacks or through feelings of fear, sadness, rage, or profound confusion. Trauma generates such tremendous psychic and physiological energy in people that they are doomed to spend their lives discharging it through intrusive thoughts, nightmares, flashbacks, and many forms of bodily tension and psychological stress, unless they are able to deal with it directly by thinking about what happened in a rational manner and by feeling some of the feelings associated with the trauma, feelings that may have been suppressed during the trauma or thereafter.

Remembering is essential to coming to some degree of emotional resolution or mental understanding of what happened and your role in the traumatic events. It's not necessary to remember every detail of the trauma. Neither is it necessary to feel every relevant feeling associated with the trauma. But you need to remember enough of what happened and feel enough of the feelings so that you can understand how the trauma affects you today.

# Why You Might Have Difficulties with Remembering

You may have difficulties remembering some of the details of what happened due to the sheer number of events occurring at the same time or because you were more focused on some aspects of what was happening than on others. Furthermore, if you were undergoing a trauma, there are special memory factors that may make remembering what happened difficult. According to Dr. Bessel van der Kolk, a trauma expert at Harvard University, traumatic memories are often stored in a way that does not permit survivors to know or to tell their stories in a narrative form. Often these memories are stored on the semiconscious or unconscious level and are split off from the conscious mind. Later on, the memories may return. However, when they emerge into consciousness, they may not return as coherent stories, but rather in bits and pieces, as fragmentary memories of the event. The memories can also return as nightmares, flashbacks, physical pain, or obsessive behaviors.

When the memories are fragmented and unconnected with one another, you might find it nearly impossible to make sense out of your inner life. Until these memories can be pulled together into at least a semicoherent story, you may have difficulty understanding yourself. You may not understand or fully appreciate the connection between the trauma and your depression, fear, anxiety, irritability, or emotional shutdown and may feel controlled by powerful and confusing inner forces (van der Kolk 1990). This feeling can actually deepen your fear, depression, and sense of powerlessness. You might feel as though you are "crazy," but your reactions are rational.

In many cases, trauma survivors, especially abuse survivors, turn to substance abuse or addiction in order to cope. However, in my experience with adult survivors of childhood physical and sexual abuse, I have found very few who could link their addiction to the abuse. Instead of seeing the obvious relationship between the abuse and their addiction, these clients tended to view their addiction as yet another indication that they were "no good" and therefore deserved the abuse. One reason for their difficulty in making the connection between the abuse and their addiction was this inability to piece together their own personal story.

# Exploring Your Memories

This section is devoted to encouraging you to uncover your memories. Regardless of the type of stress or trauma you endured, it's important for you to eventually be able to recall as much of your story as possible. You may simply be unable to remember some aspects of the story due to psychological amnesia. As you complete the exercises that follow, some of your amnesia may be lifted. You will benefit most from these exercises if you first prepare by calming yourself through deep-breathing or muscle-relaxation exercises, or both. (These techniques are described in appendix C.)

Work at your own pace. Some of the suggested exercises may be helpful; others may not. Stay with those that work for you and ignore the rest. Under no circumstances consider yourself a failure because one or more of the suggested exercises are not useful to you.

## *A Note of Caution*

Keep in mind that you should not attempt any of the following exercises if you or your therapist feel you will be unable to manage the feelings they may bring forth. Remember to consult your therapist or psychiatrist before beginning any such exercise technique—especially if you are currently taking any kind of medication. The same applies to beginning meditation exercises. Also, if these techniques bring forth intolerable memories, stop immediately.

For some trauma survivors, relaxation can be fraught with danger. Prolonged muscle relaxation and meditation may be especially risky if you have psychiatric problems other than PTSD, especially if you have been psychotic or currently suffer from either psychotic tendencies or a full-blown psychosis.

Although some survivors find great peace and freedom in practicing deep-breathing and muscle-relaxation techniques, others find such techniques counterproductive, increasing rather than decreasing their anxiety. When these individuals relax, they can only envision the trauma and little else. All the "peaceful, relaxing" suggestions commonly used in relaxation and deep-breathing techniques, which are useful and beneficial to others, are to them just a bad joke.

Jerry was an emergency room doctor who had seen many deaths. The week before he came into the mental health clinic for help, two victims of a car accident, a husband and wife, had died on the table before him. This incident shattered his professionally calm, detached front. He experienced an intense survivor guilt reaction that he did not understand. However, that night, his dream helped him understand the reason for his guilt: that night, Jerry dreamed about being four years old and seeing his father murder his mother and then commit suicide. Until then, Jerry's memories had not been triggered.

Had his counseling begun with relaxation techniques, Jerry might have spent his "relaxation" time having flashbacks of the deaths of his parents. Therefore, therapy began first with talking about the trauma, until the initial shock of recognizing it had abated somewhat. Before Jerry could even contemplate relaxation exercises, he had to have several counseling sessions. During those sessions, he learned that he would not die or cease to function if he dared to remember. He also learned that remembering would not result in the memories recurring as real-life events and that the memories would eventually diminish in intensity. He knew that if necessary he could always go back to dissociation, denial, numbing, or the other methods he had used before to keep from remembering

If Jerry's story sounds familiar to you—if you share the same fears of remembering—be sure to share your concerns with your therapist, group leader, or counselor.

## ✍ *Writing Exercise: Telling Your Story*

Describe in your journal the stressful or traumatic events that happened to you and your feelings during and after the event. Be as specific and detailed as you can. This process may bring up memories you would rather forget. It may also give rise to pain, anger, sadness, or remorse. However, your purpose in reading this book is to better understand what happened and how what happened has resulted in your survivor guilt. Through this understanding, you'll be able to exert greater control over your present and future life experiences.

Take as many pages as you need. You may want to write for ten minutes, then take a break. I don't recommend writing for more than a half-hour at a time. You can take several days or weeks to tell your story, if necessary.

If your history of stress or trauma is extensive, do not try to write down all the events that trouble you. Start with one trauma or stressful event. At a later point in time, you may want to return to this exercise and complete it for another event.

After you've described what occurred, put your journal away for a day or two. Then reread what you've written, adding to your entries any additional memories you may have recalled. Over time, your memories of the stressful events or the trauma will continue to sharpen and unfold. As they emerge, keep writing them down. If you can, keep talking about them also. Consider the exercises in this book as just a beginning. The following sections offer some additional suggestions to help you remember and tell your story:

**Read your story out loud.** Reading your story out loud to yourself (or to a trusted other) can help spark your memory. It can help you concentrate and focus on your story, because you are using your eyes, ears, and voice. Many people have found that reading their story out loud has brought to the fore details that were overlooked when they either simply thought about their story or wrote about it.

**Use prompts.** Using prompts can trigger memories. Photographs make excellent prompts. Find photographs of yourself before, after, or even during the traumatic or stressful event, or photographs of significant others from that time. With the photographs before you, ask yourself, *What was I like then? What did I feel like? What was I interested in? How did I change?* If you are looking at pictures of significant others, ask yourself, *How did this person change in their attitude or behavior toward me after the traumatic event?*

Use your judgment about the photos you choose. For example, what about pictures of people involved in the trauma or stressful event? If you were abused, is it advisable to look at pictures of your abuser or his or her accomplices? If you are a combat veteran, should you look at pictures of the dead? Or if you are an accident or natural catastrophe survivor, should you read newspaper clippings about the event?

There are no hard and fast rules—you need to trust your gut reaction. If you don't want to look at such pictures, don't. Never push yourself, and never allow others to push you, into "facing the facts" when you aren't ready or when you feel such exposure would be not only pointless but also destructive to your serenity. It isn't necessarily a matter of being ready or strong enough—sometimes it just isn't needed, or helpful. In some cases, the emotional price is just too high to pay. You can grow without ever looking at pictures of the people or places involved in your losses.

If you do want to take a look, go ahead. Feel free, however, to ask a friend to be with you, or to look at the picture in some other supportive context, for example, in an individual or group counseling session.

Start with one picture and see how you react. If it brings up too much pain, anger, or fear, or starts to create in you any of the symptoms listed in the "Cautions" section of the introduction, stop immediately and follow the directions in that section.

Among other things, photographs may help you identify some aspects of the physical conditions under which the stressful incidents or trauma occurred. These conditions can include the following:

- The season

- The temperature at the time (which may or may not have been consistent with the season)

- The type of room or other environment in which the event occurred

- The colors, textures, and smells of clothing and other physical objects present

- Your physical or psychological state of mind

You may also want to look at movies, newspapers, magazines, and objects of clothing or other artifacts, or listen to music from the era during which you were traumatized or stressed.

**Revisit the scene** Returning to the original site of the stressful events or trauma can also stimulate your memory. Under no circumstances should you consider this, however, without obtaining your therapist's or physician's approval first. There have been numerous cases of individuals completely falling apart when they returned to the scene of the trauma without adequate preparation or support. In a few cases of severe and repeated trauma, survivors lost their ability to function on the job and suffered long-term impairment in their ability to relate to others.

Thus it cannot be overemphasized that if you do decide to return to the scene of the trauma or stressful events, you need to discuss your plan with a qualified professional first. Together you can decide whether it is in your best interest to go there. You can also discuss and prepare for the range of possible reactions you might have.

**Talk to people who know about your experience.** If you plan to find and talk with people who knew you or who were present during your trauma or stressful events or otherwise have information about it, you need to talk with your therapist about how you can expect to feel before, during, and after such a venture. For example, if you hope to find the "missing link" or the "magic answer" in your search, you may be disappointed. Even if you do discover valuable information, you may find that the increased knowledge doesn't take away the pain. In fact, you need to be prepared for the possibility that, as a result of this new information, your symptoms will intensify.

Ask yourself if you're willing to deal with additional anger, grief, and possible disappointment at this point in your life. If you have many current stresses or are feeling vulnerable or overwhelmed for other reasons, you may decide to put off the plan of contacting people from the past.

If you do decide to contact individuals who have knowledge of you or of what happened, remember your goals. Do not expect these individuals to provide you with unconditional love or emotional support. They may be able to add to the information you have about yourself, the environment, and other people involved with you at the time; however, even if these people like you, or love you, it does not mean that they will be able to give you the empathic listening you would expect from a trained therapist or knowledgeable trauma survivor. In fact, you have no guarantee that you will receive any kind of supportive response from them.

Consequently, in general, it's best to ask neutral questions, such as, "I've been thinking lately about my past. I've forgotten so much that I'd like to remember. I wonder if you can help me remember what I was like when I used to live next door to you." You may also want to inquire specifically about the incident. For example, you could ask, "What is your memory of that hurricane we had in 1965?" Or, "Do you remember my Uncle Joe? I remember him as tall, with blue eyes and a lot of charm. Is that how you remember him?"

These cautions are not meant to discourage you from taking an active part in your healing. They are included merely to warn you of possible negative effects. Some trauma survivors, in their initial enthusiasm for healing, charge ahead with such plans, only to suffer as a result because they were unprepared for their emotional reactions, disappointment, and the negative reactions of others they sought out. Bear in mind also that seeking out information from others is not the same as confronting those who abused you or who you feel otherwise victimized you. Confrontations such as these are highly complex matters that are well beyond the scope of this book.

It takes a lot of courage and dedication to take the time, effort, and risk involved in returning to people and places from the past to find out what happened. Many people have found great peace in finally uncovering some of the missing pieces of their story. "It was worth the pain to find out the truth" is the feeling of many who've finally been able to use the facts they gathered to make peace with the past. And if they did not find out everything they had hoped to discover about themselves and the trauma, they still felt pride in having done all they could to heal themselves.

**Talk to other survivors or read survivor literature.** Memory can also be stimulated by talking to other trauma survivors or others who've lived through similar life stresses. You can find these individuals in various support groups or through your school, community, or workplace. Also, today there is a wealth of reading material about certain kinds of loss and trauma that can be a valuable resource for recovering lost memories. Go to the library to find books and articles on the type of stresses or trauma you endured. Works of literature can also deal with your experience. For example, the mythologies of various cultures have numerous accounts of the struggles of incest and rape survivors and those of warriors. Trauma and stress are central to much modern fiction, drama, and poetry.

**Tell your story.** An alternative to writing your story down is to record it on a tape recorder or to tell it to someone you trust. Before you do the latter, however, this individual must be prepared to make three commitments to you: First, he or she must be willing to sit and listen for however long it takes. Second, the person must agree to keep your story confidential. And third, he or she must be willing to listen to your story more than once, if this is what you need. The other person's role is simply to listen, not to make comments.

If the person commits to listening empathetically, but then begins to make critical comments or comments you feel are critical, stop, say thank you, and then find someone else to talk to— preferably a trained therapist or a knowledgeable survivor. You have enough to cope with in remembering what happened without also having to deal with the misinformed or shortsighted reactions of others.

Usually it's best to turn to a therapist or another survivor for an empathic ear. However, you must also select these listeners with care. Find a therapist who has worked with trauma survivors or with people who've undergone your type of stress. Seek out survivors who've made sufficient progress in their own healing and are willing to be there for you throughout yours.

**Engage in dancing, painting, and other art forms.** Art therapy is widely recognized as being of extremely high therapeutic value. Some of the emotional aspects of severe stress or traumatization are beyond words and are thus better and more fully expressed through other media. In addition, some people simply can express themselves better physically or artistically, through dance, painting, pottery, sculpture, or some other form of art, than they can verbally.

Start by drawing a picture that depicts what happened, maybe beginning just with a line or circle. You can then go on to draw more if you wish. Draw as many pictures as you like, with whatever tools you like: watercolors or oil paints, colored pencils or crayons.

If you decide to try a dance or movement expression, begin by finding a song or tune that somehow reminds you of the traumatic event or your feelings about the event. Then move your body to the music. If you cannot move your entire body at first, then simply tap your fingers or toes. Then gradually build up to using your arms and legs, until your whole body is involved.

Whether you decide to draw, paint, dance, or sculpt, let yourself go. This is not a talent show. You are not going to be judged for your performance. As you dance or paint, you may be able to recall the event and your feelings. Afterward, you may be able to share the experience with others you trust.

## Coping with Stuck Points

At certain stages of remembering, you may reach points where you get stuck—you can't remember anymore or it's simply too painful to go on. When this happens, stop. If you're writing, draw a line underneath what you've written and return to it later.

You should also stop if you start feeling suicidal, homicidal, or faint, or if you experience any of the other danger signs listed in the "Cautions" section of the introduction.

## ✍ Exercise: Tracing Your Addiction History

If you are addicted to alcohol, food, drugs, gambling, spending, or sexual behavior, most likely your addiction patterns reflect the stressful or traumatic event. One way to help resurrect your memories of the trauma is by writing (or recording, or telling another person) your addiction history. Use the following guidelines:

1. Write at least three pages on how your addiction has adversely affected your life. Go back to the first time you ever used your drug (whether it's food, alcohol, or drugs) or engaged in a compulsive behavior, and write how you felt about it. Then go through the rest of your life, noting the times you were practicing your addiction and how you felt about it. You can write less than three pages if that's all you want to do. But the more you write, the more you will learn about yourself.

2. Make a list of all the people in your family who suffer from some form of substance abuse or addictive behavior and/or

who are trauma survivors themselves or who endured considerable stress.

3. Go back through your journal and read what you've written about the stressful event or trauma and related incidents. What events seem to be related to your addiction?

4. Ask yourself the following questions and write down your answers:

   • How did people around you react to your addiction?

   • What was the role of the trauma or stressor in creating, perpetuating, or increasing your addictive behavior?

5. Make a list of everything in your life that prevents you from giving up your addiction (or, if you are currently clean, sober, or abstinent, write down what prevented you from giving up your addiction in the past).

6. Consider and write about how healing from survivor guilt plays a role in your recovery from substance abuse or compulsive activity.

## Professional Assistance

Ideally, you will share your written work, tape recording, or oral account of your stressful event or trauma with a mental health professional trained in these areas. A mental health professional trained in trauma work can also help you remember by using techniques such as traumatic-incident reduction therapy, eye movement desensitization and reprocessing, and hypnosis.

### Traumatic-Incident Reduction Therapy

In this form of short-term therapy, the therapist asks you to tell your story. The therapist remains relatively silent, only asking you to indicate where the trauma begins and where, in your view, it ends. The therapist then asks, "What is the significance of these events to you?" (Figley 1995)

The process is repeated several times, providing you with a rare opportunity: to tell the story in full, as many times as needed, to a willing listener. The theory behind this approach is that telling the story repeatedly provides numerous opportunities to rethink the event, to remember details that may have been forgotten but are vitally important to understanding the meaning of the trauma, and to express anger, grief, confusion, guilt, and any other feelings associated with the trauma.

## Eye Movement Desensitization and Reprocessing

Eye movement desensitization and reprocessing (EMDR) therapy helps reprocess traumatic memories both mentally and physically. In the therapy session, you're asked to remember a traumatic experience and then to identify the thoughts and feelings surrounding that experience, including the ways the anxiety and pain associated with the experience are expressed in the body.

For example, as you review your trauma in your mind, you may find that your associated thought is that you were a failure or were guilty of some immoral or incompetent act. You may also find that just thinking about the trauma creates anxiety or pain in certain parts of your body. You may experience nausea, headache, backache, pain in your legs, chest pains, hyperventilation, dizziness, muscle spasms, or tremors.

The therapist then asks you to come up with a more positive view or feeling about the trauma. At this point, you would most likely feel that the positive, alternative view of the trauma has little or no validity. Nevertheless, you have acknowledged that there could be a more positive or rational view of the trauma. Later in the session, the therapist will ask you to recall that more positive view.

The therapist then asks you to bring the traumatic memory to mind while he or she moves a finger from side to side in your field of vision. As you watch the finger, you are instructed to keep remembering the trauma and to focus on your negative thoughts and emotions. You are also asked to scan your body and be aware of where you feel the anxiety and emotional pain associated with the trauma.

This procedure is repeated until you can view the traumatic event with only a small degree of anxiety. Once you are able to do so, the therapist asks you to again bring to mind the traumatic memory, repeats the finger motions, and asks you to view the traumatic memory keeping in mind the positive feelings and thoughts that you identified earlier in the session. This procedure is repeated until you tell the therapist you can view the traumatic memory with some kind of positive feeling or thought and with minimal anxiety. During the therapy and afterward you are asked to keep a log of your anxiety and other symptoms, reactions, or thoughts you have about the session during the week. You then bring this log to the next session for discussion.

EMDR is not a form of hypnosis or "mind control." You are in control in that you can stop the process should it become uncomfortable for you. (The therapist is also to be immediately available to you between sessions.)

The exact reasons EMDR therapy works are unclear. One theory is that the EMDR process is similar to the natural healing process that occurs during REM (rapid eye movement) sleep. During REM sleep we dream, and dreaming is believed to be a way that the stresses and emotions of life are neutralized and processed. It is theorized that the rapid movement of the eyes following the therapist's finger stimulates the body's automatic healing process.

Another theory is that EMDR therapy works because it links the more rational part of the brain to the more emotional, sensual, and physical part of the brain, where traumatic memories tend to stored. By linking the right and left hemispheres of the brain, EMDR helps you see traumas more accurately and more rationally, hence eliminating much unfounded guilt and shame (Call 1995).

Another possible reason for EMDR's effectiveness is that, like the exercises in this book and other forms of trauma-focused therapy, EMDR therapy requires that you deal with the trauma directly, rather than avoid the subject. In addition, EMDR requires that you reprocess aspects of the trauma—that you try to identify positive aspects of the traumatic incident or at least reduce the amount of irrational and inappropriate guilt.

If you should decide to try out EMDR therapy, keep in mind that it is only one tool for remembering and healing. EMDR, if used, should be a part of a comprehensive therapy program conducted by a therapist familiar with you and your circumstances. For more information contact the EMDR Institute, Box 51010, Pacific Grove, CA, 93950; (408) 372-3900.

### Hypnosis

Hypnosis may sound like "hocus-pocus" to you; if so, you are correct in assessing that it's not a magic cure. However, hypnosis—the creation of a semiconscious state of deep relaxation—can be useful in bringing forth memories that are partially or totally repressed. It can be especially helpful to people abused as young children, as they tend to repress memories more than other trauma survivors.

Nevertheless, hypnosis can be problematic for trauma survivors, because it requires that you trust the therapist, and trust is not easy for trauma survivors, especially those who feel they were betrayed by an authority figure. In some ways hypnosis may even seem to create feelings of powerlessness that mimic original traumatic situations. A therapist trained in hypnosis will reassure you that the hypnosis will not put you at the mercy of the therapist. He or she will also instruct you to indicate if the hypnosis is becoming uncomfortable; the therapist will then bring you back into a fully conscious state.

If you decide to seek hypnosis, or if hypnosis is suggested to you by your therapist, be sure the therapist is well trained in this area. Also be clear about what you expect from hypnosis. Well-trained hypnotists do not make exaggerated claims about the benefits of hypnosis.

Although hypnosis may assist you in remembering your traumatic past, recalling the past and processing it are not the same thing. Once you remember a specific memory, you will still have to go on to understand its meaning to you and your feelings about it. Hypnosis is an excellent tool; but it is only a beginning.

# 8

# Mentally Reconstructing
# Your Critical Event

This chapter will guide you in mentally reconstructing the critical event that caused your survivor guilt. You already know that no amount of rethinking or logical analysis can erase your feelings of grief, anger, shame, or guilt. However, if you begin to see the critical event and your role in it in a more realistic light, you may realize that you were not as responsible for the death or injury of another as you had previously thought.

You may also realize that certain other people or organizations played a larger role than you had previously thought. Such awareness could decrease your anger toward yourself and create or increase your fury at others. If you find yourself overcome with a rush of rage, will you be able to cope with it? Will you be able to manage it, perhaps even channel it into constructive outlets, or will you turn it inward, onto yourself (in the form of addiction, depression, increased physical pain, increased obsessive-compulsive thinking, or increased paranoid thoughts), or outward, toward others (in the form of verbal and physical abuse)?

This is not an anger management book or a total treatment program for recovering from trauma or severe stress. The deep-breathing and relaxation skills described in appendix C may be helpful to you.

However, if your anger is intense, you will probably need to use some of the anger-management and relaxation skills outlined in some of the trauma-processing books in appendix B or to consult with a trained therapist.

# Recording the Critical Event One More Time

In chapter 7, I asked you to write the story of what happened in your journal and gave suggestions on how to enhance your memory. If you experienced more than one trauma or guilt-producing event, I asked you to only deal with one difficult memory at a time.

In this chapter you are going to be asked to write your story once more.

Why do I have to go over the same upsetting story over and over again? you may justifiably wonder. There are three reasons for this.

First, the more times you write about or think about what happened, the greater the chance that you will remember more of the details and the greater the chance that you will make connections between the various events that occurred.

Second, reviewing the event repeatedly may lessen its power. This principle of repetition is often used in therapy for nightmares. If you were engaged in this type of nightmare therapy, your therapist would ask you to write down your nightmare, record it on a tape recorder, or draw a picture of it. You would then be instructed to read your description of the nightmare, listen to the tape you had made about it, or look at the picture you had drawn of it at least two or three times a day, especially before going to sleep. As strange as it sounds, you'd be instructed to talk to the nightmare. For example, you would tell the nightmare how you felt about it: "Nightmare, I hate you! You ruin my nights and the next day, too!" You'd ask the nightmare questions, such as "Who is the woman in blue [or some other figure you don't recognize]?" You could even make requests of the nightmare, such as suggesting a different ending or changing some of the details.

The theory behind this kind of approach is that the more the nightmare is talked about openly, the less frightening it will become and the less power it will have over you. There are some exceptions, however. If writing, speaking, or drawing the dream repeatedly brought up increasingly traumatic memories and clients found themselves feeling overwhelmed or having any of the symptoms listed in the "Cautions" section of the introduction, then the therapist would probably have these clients discontinue working with their night-mares and concentrate on helping clients center and stabilize themselves.

This same principle holds true for you as you begin to work on the following exercises in this chapter. If you find that writing about the incident causes you to feel out of control, suicidal, or homicidal, you need to stop reading this book immediately and seek profes-sional medical or mental health care as soon as possible.

Third, although you will be writing about the same trauma or critical incident, you will not be doing so in the same way or for the same purpose. This time you're going to look at as many thoughts, feelings, and actions as you can remember and scrutinize them from the point of view of an objective observer.

Although you may think of the critical incident as a single event, there are multiple events within that event and therefore many possibilities for guilt. Even if you only committed one act, something happened *before* that act and something happened *afterward*. Also, you were not just acting, but *thinking* and *feeling*. You may have had one thought prior to the act, another thought (or two or three) during the action, and a different thought afterward. The same holds true for feelings: you might have had several feelings before, during, and after the action. Furthermore, it may be what you didn't do or didn't think that causes you agony, so you need to look at not only what you actually did, thought, or felt, but what you didn't do, didn't think, or didn't feel.

It's important to be aware of as many of the acts, thoughts, and feelings as you can remember, because you may be focusing on the one or two thoughts or feelings that you find unacceptable and forget the many more thoughts or feelings you had with which you feel comfortable. Similarly, you may be focusing on the fact that you failed to act in some way or didn't have the emotions you feel you should have had and forget about the positive things you did do and the feelings you had of which you feel proud.

For example, if you are like many who suffer from survivor guilt, you may have felt some relief when someone else was injured instead of you or a member of your family. This sense of gratitude could be the source of considerable guilt for you. However, most likely this is not the only feeling you had. You might have also felt compassion for the individual who was harmed even to the point of wishing to take his or her place. You might have felt fear, realizing that if something terrible could happen to someone you knew, that same terrible thing could happen to you. You might have felt gener-ous and giving, wishing to assist the relatives of the person who died or was injured. You might also have felt closer to your spiritual self or source or had a type of spiritual awakening.

However, if you're prone to guilt or self-blame, when you evaluate the way you felt during the incident you might give more weight to the feelings that cause you guilt than all the other feelings you experienced. For example, you may focus on the feelings of gratitude you had for your own safety (which you may see as selfish) and forget about or minimize the feelings of empathy and concern you also felt. But these other feelings might have been every bit as strong as, if not stronger than, your grateful realization that you were spared.

## ✍ Exercise: Recording the Guilt-Producing Event

Divide your journal page into five columns. (You will not be asked to complete the third, fourth and fifth columns until later.) Label them as follows:

1. What Happened

2. Reactions: Thoughts, Feelings, and Beliefs

3. Type of Guilt

4. Thinking Errors: A More Rational View

5. Strengths

You'll begin by breaking down the guilt-producing event into a chronological account of what happened, including what happened in your mind and heart—your thoughts and feelings. Be sure to include sensory details, such as what you smelled, touched, or saw, and the physical state of your body. For example, were you ill, fatigued, feverish, trembling, cold, hungry, or thirsty? Was there some other important physical condition you were experiencing?

As you write, record what you did not do, did not think, or did not feel that made you feel guilty at the time or afterward. For many people, this is the source of considerable guilt.

Put a number next to each entry so that you can refer to it in future exercises. Also, leave a space before and after each entry, since as you complete this exercise, you will probably remember another thought, feeling, action, or inaction that needs to be included.

One way to approach this exercise is to consider yourself a screenwriter who is directing a play about what happened. As the screenwriter, you need to know what the main character (in this case you) is doing, thinking, and feeling at every point during the drama.

Anyone who has watched a film knows that a character's facial expressions and body language can change several times in just a few minutes. The character may be doing the same thing, for example, rowing a boat, but the changing expression on that character's face lets the audience know that he or she is going from one emotional and mental state to another. In this exercise, it is critical that you try to remember and identify what you *thought* and *felt* as well as what you *did*.

Here's an example for you: Jane and her younger sister were walking home from the library at around 8:00 P.M. when an armed assailant coerced them into a car, drove them to a deserted building, and raped the younger sister. Jane suffers from survivor guilt because she wishes she had been raped instead of her sister. Jane feels that because she was nineteen (and not a virgin) when the assault occurred and her sister was only ten, she could have handled the rape better than her sister. This is existential survivor guilt. Jane also feels guilty for not anticipating the assailant and for being unable to escape from his grasp and his car or to stop him from abusing her sister. This is content survivor guilt.

When Jane completed this writing exercise, it looked like this:

<u>What Happened</u>

1. I ate dinner.

2. I felt anxious because I had a term paper due and needed to go to the library.

3. I also felt sad, because my boyfriend and I weren't getting along. I hadn't seen him in a while and felt lonely. Since I usually went to the library with him, the thought of going to the library alone made me even sadder.

4. I decided not to go to the library, since going without my boyfriend would probably make me feel worse than I felt now.

5. Then I started feeling guilty about not trying to get my schoolwork done.

6. I decided I couldn't let my problems with my boyfriend upset my studies, so I made plans to go to the library.

7. I told my mother I'd do the dishes later since I wanted to get to the library before it closed at 9:00 P.M.

8. When my younger sister heard I was going to the library, she asked if she could go with me. She wanted to get a book

and wanted to stop and get an ice cream cone on the way home.

9. I felt annoyed at the thought of having to drag my little sister along when I was feeling pretty bad myself. I also felt I wouldn't be able to get much work done if I had to watch out for her.

10. I told her I wouldn't take her this time but I'd take her next time. But she pleaded and I didn't have the heart to refuse her request. After all, it wasn't her fault I felt irritable because I was having problems with my boyfriend.

11. We walked to the library.

12. I found what I needed, and at around 7:00 P.M. I started getting tired and wanted to go home.

13. I told my sister it was time to leave, but she didn't want to go.

14. I insisted that it was time to leave. I didn't want to tell her the truth, that I was tired, because, knowing her, that wouldn't have convinced her. Instead I told her that I was worried that it was getting late and I didn't want to be on the streets after dark.

15. My sister didn't go for it. She pointed out that home was only ten minutes from the library and it was summer. So there would be light until around 8:30 or 9:00. She begged to stay for another half-hour. We agreed to leave at 8:00.

16. I resented the power my sister had over me, the kind of power little girls can have over older sisters and others in the family, at least my family. Because she was the "baby," she got more attention and was able to get her way much more than I ever did. Also, I was jealous because she has big blue eyes and I don't.

17. I was too tired to do any more research for my term paper, so I sat in the magazine section and looked through some magazines. I read several articles, one about losing weight, another about using vitamins to help get over illnesses and injuries.

18. I was so tired I started falling asleep while reading.

19. I got really mad at my sister for pressuring me to stay.

20. I went to my sister and insisted that we leave.

21. She started arguing with me, and I gave in to her again.

22. We left the library at 8:00. She started complaining about having to leave early. I lost my cool and called her a spoiled brat and told her she should be grateful to have a sister like me who was willing to take her places and wait around for her even when I was tired.

23. The rapist came out of nowhere and grabbed me and my sister. When he raped her it was still light out.

## Stuck Points: Blocking

Jane was able to remember many of her thoughts, feelings, and actions prior to the actual abduction and rape. However, her account of the actual trauma was extremely brief and sketchy. Obviously Jane had reached a stuck point when it came to remembering the moment-to-moment details of the most fear-provoking aspects of the event. When I asked Jane to describe the block, she replied that whenever she tried to describe this part of what happened, she would feel her body become overheated and she would then feel dizzy and spaced out. When I asked what she was feeling, she replied, "Guilt and shame."

Stuck points, or blocking, can occur for two reasons. The first is that the emotions associated with the particular event are so powerful, painful, or shameful that the individual feels he or she will not be able to manage them and will lose control of his or her behavior or reason. The second is that the particular event challenges a cherished belief or ideal, creating a mental or moral dilemma for the individual that she or he feels is unresolvable.

Jane, for example, found it impossible for her to reconcile her view of herself as a good sister and loyal family member with her voyeurism during her sister's rape. She felt so guilty and so ashamed, she couldn't bear to think about what happened, let alone put it on paper. Yet with encouragement and support, Jane was able to make some progress in dissecting what had happened that terrible evening that changed her and her sister's lives forever.

If you find yourself stuck or blocked in remembering what happened or in identifying your thoughts and feelings, if your account sounds more like a lab report than the drama of a person under siege, if you find you are unable or unwilling to record any emotions about what happened, or if you find yourself jumping over certain events or minimizing certain thoughts or feelings you had, I strongly recommend that you share what you have written with a therapist who is familiar with trauma issues or guilt and grief work. A trained therapist can provide you with the guidance and support necessary for you to uncover and face certain thoughts, feelings, and events that were traumatic or extremely stressful for you.

The more stressful and traumatic the events you went through, the more painful the feelings you experienced, the more internal conflict created by the traumatic events, and the more socially unacceptable your thoughts, the more likely it is that you will struggle as you attempt to write down what you did, thought, and felt. But without some awareness of the feelings you were having, you won't be able to complete any of the additional exercises in this book, since they are geared toward better understanding your feelings.

To be as complete as possible about what happened, including what happened inside your head and your heart, is a major accomplishment. It bears repeating that you can take as long as you need to complete the story and that it's perfectly normal and even desirable for you to return to what you have already written and add more details.

After Jane sought help, she was able to record a few additional events, including the following:

24. When the rapist shoved us into his car, he locked the car doors with automatic locks and started driving. I thought about trying to smash the car window so I could get out that way to look for help. But, coward that I was, I was afraid of getting cut.

25. When the rapist started undressing my sister, I thought about asking him to take me instead, but I didn't. I let him go ahead. A part of me was really glad he chose her, not me, because I was already unhappy enough in my life.

26. When the rapist started having sex with my sister, I was frightened and nauseated. But, as much as I hate to admit it, I was curious about what he was going to do and how my sister, who had never had sex, would react. I watched him and her as if I was watching a movie. A part of me was detached.

27. When I started looking around for ways to escape, the rapist saw my eyes darting and told me he'd kill my sister if I tried to get away.

It was some of these later revelations that caused Jane the most guilt. The same may be true of you: what's hardest to think about or write about may hold the clue to what feelings, thoughts, or events are causing you the most emotional pain and the most guilt. It may seem like overkill, but it is probably worth your while to go back and review what you have written one additional time and ask yourself if you left out any thought, feeling, or act. Read what you've written out loud (to yourself or to someone you trust) and add any additional details that reading out loud has brought to the fore.

For example, when Jane reviewed what she had written in item 24, she realized that another reason she didn't try to smash the car window and get out to search for help was that she didn't want to leave her sister alone. Her revised entry was:

> 24. When the rapist shoved us into his car, he locked the car doors with automatic locks and started driving. I thought about trying to smash the car window so I could get out that way to look for help. But, coward that I was, I was afraid of getting cut. I was also concerned about leaving my sister alone.

She also remembered that while at the library she began flirting with a young man. She enjoyed the flirtation but felt somewhat guilty about it since she hadn't formally broken up with her boyfriend. When she and her sister were abducted, her first thought was that their attacker was the young man with whom she had flirted at the library. For a split second, she felt that her flirtation had caused the attack. One look at the attacker, however, indicated that this was not the case.

This split-second guilt was largely unconscious until Jane completed this exercise. Even though it was a minor guilt and one that Jane hardly ever thought about, it contributed to her sense of self-blame and self-hate. The nagging feeling that "there was something else I did wrong" that had haunted her now had a name: that "something else" was her minor flirtation. By having been able to identify the guilt in the light of day (as opposed to the dark of the unconscious or semi-conscious), Jane was able to see that minor flirtation for what it was—a minor flirtation with no harmful consequences—rather than for what she suspected it to be—a secret character flaw or massive personal failing that resulted in her sister being harmed.

## ✍ Exercise: Identifying Reactions— Thoughts, Feelings, and Beliefs

After you have described the event in detail, in the next column, "Reactions: Thoughts, Feelings, and Beliefs," write down what you believe or think and how you feel about what you did, thought, or felt as it's described in column 1. Write at least two or three sentences about how you feel today about the particular action, thought, or feeling you identified in column 1.

Consider the following questions: What are your feelings about the action, thought or feeling you described? Are you proud, ashamed, happy, guilty, or afraid of how you thought, felt, or acted? What do you think or believe about what you did, thought, or felt? Do you feel your actions, thoughts, and feelings were reasonable under the circumstances, or do you have some other point of view? Are there thoughts, feelings, or acts for which you feel you deserve to be applauded? For which you feel you deserve to be punished?

If you had more than one type of reaction to the action, thought, or feeling you identified, be sure to list them all. It's quite possible, and normal, to have several reactions to the same event, some of which may seem to contradict each other.

For example, Jane's entries in the second column were as follows:

1. No reactions to eating dinner.

2. I'm mad at myself for being nervous about my term paper. If I wasn't anxious about getting it done, I would've never gone to the library, and the rape wouldn't have happened. I should have more faith in myself that I can get my work done on time and not worry so much. If I didn't worry so much, the rape wouldn't have happened.

3. I should've been able to manage missing my boyfriend on my own. If I was a stronger person, the argument with him wouldn't have bothered me so much and I would never have agreed to take my sister to the library with me.

4. Same as 3.

5. Once again, I was stupid to feel so responsible about that term paper. It could have waited another day or two.

6. At the time, I felt proud of myself for going against my feelings and deciding to go ahead with my work. But now I think my reluctance to go to the library was a sign that something bad was going to happen. I should've gone to bed and cried over my boyfriend and not tried to prove to myself that I was tough.

7. My mother should've stopped me from going to the library. If she was a good mother she would've seen how upset I was

and made me stay home. That way there would've been no rape. But no, as usual, she wasn't paying attention to me.

8. No reaction.

9. I should've paid attention to my feelings. If I had, I wouldn't have taken her along.

10. Same as 9.

11. I should've driven to the library. It was such a beautiful evening, though, I thought it would be nice to walk. Besides, I ate too much at dinner and wanted to walk some of it off.

12, 13, 14, 15, and 16. I should've insisted that we go home. If we had left earlier, the rape might not have happened. I made the same mistake I made before—giving in to her.

17. I believe I should've known that the vitamin article about illnesses and injuries was a sign that something bad was going to happen. I should've called my mom for help. Oh no, she probably would have thought I was crazy; but my dad would have come and picked us up.

18. If I'd been more alert, I might have seen the rapist when we left the library. But I was already sleepy before we left. I feel guilty about being sleepy so early. That's not normal.

19. At the time I felt guilty about getting mad at my sister. Now I see I was right to be mad at her. We should've left when I wanted to.

20 and 21. Same mistake—giving in to my sister. My problem is I'm not assertive enough. It causes problems with both my sister and my boyfriend. They both push me around.

22. If I hadn't lost my cool and started scolding her, I might've noticed the rapist.

23. I believe I'm a really bad person. I wasn't able to save my sister from getting raped. I'd do anything to go back and be raped for her. I could have taken it. After all, I was nineteen, not a virgin, and would have been better able to handle matters. I was wrong to be jealous of my sister for being prettier than I am and wrong to resent having to take care of her. I was too wimpy to be firm with her and make us leave on time, and I was too wimpy to fight off the rapist.

24. I'm a coward and a wimp for not smashing the car window, grabbing my sister, and trying to get both of us out of the car. I could have at least pushed her out of the car window, and then she wouldn't have been raped. But then she might have gotten badly cut going through the window or badly injured when falling into the street. If I had tried to go through the window I might've gotten cut. My face would have been all scarred and then I'd look horrible. I might've broken some bones tumbling out of a moving car. But I'm larger than my sister. I could have taken the cuts. But I didn't do anything. I just sat there and let him drive on. I could've tried to hit him or I could've taken off my clothes and tried to tempt him into raping me. Then my sister might have been spared. At least she'd have had a chance to run away while he was raping me.

25. I feel very selfish about this. Here I am, the big sister who's supposed to take care of her little sister, and all I was thinking about was my own happiness. "Me first. Me first," that's what I was thinking. How disgusting!

26. I feel that watching that man have sex with my sister and enjoying it sexually is a sin. It makes me a terrible person. I deserve to be punished. I can't tell anyone about this part of it. My mom would be horrified and my father would disown me. My boyfriend would dump me and my sister would feel so utterly betrayed.

27. The rapist said he'd kill me, but at the time I wasn't sure if he meant it. A part of me felt he meant it, to scare me into staying still. But it might have been a threat. If it was just a threat, then there was a chance I could've gotten help. But, chicken that I was, I took the easy way out and did nothing.

## ✍ Exercise: Separating Guilt from Other Emotional Issues

Review your journal entries under the column "Thoughts, Feelings, and Beliefs." On a separate piece of paper in your journal, write the heading "Feelings during the Event." Make a list of the various types of feelings you experienced, for example, guilt, anger, self-doubt, numbness, or confusion. Leave plenty of space between each item that you list.

Jane's entries on this page included the following:

1. Anger at my mother: I felt my mom was not helpful the night of the rape, but then I've always felt that way—especially with regards to me. I feel she loves my little sister more and am frustrated with her because she doesn't pay much attention to me.

2. Jealousy of my sister: I was jealous of my sister's special place in the family and her good looks.

3. Loneliness: I wondered if I'll ever have a good relationship with a man.

4. Anxiety: I doubted my ability to complete projects.

5. Guilt: I felt guilty about not protecting my sister. [Jane had many other guilts as well.]

For each emotional issue you list, write a sentence or two about how that issue is related to your guilt feelings. Some of your issues may not be intertwined with guilt, but others may be. Take some time to think before you reply.

For example, under the topic of jealousy, Jane wrote: "I know it doesn't make sense, but I feel that my jealousy of my sister caused the rape. If I wasn't jealous of her and didn't feel ashamed and guilty about being jealous, I probably would've put my foot down about her not going with me to the library or staying late. Because I feel guilty about being jealous, I try to make it up to her by giving in to her when I shouldn't."

Under the topic of anger at her mother, Jane wrote: "My frustrations with my mother go way back. I'm blaming her for not paying enough attention to me, but really that had nothing to do with what happened. I have to keep my frustrations with my mother separate from my guilt about what happened to my sister."

## ✍ Exercise: Separating Survivor Guilt from Other Types of Guilt

You should now be able to separate some of your guilt issues from other issues the trauma or critical incident raised for you and to see how they are related, if they are in fact related.

Review the definitions of the various types of guilt in chapter 1 and your self-assessments for various guilts, for example, infantile guilt, shadow guilt, and guilt of being. Also review the definitions of existential and content survivor guilt and your self-assessments for these types of guilt.

Return to your entries in column 2, and make a list of the numbers of every entry that involves guilt. Then, in column 3, "Type of Guilt," answer the following questions for every entry for which you've noted guilt feelings:

1. What type of guilt is this? (Refer to chapter 1.)

2. Is this an instance of existential or content survivor guilt? (Refer to chapters 2 and 3.)

3. Is there more than one type of guilt present? If so, which ones?

On a separate piece of paper in your journal write the heading "How Other Types of Guilt Affect My Survivor Guilt." For each of the instances of survivor guilt you noted in column 3, "Types of Guilt," write two or three sentences about the relationship of your survivor guilt to any other types of guilt that were present.

For example, for item 26 Jane wrote: "Feeling guilty for enjoying watching people have sex is religious guilt for me. My religion teaches that is wrong. I also violated my parental expectations that I be relatively disinterested in sex until marriage, which I already felt guilty about because I'm not a virgin. So my guilt for not being a virgin got mixed in with my guilt for how I felt watching my sister get raped. That makes my survivor guilt stronger."

Once you've done this for each entry, answer the following questions in your journal:

1. Has identifying the various types of guilt you experienced been an easy or a difficult process for you? What feelings have you experienced while completing this exercise?

2. Did any of the new awareness you acquired make you angry? If so, how do you plan to deal with that anger? It is important to have a plan for coping with the anger, lest the anger be directed inward on yourself or outward on other living beings. If you haven't done so already, this might be a good time to seek the help of a trained mental health professional.

3. As the result of breaking down your guilt into the various types of possible guilt, do you feel in more or in less control of your guilt feelings?

4. As the result of completing this exercise, has there been any change in your feelings of guilt? For example, do you feel more guilty or less guilty? Write two or three sentences

explaining how completing these exercises has affected your burden of guilt.

5. Can you identify three things you learned about yourself by completing this exercise? Write a sentence or two about each of your self-revelations.

# Defusing Survivor Guilt

The exercise that follows is crucial to your healing from survivor guilt. It's a difficult exercise, because it will require you to reevaluate what happened in light of the bigger picture. This exercise is not intended to excuse what you believe to be inexcusable or to make light of any strong feeling you experienced. The purpose of the exercise is to help you put your actions, thoughts, and feelings into a perspective that takes into account the numerous factors at play during your critical event.

In the forthcoming exercise, you are going to use the description of common thinking errors on the following pages as a way to examine the rationality of your guilt. First you'll review each feeling, thought, or action in column 1 of your five-column list about which you feel guilty. Then you'll ask yourself each of the questions in the "Thinking Errors" exercise about each of the guilt-inducing entries in column 1. Not all of the questions in the exercise will apply to each of the entries in column 1.

## *Common Thinking Errors*

These thinking errors are based on the work of trauma specialists who have researched the effects of trauma on human functioning and on the work of cognitive therapists, such as Kubany (1997), Beck (1976), Resick and Schnicke (1992), and Smyth (1994), who have written extensively on the process of helping people sort out their rational from their irrational thoughts and beliefs.

Kubany has identified several thinking errors that can be divided into three categories:

- Category One: Thinking errors that lead people to make erroneous conclusions about their *degree of responsibility*. This category includes thinking errors that cause people to believe they could have or should have been able to predict the future or know the outcome of events before they happened.

- Category Two: Thinking errors that lead people to draw inaccurate conclusions about justification for their *decisions or actions.*

- Category Three: Thinking errors that cause people to make inaccurate conclusions about the *morality of their behavior.*

Each of these categories of thinking error will be explained in more detail on the following pages. (Some of the thinking errors to be described have already been presented in chapter 3, but will be briefly presented again as a matter of review.)

## Category One: Degree of Responsibility

Four types of thinking errors fall into this category:

*Hindsight bias.* Hindsight bias (also see chapter 3) involves believing you could've known what was going to happen before it was possible to know or believing that you dismissed or overlooked clues or signs that "signaled" what was going to occur. Because you believe you should have known certain things or should have acted on clues or signs, you decide that you, to some extent, caused the tragedy.

For example, Raphael, a soldier, asked his commanding officer (CO) to be relieved of guard duty one night. He wasn't feeling well and had a "bad feeling" about being on duty that evening. Raphael had never asked for any favors before and was an especially skilled and dedicated soldier. But the commanding officer refused his request. His men were always having "bad feelings." After all, they were in a war zone. It would be abnormal for them not to have bad feelings.

For a brief moment, the CO considered taking Raphael's place that evening, but decided against the idea. If he gave in to one soldier's request, then in fairness he'd have to give in to the requests of others, and he could not do that without seriously compromising his ability to perform his duties and creating chaos.

The CO refused Raphael's request, only to find out the next day that Raphael had been killed five minutes after assuming guard duty. To this day, the CO feels that he killed Raphael and should've died in Raphael's place.

The CO is engaging in the thinking error of hindsight bias. He had no knowledge of what was going to happen on guard duty that evening. He feels guilty for not respecting another person's intuitive feeling (or in other instances, a hunch or premonition), yet the norm is for people to base their actions on high probability outcomes, not low probability outcomes, which is the standard for hunches, intuitive feelings, or premonitions.

In the CO's experience, hundreds of men had "bad feelings" on certain days, and there was little relationship between a man's bad feeling and his fate in battle. Some soldiers with premonitions that they were going to die that day actually did die, but others did not. Conversely, some who were confident of returning alive were killed, whereas others with confidence returned alive and uninjured.

It has been suggested that people tend to view thoughts or intuitions they had but disregarded as omens, premonitions, or warning signs because this gives them a sense of control or mastery in situations where they did not have enough control to prevent the death or injury of another (Kubany and Manke 1995; Opp and Samson 1989; Krystal 1971). It has even been suggested that in some cases people change their memory of the event to include omens and premonitions in order to avoid feeling helpless or powerless (Terr 1983).

*Believing that you were totally responsible for the event or overrating your role in what happened.* There is a tendency for people with survivor guilt to exaggerate the importance of their role during a traumatic or stressful event. However, you are rarely the sole cause of a negative or devastating situation. For example, the emergency room nurse who felt such intense survivor guilt about patients who died while under her care that she frequently dreamed of dying in her patients' place needed to realize that a host of factors determined the quality of patient care.

Certainly her competence on the job was a factor, but there were other factors involved. These included the competence of other staff members; the organization of the hospital as determined by the administrators, state and federal laws, and medical boards; the potency of the medications; and the reliability and quality of support services, such as electricity and gas. Just as she would not take sole credit for helping to save a patient's life, she could not, realistically, take sole credit for causing the death of a patient unless, of course, she purposely murdered the patient.

Kubany (1997) suggests that clients list all the causative factors involved in the incident that troubles them and then assign a percentage to the actions they feel they contributed to the negative outcome. For example, in reflecting on the death of a pregnant woman, the emergency room nurse noted that many factors were involved, including the following:

1. In the rush to take care of her, I made a mistake in the amount of oxygen I administered.

2. The emergency room intake staffperson failed to recognize that the woman was almost in a state of toxic shock and consequently didn't make her case top priority.

3. The staff who trained intake staff to assess the severity of a patient's illness did not adequately train or supervise this particular intake worker.

4. The waiting area was very warm because the hospital's air-conditioning unit had broken down, and the intake staff confused the woman's sweating from her medical condition with the sweating that could be expected from having been sitting in a hot emergency room. The air-conditioning unit was defunct due to funding problems and the decision of certain authorities to delay repair of the unit and repair other parts of the hospital instead.

5. No one from the woman's family was with her. This was an out-of-wedlock pregnancy, and the woman was too ashamed to ask her family for help. The father of the child had insisted on an abortion. Since she refused this request, he refused to be helpful to her during the pregnancy.

By the time the nurse completed her list, she had written down over fifty factors that contributed to the young woman's death. One of the factors was the young woman herself. Because of her shame at being pregnant, she had not sought medical care. The dead woman herself needed to be given some responsibility for her own death because she'd acted irresponsibly by not seeking medical attention when she first became pregnant and when she started experiencing medical problems. Instead she waited until the last minute to seek help. Had she come for help a few weeks earlier, there was a much greater chance she could have been saved.

I asked the nurse the following question: "You've just laid out all the various causes of the woman's death. If the total percentage is 100, what percent was your contribution to the woman's death?"

The nurse decided that she had made a 7 percent contribution to the woman's death. She still felt some survivor guilt, but the degree of that guilt had been reduced by coming to appreciate the numerous forces involved in the death of the woman. Just as it would've been grandiose of her to say that she and she alone saved the woman (had the woman been saved), it would've been a sign of childhood omnipotent guilt for her to claim that she and she alone had caused the woman's death.

*Confusing the possibility that you could have prevented the negative event with the belief that you caused the event.* Kubany writes that many people "mistakenly equate beliefs that they 'could have prevented' a traumatic event with beliefs that they caused the event. Even if such individuals 'could have prevented' the traumatic outcomes, it does not mean that they actually caused them" (1997, 6). It's easy to think that because you could have or might have done something to save a person from harm, that you caused the harm. In the example of the emergency room nurse, it was important for her to realize that even though she might have done something to save the young woman's life—for example, she could have been more careful in administering oxygen—this doesn't mean she intended or caused the death. The young woman died of a medical problem, which medical intervention failed to reverse, not because the nurse, or any other medical person, wished or decided that the young woman needed to die.

*Confusing your sense of responsibility due to your role with the idea that you had the power to avert a negative outcome.* There is a difference between feeling responsible about your role, as a parent, physician, teacher, police officer, military officer, or some other role involving the care and protection of others, and having the ability to prevent disasters and terrible events from occurring. Just because you are in the role of a teacher or a parent doesn't mean you have the power to protect your students or children from all harm. If you had the power to protect them from negative events, such as a car accident, then you should also have the power to create positive occurrences for them, such as arranging for them to meet the love of their life. Although highly desirable, that kind of power simply does not exist.

While your reasoning may quickly tell you that you can't orchestrate a series of blissful events for your child (or student, or protégé), if you suffer from survivor guilt, you need to use that same reasoning to remind you that you can't always shield your child (or student or protégé) from life's harms. (You may want to review the section on role responsibility in chapter 3.)

## Category Two: Decisions or Actions

*Disregarding the power of certain scientifically proven physiological and emotional human reactions to extreme stress.* Under conditions of trauma, time is limited and confusion reigns. Seldom is there the luxury for extended gathering of facts, consultation with experts, and careful weighing of options. Also, as described in the section on Fight/Flight/Freeze reactions in chapter 3, under conditions of trauma, a person's auditory and other sensations can be altered and their mental capacities can be negatively affected. These reactions are not voluntary.

*Evaluating what you did based on information you only knew about or options you only thought of after the event was over.* Kubany (1997) stresses that it isn't fair to judge the decisions you made based on options you thought of later, after having considerable time to contemplate what you might have done or after having had time to study the situation or discuss it with others. You can only weigh the merits of what you did against the alternatives you thought of at the time.

For example, a mother whose son committed suicide years ago wishes she had died in his place and feels guilty because she didn't take him to a psychiatrist who would have prescribed him a new antidepressant that had a reputation of helping many difficult cases of depression. "If only I could have gotten him this new drug, he might have been saved," she laments. However, at the time that her son was still alive, that drug had not yet been put on the market.

*Judging your actions against idealistic fantasy options.* It isn't fair for you to judge yourself for what you did or didn't do against impossible choices. While we all wish for miracles to provide a magic rescue out of a horrible situation, the hard truth is that there are situations where it's impossible to preserve the life, health, or integrity of all involved. (Review the section on childhood omnipotent guilt/superman/superwoman guilt in chapter 1.)

*Considering only the possible positive consequences of an alternative action.* If you're feeling guilty because you acted one way and wish you'd acted in another way, you need to ask yourself if you've fully examined the full range of possible outcomes of the wished-for alternative. Are you focusing only on the possible positive results of this path and minimizing the possible negative consequences?

For example, a formerly abused wife feels she made the wrong decision by running away from her violent husband without a plan and without emptying out their joint account. After she filed for divorce, her husband refused to give her any of their joint property, and she was unable to acquire a court order mandating that she be given what was legally hers.

"It's my fault the kids and I are struggling right now. I have to work two jobs to make ends meet. Meanwhile, the kids are being neglected, right when they need me the most. If only I left in a reasonable way, rather than like a frantic fool, or at least stolen money out of the joint account, like my ex-husband did, the kids and I wouldn't be having the stress we have today."

This woman was looking only at the potential positive outcomes of seeking legal help or grabbing whatever moneys she could prior to leaving her husband. When you judge the soundness of the decisions you made under conditions of stress and trauma against alternative options, it's crucial that you scrutinize the decisions you didn't make as thoroughly as you do the decisions you did make. This includes brainstorming some of the possible negative outcomes of the options you didn't choose. She failed to appreciate that if she had sought legal help, her husband might've found out and punished her (or one of the children) so severely that she might have never left. Also, if she had stolen money from the bank account, she would have been violating a religious principle that was very important to her. Such a violation would have severely damaged her self-esteem and diminished her personal sense of power, which would have impaired her ability to work and to function as a mother. Furthermore, if she had stolen the money, her husband might have become so angered that he might have hunted her down and killed her as he had threatened to many times in the past.

When this woman was able to consider some of the possible negative consequences of the alternative she thought was so much more desirable than the path she had chosen, her guilt level was reduced.

## Category Three: Morality of Behavior

*Judging yourself on the basis of what happened rather than on what you intended to happen.* You may feel guilty about something you did, thought, or felt not because any of these went against your moral standards, but because the outcome was unexpectedly disastrous. For example, a woman who was ill asked her boyfriend to pick up her prescription medication on the way to visit her. The boyfriend entered the drugstore at the precise moment that a burglary was going on and was shot three times. The woman feels guilty, even though she did not intend for her boyfriend to be harmed and she had no foreknowledge of the burglary.

*Being unaware of or unwilling to accept that certain emotional and biological reactions to trauma or extreme stress are involuntary and can't be controlled by personal determination or willpower.* As outlined in chapter 3, trauma, and even extreme stress, can give rise to fight/flight/freeze reactions, dissociation, hypersexuality (or the converse, disinterest in sex), and a host of other reactions. Such reactions are not under your control. If you persist in blaming yourself for having a numbing reaction or an adrenaline surge, then you're practicing superwoman/superman guilt, because you feel you are above normal human experience.

Another strong emotional reaction is feeling glad that you are alive and well in situations where others are being harmed or killed. All living beings are born with an instinct to survive. Perhaps you feel guilty for feeling grateful that you're safe relative to others; however, your instinct to survive is not a matter of personal choice. You were born with it. People who lose their will to live, for example, people who suffer from suicidal depressions, are considered to be suffering from a grave mental disorder.

*Judging your behavior by comparing it with a fantasy positive alternative that simply was not available (related to catch-22 guilt).* Trauma has been defined as a situation where all of the alternative courses of action are unacceptable or painful. If you are in a traumatic situation, the choice of safety and happiness for all is not available. The best choice is the choice with the least negative consequences.

*Using only your emotional reaction as a guide to the soundness of your decisions or actions.* Another common thinking error is judging the merits of a particular action or idea by your emotional reaction to it. Feeling one way or another about a certain course of action is not necessarily an indication that pursuing that course of action is in your best interest. For example, because of your survivor guilt, you may feel you owe special favors to someone who holds a relatively disadvantaged social position compared with yourself. However, this feeling is not sufficient reason to automatically conclude that special treatment is in your best interest, or the best interest of the other person.

## ✍ Exercise: Common Thinking Errors and Looking at the Bigger Picture

Use the questions that follow to evaluate each instance of guilt you have listed in column 3. Using these questions as your guide, identify any thinking errors present regarding the guilt listed. Write the name or number of the thinking error in column 4, then write two or three sentences about how this thinking error colored your perception and feeling of guilt.

**Thinking Error 1. Hindsight Bias:** Is your guilt the result of hindsight bias, where you judge what you did, thought, or felt (or didn't do, think, or feel) on the basis of information that was not available to you during the event? Is your guilt based on omens and premonitions present during the event that have no scientific basis and that you probably would've disregarded or never thought of twice if events had turned out more positively?

**Thinking Error 2. Believing you were totally responsible or overrating your role in what happened:** Do you feel you and you alone caused the negative event or that you were the prime cause of the death or injury of another person? What were the other forces at play?

Before you complete column 4, you may need to work on this thinking error on a separate page of your journal. On a fresh piece of paper, write the heading "Causes." Make a list of all the other people and forces involved in causing the death or injury. Try to organize this list in sequential order. Include not only immediate causes but also more distant causes. For example, the sibling of an abused child who feels guilty about not having been able to stop the abuse needs to remember immediate causes, such as fear of punishment, as well as more distant causes, such as the difficulties involved in enforcing laws against child abuse. A medic who feels guilty about not having saved more lives on the battlefield needs to take into account not only the immediate conditions of the front line but also the fact that elected officials were responsible for declaring an armed conflict, that the American public was responsible for voting into office people who made this decision, or that his medical training did not adequately prepare him for many war-related medical emergencies.

If you tend to see yourself as the central cause of the negative event, you may need help in obtaining a complete list of causes. If this is the case, you may want to share your list with your therapist, a trusted friend, or a trusted member of your recovery program. Consider also the following question: have you taken on so much responsibility that others, for example, certain aggressive people or institutions, are exonerated from responsibility?

After you've generated your list of causes, give each cause a percentage of responsibility. What percentage of the cause belongs to you? Has this exercise altered your original view of your role in the negative event?

**Thinking Error 3. Confusing the possibility that you could have prevented the negative event with the belief that you caused it:** Do you feel you could've done something (or something more) that would've averted negative consequences? Even if you could've effectively prevented the death or injury of another, this doesn't mean you *caused* the death or injury.

**Thinking Error 4. Confusing your sense of responsibility due to your role with the idea that you had the power to avert a negative outcome:** Did you hold an official position or some other responsible role at the time of the tragic event? What responsibilities were associated with your position? Most likely no official description of your responsibilities included the ability to avert disaster. Yet because of the nature of your role, you may unrealistically feel it was your duty to avoid all and any negative outcomes.

**Thinking Error 5. Disregarding the power of certain scientifically proven physiological and emotional human reactions to extreme stress:** Did you act, feel, or think (or not act, feel, or think) in a way that made you feel guilty due to involuntary biological reactions to trauma or extreme stress, such as fight/flight/freeze reactions? Do you feel that you should've been able to "overcome" involuntary biological responses to trauma on the basis of your strength and willpower? Do you feel that you are beyond the limitations that affect most people? Is such thinking an instance of childhood omnipotent guilt or superman/superwoman mentality?

**Thinking Error 6. Evaluating what you did based on information you only knew about or options you only thought of after the event was over:** When you evaluate what you did during those difficult moments, are you judging yourself on the basis of information you have now, which you didn't have at the time, or on the basis of possible courses of action you thought of after the event was over? It isn't fair for you to judge the effectiveness or morality of what you did or did not do during the crisis based on knowledge you did not have at the time or based on options you had the opportunity to think of after consulting with others or after the benefit of having time to contemplate additional possible courses of action.

**Thinking Error 7. Judging your actions against idealistic fantasy options:** It is human nature to wish for happy or miraculous endings to difficult situations. But there are many instances in life where a just or happy ending is simply not possible. Are you judging your actions against wished for or miraculous options that could not possibly exist?

**Thinking Error 8. Considering only the positive consequences of an alternative action:** When you think of what you might have done differently that would have resulted in a better outcome, are you considering only the possible positive consequences of these other courses of action? You need to take into account possible negative consequences of having done, thought, or felt something other than you did, thought, or felt.

**Thinking Error 9. Judging yourself on the basis of what happened rather than on what you intended to happen:** Is your guilt based on what happened rather than what you planned to happen? Are you making the mistake of condemning yourself for doing, thinking, or feeling something due to an unforeseen or unintended outcome rather than on the basis of the goals you had in mind?

**Thinking Error 10. Catch-22 guilt:** Do you feel guilty because you violated a personal standard of right or wrong? Which standard did you violate? Did you violate this standard due to threats or coercion or to protect the life and health of others? Did you violate one of your standards of right and wrong in order to uphold another standard?

Physical survival, psychological integrity, and economic stability are not commonly thought of as personal standards, but they are part of the standard of valuing human life. If you acted to protect your body or health, your self-esteem and self-respect, or to prevent economic disaster, then you were acting out of the need for self-preservation. Be sure to take into account the standard of self-preservation as you reply to questions about personal values.

Were you in a catch-22 situation where all the alternatives available to you involved violating a personal standard of right and wrong? Write at least three or four sentences about how the options available to you all involved disregarding a value you held dear. Keep in mind that under such conditions, the least bad choice is the best choice (Kubany and Manke 1995). If moral or atrocity guilt is an issue for you, you may need to create a separate section of your journal labeled "Catch-22 Guilt" and devote several pages to writing on this subject.

**Thinking Error 11. Using only your emotional reaction as a guide to the soundness of your decision or actions:** Emotions are important, and you need to pay attention to them. However, emotions alone are not the sole criteria for assessing the soundness of your decisions or actions. Are you using your emotional reactions to what you did, thought, or felt as the measure of the reasonableness of your behavior? It is possible to have made one of the best decisions possible under trying circumstances yet still feel fear, confusion, guilt, or anger about what you did or did not do. Having distressing emotional reactions to what you did may be a sign to you that what you did was wrong. But your emotional reactions alone can't be the determiner of the soundness of your decisions or behavior. You need to evaluate what you did based on the options available. If the situation was traumatic or extremely difficult, it is possible that you would have negative emotional reactions to your behavior no matter what you did.

**Thinking Error 12. Childhood omnipotent guilt/superwoman/ superman guilt:** Does your guilt reflect a belief that you had superhuman abilities or insights? Is this guilt an instance of childhood omnipotent guilt or superwoman/superman guilt?

**Thinking Error 13. Failure to meet societal expectations or the expectations of others:** That everyone didn't give you approval or affection for what you did (or did not do) is not a sign that you committed a wrongdoing. It's virtually impossible for any of us to receive the approval of most or all people, especially under conditions of stress or trauma.

**Thinking Error 14. If I had died, the other person would have lived. If I had been made to suffer, the other person would have been spared:** In most life situations, even traumatic situations, it's difficult if not impossible for you to change places with someone in order to spare that person death or injury. In certain extreme situations, such as war or family violence, you may be presented with some opportunities to take the place of another who is condemned to death, torture, or abuse. In the case of incest, for example, suppose you could offer yourself to be abused so that a sibling would be spared. This may work, but there is no guarantee that the abuser will not harm both you and the sibling you are trying to protect.

Do you ever wish, dream, or fantasize that you could have traded places with the person who suffered or who died? Do you ever replay the situation of injury or death putting yourself in the place of that person? Stay with your dream or fantasy and carry it as far as it can go. Imagine the scene of injury or death as precisely as possible and ask yourself whether, realistically, if you had died, the other person would still be alive and well. What might have really happened if you died or were injured in the person's place? Might the person have died or been injured anyway or shortly thereafter? Would your taking the person's place really have averted the tragedy?

In situations such as normal bereavement, illness, suicide, homicide, and many accidents, it's virtually impossible for you to serve as a substitute. Even if you made yourself ill or killed yourself, that would not necessarily restore another person to health or spare that person from death.

Here's how Jane did this exercise: She reread what she wrote for each event in column 1 that involved guilt (as she specified in columns 2 and 3). Then she reviewed the various thinking errors and decided if her thinking reflected one or more of these thinking errors. She wrote the names (or numbers) of the thinking errors in column 5. For each thinking error, she wrote at least one sentence describing how her thinking reflected that thinking error and another sentence that reflected a more rational view of the guilt-evoking event recorded in column 1.

An example of one of Jane's entries is on page 216.

## ✍ Exercise: Identifying Strengths

Congratulations. You've done quite a bit of work already in completing columns 1, 2, 3, and 4. The last part of the exercise will help you synthesize all that you have done. In column 5, you'll write two or three sentences identifying strengths you exhibited during that particular event.

For each of the events you listed in column 1, identify those thoughts, actions, or feelings on your part about which you feel some pride. Don't worry about seeming conceited. Just make a list of all the positive qualities you can think of.

You may want to begin as follows: "As a result of the way I acted, thought, or felt during those difficult times, I now see myself as . . ." Consider the following list of possibilities as you complete column 5: brave, clever, intelligent, resourceful, caring, loyal, moral, emotionally strong, physically strong, spiritual, focused, or original.

If there's anything else positive about what you did, thought, or felt (or didn't do, think, or feel), be sure to list that in column 5 as well.

## Getting Feedback

At this point, as at other points in the healing process, it would be extremely helpful for you to take your writing about your survivor guilt to a therapist or support group to get feedback. If you are like many who suffer from survivor guilt, you may have a distorted view

| What Happened (entry 3) | Thoughts, Feelings, Beliefs | Types of Guilt | Thinking Errors |
|---|---|---|---|
| I should've been able to manage missing my boyfriend on my own. If I'd been a stronger person, the argument with him wouldn't have bothered me so much and I would have never agreed to take my sister to the library with me just because I was lonely. If she hadn't gone along, she wouldn't have been raped. | I'm a weak person. I'm an overly dependent person. I was weak to feel so bad about my boyfriend and then weak again in not being able to save my sister from assault. I should've been raped instead of her because I was older and could handle it better. It isn't fair that she, a virgin, was hurt and I, who have sexual experience, was not. | *Failure to Meet Societal Expectations Guilt:* My friends all think that women shouldn't need men anymore and that girls who fall apart when their boyfriends argue with them are weaklings. My women friends would condemn me as some kind of archaic freak for being so dependent on my boyfriend. That is no longer the "in" thing to do. *Survivor Guilt:* I wish I had suffered in my sister's place. *Responsibility Guilt:* Because I am the older sister, I'm responsible for the welfare of my sister and therefore I'm to blame if she is hurt. My family expects this of me and I expect this of me also. | *Thinking Error 3:* It's illogical for me to think that just because I might have been able to prevent the rape (by not taking my sister alone, by miraculously fighting off the rapist) that I caused the rape. The rapist caused the rape, not me. I didn't rape my sister; he did. *Thinking Error 13:* I feel guilty for not living up to my girlfriends' expectations, but this guilt seems foolish to me now because it isn't based on the truth. The truth is I need my boyfriend and it hurts not to have him anymore. To pretend I'm tougher than I am is a lie. It's a mistake for me to try to be a fake. It's also a thinking error to think that not living up to my girlfriends' expectations had anything to do with the rape. They are unrelated problems. *Thinking Error 14:* Even if I had the chance to suffer instead of my sister, there was no guarantee that the rapist wouldn't have harmed both of us, or that at some later point in time he would have come back for her. |

of the options available to you while the trauma or stress was occurring. Most likely, you had fewer choices in the situation than you imagined. Others can help point out to you certain realities of the situation that you might've overlooked. You can also share with them your feelings about your survival behaviors, including your guilt or any feelings of pride, shame, or sadness.

Although it's true that sharing your secrets with others can be extremely cathartic and therapeutic, you may not want to share everything you've written. You have the right to be selective about what you share. Under no circumstances should you allow others—peers, therapists, or your doctors—to pressure you. Being overtly, or subtly, forced into talking may only repeat an element of your painful past, and so may ultimately be counterproductive. Also, it's doubtful that sharing is therapeutic when it is coerced.

After you've obtained feedback, you might want to make some additions to columns 4 and 5.

# 9

# Exercises for Coping with Guilt

Despite all your efforts, there may be areas about which you still feel guilty, so that no matter how rational you try to be about what happened, you're left with a profound feeling of remorse and sorrow that all the reasoning in the world cannot erase. In this chapter, you'll deal with the guilt that is still there in two ways: First, you'll learn how to train your mind to see the events and your role in them in a more realistic fashion. This will mean countering some of the irrational thinking patterns you've practiced so often with more rational thoughts. Second, you'll learn to take other forms of action to put the energy involved with your guilt to constructive use.

## Countering Irrational Guilty Thinking

If you've read the previous chapters and answered the questions in the exercises in these chapters, you need to congratulate yourself. You've just completed a tremendous amount of work. Most likely recording the details of what happened to you and reviewing these events several times was a painstaking and emotionally wrenching process. During the process of reexamining your guilt, you probably experienced your guilt, as well as other painful feelings, deeply and repeatedly. Confronting your guilt is an act of immense courage, since the usual tendency is to avoid it at all costs.

You may have expected to be fully released from your burden of guilt at this point. However, as I've stated repeatedly, reexamining your guilt from a more rational point of view is not a prescription for eliminating or erasing all guilt or the feeling of hopelessness and loss that attends survivor guilt.

When you think of the trauma or the critical incident you've been writing about, it's normal for you to revert back to the way you thought before and feel the way you used to feel before you picked up this book. Your first response may be to feel as guilty as you did prior to any attempt to work on your guilt feelings. This doesn't mean you've failed in the way you worked on your guilt or that all your efforts in reading this book, working on the exercises, or talking to a therapist or others in a recovery effort have been a waste of time. It simply means that in order to make your more rational perspective stick, you have more work to do. You'll have to make active and repeated efforts to counter your irrational self-blaming thoughts with the rational perspective you've developed and written about so extensively in the previous chapter.

If you've spent many years feeling guilty for irrational reasons, then you can't expect to automatically discard the old irrational ways of thinking and instantly begin thinking more rationally. In essence, you will have to carry out a debate in your head. The old point of view will dominate for a while, despite your new learning. When the old accusations come up, you will have to remind yourself of all you have learned about the various types of guilt, the nature of traumatic and stressful circumstances, and the various thinking errors.

When you begin to experience those familiar guilt feelings again, you need to ask yourself the following question: *What am I feeling? Is it guilt, grief, or hopelessness?* When your mind starts to berate you for something you did or didn't do, something you felt or didn't feel, or something you thought or didn't think, you'll need to learn to catch yourself. This is not easy to do. However, once you've interrupted your irrational thinking once, it'll be easier to do it twice, then three times, and then some more.

Your goal is to be increasingly able to observe yourself thinking the old irrational ways and say to yourself, *Wait a minute. Didn't I already figure out that I could view this in another light? I don't need to feel guilty about this the way I used to.*

If, in sorting out rational from irrational guilt, you've found that some of your guilt is unfounded and that some of your survivor guilt has been intensified by other guilts, for example, shadow or religious guilt, that had little to do with the other person's death or injury, then you need to remind yourself of this, over and over again, until thinking rationally becomes as automatic as blaming yourself irrationally. At first, talking back to yourself may seem strange, and new, but it is necessary for you to heal. Over time, if you continue to review what you've written in your journal and reflect on it, and if you continue to remind yourself of the more rational perspective on your guilt that you have worked to achieve, your guilt should lessen.

## *Positive (but Rational) Self-Talk*

Reprogramming your mind to think rationally about incidents that cause you to experience survivor guilt is not an easy process. Figuring out a more rational way of looking at what happened and your role in it and recording a more rational view of each aspect of what happened is only the beginning of winning the war that is raging in your own mind: the battle between automatic, irrational, guilt-evoking thoughts and more rational, less guilt-evoking thoughts.

If you automatically tend to think irrationally about your guilt-producing events or have felt guilty about certain matters for many years, then you can't expect to automatically think more rationally right away. You will have to work at it.

This means that whenever an irrational, guilt-evoking thought pops into your mind, you will have to counter it with a more rational view. Although this may seem like an overwhelming task, consider the costs of feeling unnecessarily guilty. It may take more effort, time, and concentration to work on your thinking than you planned. However, consider how much time and emotional energy is consumed by feeling guilty and by making amends for the destructive ways in which you handle your guilt.

Nothing is easy in life, especially change—even positive change. When you feel upset about having to spend more time reprogramming your mind to think rationally, consider how much time you would spend drinking (and recovering from a drinking binge), overeating (and recovering from the binge), arguing with someone (and then having to make up with that person or make different arrangements because that person feels alienated from you), sinking into depression (and losing time from work or damaging your social life), or reacting in some other predictable way to strong guilt feelings. In the long run, it's faster, easier, and perhaps less expensive (in terms of doctor's visits, lost productivity, and other costs) to invest the time in working on your mind than to not make the effort to benefit from all the hard work you have put in already in reading this book and working on the exercises.

### ✍ Exercise: Practicing Rational Thinking

Select the three aspects of your critical incident that have created the most guilt in you. In your journal write out the more rational view of these incidents and the strengths you exhibited. For each aspect, stand in front of a mirror and repeat the following to yourself three or four times, or until it is almost automatic:

> During the trauma or stress, _____ happened. Whenever I remember this, I usually think _____ and feel guilty. When I start feeling guilty about _____, I need to remind myself that I'm thinking incorrectly. Instead of practicing the thinking error that [insert a description of the relevant thinking error], I need to view the situation as follows: [insert rational thought]. I also need to remember that I displayed the following strengths [list strengths] and need to give myself credit for these. Just as it would be a mistake for me to concentrate on all the good things to the exclusion of the things I feel guilty about, it would be a mistake to focus entirely on the negative and totally exclude the positive.

I also highly recommend that you state your rational and irrational thoughts about certain incidents out loud to trusted friends, members of your recovery or support group, or to your therapist. You need to make the rational thoughts as much a part of you as your irrational thoughts used to be. Once again, this will require practice.

## Accepting Guilt

An important part of coping with your guilt involves learning to forgive yourself for past actions or behaviors.

### ✍ Exercise: Self-Forgiveness

Forgiving yourself for some of your choices, behaviors, and feelings during the traumatic incident or stressful events you experienced is crucial to your healing. You may find forgiving yourself as hard as or harder than making some kind of peace with some of the individuals, institutions, or natural forces that caused the harm. (Please notice I didn't say "forgiving" the person or force that created the loss or injury, but instead "making peace with.")

To begin forgiving yourself, in your journal, answer the following questions:

1. Go back over your description of the critical events in column 1 of the exercise in the previous chapter. For which behaviors, attitudes, and feelings do you still castigate or blame yourself?

2. What would it take for you to forgive yourself for some of these behaviors, attitudes, and feelings?

3. Is it possible for you to do whatever you've listed so that you can forgive yourself? If so, what is keeping you from pursuing whatever you need to make peace with this part of your past?

4. Is there information you need that you might never be able to obtain before you can forgive yourself? If so, your options are to try to forgive yourself anyway or to continue to punish yourself. Who are you helping and what good are you doing in the world by punishing yourself? Who would you harm if you forgave yourself?

## ✍ Exercise: What If It Were Someone You Love?

Think of the names of family members and friends, people you dearly love. If you can't think of anyone you truly love, imagine a child of about ten or eleven. Now rerun the story of your trauma or stressful events as if it were an imaginary movie, but make the star one of the people you love or the young child. Have the person do, think, and say exactly what you did during the trauma.

Make notes about what you condemn or blame the person for. Are you being kinder to that person than you were to yourself? Would you be able to forgive a loved one for some of the actions or inactions you blame yourself for? If you can forgive that person, why is it you can't forgive yourself for the very same behaviors, attitudes, and feelings?

## *Double-Dialoguing*

In the following two exercises, you will be asked to communicate with the person (or people) who died or was injured about whom you feel survivor guilt. If there is more than one person, you may need to complete this exercise separately for each individual for whom you carry survivor guilt.

## ✒ *Exercise: Exchanging Letters with the Dead or Injured*

Write a letter to the individual who died or was injured. This letter should be at least one page. Tell him or her whatever you want: more facts about what happened, how you feel about what happened, or how his or her death or injury has affected your life. You may also want to ask that person how he or she feels about what happened. Be sure to point out how you've been paying penance or harming yourself (or others) as the result of the person's death or injury and ask the dead or injured how much longer you need to go on punishing yourself or others for what happened. A good question to ask is, "How will I know when I've punished myself (or others) enough for what happened to you?"

Now imagine that you are the other person and write a letter back to yourself. Be sure to have the injured or the dead respond to your question about what type of penance you should be doing and how long you should be involved in punishing yourself (or others) for what happened.

## ✒ *Exercise: A Dialogue with the Dead or Injured*

You can complete this exercise in addition to, or instead of, the letter-writing exercise. Ideally this exercise can be completed with a trained mental health professional or a trusted friend who is psychologically aware and can be supportive.

Place two chairs facing each other. In one chair, put a picture of the person who is dead or injured, or write the person's name on a piece of paper and put it on the chair. Any symbol of that person, for example, a favored object, will do. The point is that that chair is to represent the person about whom you feel survivor guilt.

Place yourself in the chair opposite and talk to him or her. Tell him or her how you feel, what happened during the event, and what has happened since. Feel free to ask the person how he or she felt about what happened and how he or she feels about you. Be sure to talk about how his or her death or injury has affected your life and, very important, ask him or her what you should do about punishing yourself or making amends for your failings and wrongdoings. Also ask if he or she wants you to memorialize his or her death or injury in some way, for example, by starting a scholarship fund in his or her name, writing a letter to the newspaper about the death or injury, or arranging for a special religious ceremony in his or her honor.

Now switch chairs and sit where the dead or injured is supposed to be sitting. Answer the questions you have asked the person who is dead or harmed. (If you're working with someone else, you won't need to switch places.)

Once again, sit in your chair and respond to what the dead or injured person has shared with you. You can then sit in his or her chair and respond to what you have just said.

You can keep up this process as if you are having a dialogue or conversation as long as you like or need to. You can stop it for a while, then continue at a later point in time.

This exercise, and the letter-writing exercise, may fill you with many strong feelings. If you become overwhelmed, remember to heed the cautions listed in the introduction. However, if you are simply feeling strong feelings, the kind of feelings that should go along with something as important as the death or injury of another human being, there is no need for alarm. It's good that your strong feelings of missing, caring, anger, or guilt come to the surface and be expressed. You may feel that these feelings have "broken you," but ultimately there can be power in being broken. This may sound like a contradiction, but in this phase of the healing process, as in other parts of the therapeutic process, contradictions reign.

The suggestion of dialoguing with the dead or injured, in written or oral form, has its innate contradictions also. In facing your guilt and grief, and perhaps letting them flood your consciousness, you will ultimately be able to cope with them better and they can become the source of positive change and creative contributions.

## ✍ Exercise: Reversing Positions

In this exercise, you are asked to change places with the dead or injured for whom you carry survivor guilt and begin a dialogue about what happened and its effects. You can complete this exercise in written manner, by writing letters, or orally, by talking out loud, as in the empty chair technique described above.

Imagine that you are the person who died or was injured and the person who died or was injured is you. That person acted, felt, and thought as you did during the traumatic event. Have that person write you a letter that explains what happened, outlines what he or she felt guilty about, and describes the impact of what happened on his or her life since the traumatic or critical incident.

You then reply to that letter, as if you were the one who was injured or who died. Be sure to discuss how you feel about what happened, what you expect the other person to feel guilty about (or not feel guilty about), how you would like that person to punish himself or herself and for how long, and what you would like that person to do in your honor or in your memory.

You may exchange letters in this manner until you have a deeper understanding of your guilt, some sense of what actions you might take to help channel your guilt in constructive ways, and some idea of what you need to do and for how long in order to alleviate your guilt.

# Making Amends

Just as you might apologize to someone you feel you have harmed, you may want to make amends to people you feel you have harmed, or, if those persons are not available, you may want to make some other form of amends or restitution. Making amends can help alleviate your feelings of guilt. While you may feel that whatever amends you make are inadequate, because they can't reverse the damage, making amends can still help not only lessen your guilt but also leave the world a better place.

Some individuals with survivor guilt state that they would like to make amends. However, because they can't bring back the dead or reverse some other grievous harm they feel they were responsible for (erroneously or not), they reason that it's useless to make any amends or restitution. In my professional opinion, this is an excuse. There is always something you can do to make amends, even if it is not perfect or powerful enough to change the past.

In twelve-step programs such as AA, Al-Anon, OA, and NA, the eighth and ninth steps concern the process of making amends. First you make a list of people you have harmed. Then you make amends to such people, except when to do so would injure yourself or others. In working through these steps, twelve-step members consult with their sponsors, other program members, spiritual or religious advisors, and others. It is critical that making amends is not a form of immoderate self-punishment and does not create more harm than good. Even if you are not a member of a twelve-step program, you may find some guidance and suggestions in the twelve-step literature regarding the process of making amends. (Hazelden Educational Materials offers several pamphlets and booklets on the process of making amends. You can call 800-328 9000.)

One suggestion is to start by making one amend and then evaluate it. How did it feel to make the amend? Were there any unexpected positive or negative results of making this amend? How can the information you gained by making one amend help you in deciding whether or not or how to make any future amends?

Another suggestion is to make an amend that promotes the value that you feel you violated and about which you still feel guilt. For example, if you feel guilty about having killed, an appropriate amend might be to take action that promotes life. If you have killed or harmed animals, you may decide to make some kind of contribution of time or money toward helping animals.

If you don't feel you violated any particular moral standard, but suffer from survivor guilt because someone died of a certain illness or situation, you might cope with your survivor guilt by becoming involved with or somehow contributing to organizations that help others who died of that illness or because of that situation. For example, Jane, who felt guilty about her sister being raped, began to volunteer some time at a rape crisis center and arranged for rape awareness programs to be held at various schools. Even though Jane's therapist, friends, and even her raped sister, did not hold Jane at all accountable for the rape, and even though Jane worked on her guilt issues following the suggestions in this book, she still felt some survivor guilt. Rather than sitting with that guilt and letting it fester into a depression or explode into anger at others, Jane chose a constructive outlet for it.

If you have guilt, even if others think you "shouldn't" have it and even though you have reduced your guilt by correcting your thinking about what happened, I recommend that you put that guilt to work. Let the energy of your guilt be used for a good purpose, however you define that purpose. One way to cope with guilt is to take some control over it by translating it into a form of action you can take.

How you structure your amends, how many amends you choose to make, and how many amends you think are "enough" are matters for you to decide. There are no "rules" here. You can try making some kind of limited amend and see how it works for you.

# ✍ *Exercise: Making Amends*

In a fresh page in your journal, write the heading "Amends" and answer the following questions to the best of your ability:

1. As the result of taking a close look at your guilt, do you feel the need to make amends for what you perceive to be a wrongdoing (or a wrong feeling or wrong thought)? If you don't, then there is no need to continue reading this exercise. Skip this exercise and go on to the next section of this chapter.

2. In your dialogues with those who were injured or died, did you remember to bring up the topic of amends? If not, then go back and complete one of these exercises and include the issue of amends.

3. When you talked about, or thought about, the issue of what you needed to do and how long you needed to do it in order to make up for the past, what was decided?

4. Make a list of the people or organizations you feel you have harmed.

5. Select three people from this list and write down two or three ways you could make an amend or restitution toward these people. Consider some of the ideas for amends that might have come up when you were writing letters to and talking with those toward whom you feel survivor guilt. Make sure the amends you have chosen will cause no harm to you or to others. You may want to consider a type of amend related to the nature of your guilt.

6. Discuss the advisability of these amends with your therapist, a trusted friend, or a religious or spiritual advisor.

7. Select the least complicated and least costly amend that you and others deem suitable and set a time and place to make that amend.

8. Write two or three sentences about how you feel about making the decision to make an amend. How did it feel to make a decision to take positive action as the result of your guilt?

9. Make the amend, keeping in mind that you are making this amend for yourself as well as the other person.

10. How did it feel to actually make the amend? Write two or three sentences about your reaction to making the amend.

How did it feel to take positive action as the result of your guilt? Is this something you would like to do again? Focus your writing on your feelings, not the reactions of others.

11. Is it possible that others feel the same kind of guilt or concerns you do? Would you consider trying to find people who, like yourself, would like to honor the dead or injured or take steps toward preventing the kinds of deaths or injuries they witnessed and about which they carry survivor guilt?

12. Do you wish to make more amends? Write two or three sentences about why you want or do not want to make more amends. If you decide to make more amends, follow the process outlined in this exercise of thinking about what you want to do and why and obtaining feedback from others. Also, every amend needs to pass the test of not being harmful to yourself or others.

Do not hesitate to ask others for suggestions or feedback. Making amends is not as simple as it seems. Many factors need to be considered, and often considerable creativity is needed to find an amend that works for you as well as any others involved. Brainstorming with others or asking others for feedback is a good way to stimulate your own thinking. Even if others don't have a viable suggestion, just talking about the issues involved may help you make your own best decision or spark a new idea in your head.

## Standards of Recovery

How will you know if you are making progress in healing?
Here are some questions to consider:

- Are you increasingly honest about your guilt feelings?

- Are you increasingly able to feel your guilt without running from it, without trying to hide it with alcohol, drugs, food, overspending, or compulsive sexual activity or without trying to displace it onto others in the form of verbal or physical abuse?

- Are you increasingly able to counter your irrational thoughts with more rational thinking?

- Are you increasingly able to see some of the complexities involved in the situation that created your survivor guilt instead of viewing the situation as a simple case of your inadequacy, failure, or sinfulness?

- Are you taking action against the guilt you still carry by making amends or trying to find constructive outlets for your guilt?

- Are you more able to talk about some of your guilt feelings with certain select others?

Answering "yes" to any of the above questions is an indication that you are making progress.

## The Bottom Line: Self-Care

Another criterion for recovery is your degree of willingness to take care of yourself. This last criterion of progress, self-care, is crucial. Harming yourself or allowing yourself to deteriorate as means of punishment for survivor guilt is not a healthy way of coping with guilt. Sometimes when the guilt comes, and along with it grief, anger, and other powerful feelings, your ability to counter irrational thinking may weaken and the forces of destruction within you may clamor for expression. It is at these times that what is necessary is endurance, as well as a pure and simple commitment to self-care.

## ✍ Self-Assessment: Self-Care

The following questions will help you assess your degree of self-care by examining the degree to which you have created safety in your life and by identifying areas you still need to work on. Circle the appropriate response: yes, no, or sometimes (if applicable).

### The Million-Dollar Question

1. Do you feel you deserve good treatment?
   Yes   No

### Basic Health Needs

1. Have you had a physical checkup in the last year?
   Yes   No

2. Do you see your physician when you have or suspect a medical problem?
   Yes   No   Sometimes

3. Do you have a plan to take care of yourself in case of a medical or psychiatric emergency?
Yes   No   Sometimes

4. Do you see a dentist regularly or as needed?
Yes   No   Sometimes

## Regulation of Basic Body Functions

1. Do you try to regulate your eating?
Yes   No   Sometimes

2. Do you include exercise in your life (if medically permissible)?
Yes   No   Sometimes

3. Have you made attempts to try to regulate your sleeping via medication, avoiding caffeine or overstimulating substances and activities prior to bedtime, trying to get to bed at the same time every night, or arranging room temperature so that it is comfortable for you?
Yes   No   Sometimes

## Control of Self-Destructive Behavior

1. Are you abusing your medications by not taking them as prescribed; combining them with other medications, drugs, or alcohol without consulting a doctor; or overdosing?
Yes   No   Sometimes

2. Do you self-mutilate, for example, cut yourself, bang your head, pick at scabs and sores, burn yourself, pull out your eyebrows, eyelashes, or hair?
Yes   No   Sometimes

3. Do you engage in impulsive risk-taking behaviors, for example, cruising around dangerous neighborhoods looking for a fight, driving in a reckless manner, picking fights with people larger than yourself, or making yourself vulnerable to attack in other ways?
Yes   No   Sometimes

4. Do you have control over substances such as food, alcohol, or street drugs?
Yes   No   Sometimes

5. Do you have a plan as to how to handle suicidal feelings?
Yes   No   Sometimes

6. Do you practice safe sex?
Yes   No   Sometimes

## Control of Symptoms

1. Do you have increased control over your anger today, as opposed to five years ago?
Yes   No   Sometimes

2. Do you have increased control over your guilt feelings today, as opposed to five years ago?
Yes   No   Sometimes

3. Do you have increased control over your depression today, as opposed to five years ago?
Yes   No   Sometimes

## Safe Environment

1. Is your housing safe?
Yes   No   Sometimes

2. Have you taken steps to make your home as safe as possible?
Yes   No

3. Is your car or vehicle safe?
Yes   No   Sometimes

4. Do you associate with dangerous people?
Yes   No   Sometimes

5. Do you associate with exploitative people?
Yes   No   Sometimes

6. Do you associate with impulsive, risk-taking people who might pressure you into some destructive activity?
Yes   No   Sometimes

7. Do you have an emotional or social support system? If your family of origin is not supportive or interferes with your recovery, do you have emotional ties to other people who can help you when you need support?
Yes   No   Sometimes

## Financial Security

1. Do you try to budget your money to the best of your ability?
Yes   No   Sometimes

2. Do you gamble compulsively?
Yes   No   Sometimes

3. Do you have adequate insurance coverage for your car, home, or other possessions?
Yes   No

## *A Commitment to Self-Care*

Review your answers to the questions above. Are there areas where you fail to take care of yourself? In your journal, title a page "Self-Care" and make a list of all the areas where you need to improve your self-care. Leave several lines blank after each entry. After each item you have listed write two or three sentences about how you plan to improve your self-care in this area. Be specific about what you will do and when you plan to do it.

If you've read this book and worked on the written exercises, you need to congratulate yourself for having completed a tremendous amount of work. Time, energy, and thought were required for you to examine your survivor guilt so thoroughly and honestly. Even though it may not be apparent immediately, your many efforts to better understand your survivor guilt and see it in a more rational context *will* bear fruit.

It takes time to change the ways you view yourself and your survivor guilt and to change the ways you cope with such a profound feeling. If you're like most people, you've probably spent hundreds, if not thousands, of hours practicing some of the thinking errors described in this book and coping with survivor guilt in an indirect or destructive manner. A history of unnecessary self-blame, illogical thinking, and dysfunctional coping mechanisms cannot be eradicated easily or quickly. But, with practice and time, you can build a new history, and the old, hurtful ways of thinking and behaving can diminish. Eventually, they will fade away.

Your survivor guilt should lessen not only because you have taken the time to examine it thoroughly from a variety of angles, but also because you have taken other actions, such as finding ways to honor the dead, making amends, and taking better care of yourself. Nevertheless, neither this book or any other counseling effort can remove your grief for your losses or be a cure-all. The damage wrought by the past cannot be completely undone. Grief, conflict, anxiety, and survivor guilt may always be a part of your life. But they no longer have to dominate or destroy your life. Your greater understanding of your survivor guilt and your ability to see it in a more logical manner will give you the strength to bear the grief and any other suffering involved. Also, you will now have ways of taking the energy involved in survivor guilt and using it to good purpose.

# Appendix A

# Getting Help: Survivor Groups and Therapy Programs

Healing from survivor guilt is something no one should have to go through alone. Indeed, in many cases doing so is almost impossible. Virtually anyone who suffers from guilt can benefit from the right kind of help. Notice, however, that I said "the right kind." The quality of a survivor group or therapy program—whether individual or group—must not only be good, but also must suit you as an individual. In order to find the right program, you must carefully evaluate your options.

## Finding a Therapist or Treatment Program

One of the most important tasks you'll be faced with in helping yourself to heal is selecting the therapist or therapeutic program that will best meet your needs. This section is devoted to helping you decide which kind of counselor, program, or support group is right for you. Unfortunately, there are many therapists and programs that should be avoided. For example, in recent years PTSD—especially as it relates to rape and childhood sexual abuse survivors—has received considerable media attention. As a result, some therapists and programs have simply jumped on the bandwagon. They may present themselves as able to offer help to trauma survivors even though the only training they have is a couple of workshops and, perhaps, some extremely limited experience.

In choosing a therapist or program, you have the right to shop around and ask questions. To do this you may need to overcome the passivity and low self-esteem that plague so many people with survivor guilt. But it's vital to convince yourself that you deserve the therapist or program that is best suited to your needs.

There is a minimum set of criteria for effective survivor guilt therapy. Effective therapists and therapeutic programs (for you as a person suffering from survivor guilt) must do the following:

- Be acquainted with the different types of guilt, especially survivor guilt, and the way they interact

- Be familiar with faulty thinking patterns that can lead to irrational guilt

- Be able to allow you to continue to feel guilty about whatever you feel guilty about, whether or not that guilt is seen by them as rational or irrational and to help you deal with the pain of that guilt and find ways to cope with it constructively

- Be familiar with the grieving process

- See the stressful event as real and important in itself, apart from any preexisting psychological problems and any current social, family, or personal pressures

- View you as a person who is capable of being healed—not as a willing participant in the loss or trauma or as a hopeless psychiatric case

- Educate you about the nature of guilt, grief, stress, trauma, and the healing process itself

- Either teach you coping skills, such as assertiveness, stress management, relaxation techniques, and anger management, or make appropriate referrals for you to receive such help

- Use medication and behavior-management techniques when appropriate, but not to the exclusion of examining your present and past with the goal of understanding what occurred and your feelings about those events

- Be aware of the effects of sex-role stereotyping, racism, and blame-the-victim attitudes on the healing process

## *Where to Begin*

To begin the process of selecting a therapist or program, compile a list of names. Get recommendations from friends, doctors, other trauma survivors who've had positive experiences, and hospitals with specialized programs for trauma survivors.

The Anxiety Disorders Association of America maintains a listing of member therapists and self-help groups by area. Call (301) 231-9350 anytime to listen to a recording, or call between 9:00 A.M. and 5:00 P.M., Eastern time, Monday through Friday, to speak directly with an ADAA staff member.

Veterans Outreach Centers, or Vet Centers, specialize in the treatment of combat-related PTSD. However, Vet Centers' staff members are often familiar with private therapists and programs that serve survivors of other types of trauma. You may want to contact your local Vet Center for a referral. Check the telephone directory, or call your local Veterans Administration hospital or medical center, or any veterans service organization, for example, the American Legion.

Other potential sources of referrals are university health or counseling centers (if you are a student) and local mental health and social service agencies, which are usually run by either the city or the county. If you contact one of these organizations, be sure to inquire if the therapists and programs listed are identified by specialty, such as trauma, addiction, eating disorders, and so on, and contact only those therapists whose specialty area(s) matches your needs.

You can also check your phone directory or local library to see if there is a statewide association of psychologists, psychiatrists, or social workers. These might, for example, be listed as "Maryland Psychological Association" or "Psychological Association of Pennsylvania." Many of these statewide organizations list therapists by specialty.

If you're a victim of crime, the police may also have a useful referral list. Victims of sexual assault and/or domestic violence can also telephone local rape crisis hotlines, battered women's shelters, and local chapters of NOW (the National Organization for Women) for referrals. Other women's organizations may also have lists of qualified professionals. Your telephone directory, local library, or social services agency should be able to provide you with the phone numbers of these organizations.

The following organizations can provide child abuse survivors, including those with multiple personality disorder, referrals to qualified therapists:

American Professional Society on the Abuse of Children (APSAC), 407 S. Deerborne, Suite 1300, Chicago, IL 60605; (312) 554-0166.

Childhelp USA, 1345 N. El Centro Ave., Hollywood, CA 90028; (800) 422-4453 or (323) 465-4016.

VOICES in Action (for incest survivors), P.O. Box 148309, Chicago, IL 60614; (312) 327-1500.

The agencies and organizations listed under the various headings in appendix B may also be able to provide referrals.

# The Screening Process

When you've come up with the names of at least four or five good prospects—ones whose specialties seem to fit your needs—interview each of them by phone. (If you're considering a program, you'll interview a program representative or staff member.) Before asking about the therapist's or program staff's qualifications, find out about fees, whether there are any openings, and whether the available time slots would be workable for you. Eliminate therapists and programs that are geographically inaccessible and those whose fees are prohibitive. When discussing fees, remember to ask about the possibility of a sliding scale, how payments are to be made, and what happens if you miss an appointment.

If the therapist or program meets your needs for these criteria, then inquire about training, experience, and focus. You might expect that a traumatic event such as the one you experienced would be seen as both important and real by any professional; yet there are schools of thought in the mental health field that regard trauma as relatively minor compared with other problems.

Also, since coursework on trauma and resulting psychological problems is not required training even for licensed social workers, psychologists, and psychiatrists, it's critical that you inquire about the background of any potential therapist or the staff in any therapeutic program. Don't be afraid to ask how many workshops the therapist or staff members have attended or how many books they've read on guilt, grief, loss, chronic illness, stress, post-traumatic stress disorder, clinical depression, addiction, and related subjects

You can also ask how the therapist keeps up with the latest developments in the field of stress and trauma, and whether he or she has colleagues available for consultation who are experts in guilt, grief, stress, and trauma.

You needn't sound hostile, but don't avoid asking the hard questions for fear of offending, either. Remember, your mental and physical health are at stake. You might want to preface your questions by telling the therapist or counselor that you are faced with a bewildering array of alternatives now and you want to make the best choice for yourself. Consider asking such questions as the following (if you are considering a program, you would ask these questions in terms of the program's staff):

- How long have you been in practice?

- Are you a member of any professional organizations?

- How many trauma survivors have you seen in therapy?

- What is your background in the area of stress and trauma?

- What, in your view, constitutes the healing process for someone with survivor guilt?

- What experience have you had in treating people suffering from depression/eating disorders/alcoholism? (Gear your questions to your particular problems.)

- How much and what kind of training have you had in these areas?

- What approaches would you take toward healing an eating disorder/alcoholism/suicidal behavior/depression? In the case of an eating disorder, would you work with a nutritionist or dietitian? In the case of clinical depression, do you have a psychiatrist with whom you consult on issues of medication?

- What would you do if I became suicidal?

- What is your view on self-help groups or other group therapy?

- Do you also conduct family therapy? If not, do you work with a family counselor? (Ask this only if you want family counseling as well.)

- What is your format for communicating with your clients outside the session? Under what circumstances would you contact your clients by mail? By phone?

- What limits do you impose on contact with clients? Do you accept phone calls outside of regularly scheduled sessions? Would you accept these calls at your office only or also at home? Is there a charge for time spent on phone calls?

When you've narrowed your list down to a final two or three therapists or programs, visit them. In the past, many therapists gave an initial consultation free of charge or at a reduced rate. Today most therapists charge the full fee for their time at the initial consultation. Despite the cost, it's essential that you meet with the therapist face to face before making your selection. (Programs usually have a provision for a similar type of interview.)

After this initial interview, think about these questions:

- Does the therapist or counselor seem warm and supportive?

- Is he or she respectful toward you?

- Do you feel as if you could talk with this person about your inner feelings about the trauma?

Most important, what is your gut feeling about the therapist? Qualifications are important—and you should only be considering qualified therapists at this point—but the final decision may be a matter of finding the best emotional match for you. Pay attention to your feelings. If you have strong negative feelings toward a particular therapist after the first interview, it probably isn't a good match. If you are ambivalent, you might consider meeting with the therapist an additional time before making your decision.

Special note for women: Many psychologists—both men and women—call themselves "feminist" or "nonsexist," but you need to decide for yourself if they actually are. Also keep in mind that just because a therapist is a woman does not automatically make her a nonsexist therapist.

You do not have to choose a woman therapist in order to find one who is unbiased. There are many male therapists who are committed to nonsexist treatment and provide excellent counseling. In general, though, it takes considerably more effort for a man to truly understand the influence of sex-role stereotyping on a woman than it does for a woman.

## Evaluating the Course of Therapy

Once you've selected a therapist, you can start your therapy on a trial basis. Make a commitment to work with the therapist for a month, six weeks, or some other limited time period; then reassess your choice. How do you seem to be faring? How effective has the therapist been in addressing your survivor guilt and secondary symptoms (such as alcoholism or depression)? What is the therapist's assessment of your progress and prospect for healing?

If the therapist you've selected turns out to have been a poor choice, use the knowledge you've gained to make a better one. The wrong therapist can do more harm than good. However, as you make your decision about whether to continue with the therapist, bear in mind that the course of therapy is not always smooth: backsliding, regression, and hostility on your part may all be part of healing. Stop seeing the therapist only if you believe that he or she is actually doing you harm, or if you feel that your prospects for progress with this individual are very slim.

A case in which you would definitely want to look for another therapist would be one in which the therapist blamed you for what happened. You do not need more guilt, blame, or shame than you feel already. Even if you had nothing to do with causing the stress or trauma, and could have done nothing to prevent the events that so trouble you, on some level you probably feel guilty—such is the irrational nature of survivor guilt. If, as a result of the therapist's statements or nonverbal reactions, you continually leave the office feeling more debased, ashamed, and unsure of yourself than before, it's probably time to search for another therapist.

You should also question staying with a therapist who judges you to be "deficient" because he or she subscribes to one of the following myths:

- Having a good moral character and strong personality structure can make you resilient to stress and trauma.

- You sought the stress or trauma to gain attention, to meet your masochistic needs, or to fulfill some other neurotic need.

- The stresses, losses, or traumas you experienced play a minor part in your problems compared with the mistakes you've made as a human being.

Since you are human, you probably have made mistakes in your life, even during the events that caused your survivor guilt. You probably do have areas in which you need to grow and inner conflicts you need to explore. Your therapist may want to help you better understand these mistakes and problem areas. However, this should be done in a manner that respects your dignity and good intentions. It is not only humiliating but in the long run also self-defeating and ineffective for a therapist to try to change any of your problem areas through tactics of guilt and shame.

# If You Are Referred to a Psychiatrist

If you have a clinical depression or your psychological symptoms are severe, your therapist may refer you to a psychiatrist, who can prescribe medication. If and when you go to a psychiatrist, he or she will probably do a complete medical and psychiatric evaluation. You should be prepared to list your symptoms, their duration and frequency, and any other observations you have about your symptoms. In addition, you have the right to expect the psychiatrist to explain your diagnosis and the medication in detail. You might want to ask the doctor these questions:

- What is my psychiatric diagnosis?

- What are the various types of medications that have been found useful for this diagnosis?

- What are the potential benefits and the possible negative side effects of each of these medications?

- Are there any initial side effects that should disappear in time, such as nervousness or extreme fatigue? If so, how long should I wait for the initial symptoms to disappear before I call the office?

- Why is this particular medication being selected over another?

- How much research has been done on this particular medication, and what is the probability that this medication will be helpful?

- How long does it typically take for this medication to have an effect?

- If I were to overdose on this medication, would I die?

- Should I give myself the daily medication, or should somebody else have the responsibility of giving it to me?

- What if I forget to take the medication at the prescribed time? Should I take it later in the day or wait until the next day? If I skip a day, should I double the dosage the next day or not?

- What should I do if I throw up the pill for some reason?

- Will this medication interact with other drugs, such as alcohol? If so, will the effect be harmful or possibly deadly?

- Will the drug be administered in ever-increasing doses?

- How will you determine if the dosage needs to be changed? Will blood tests be required? If so, how often?

- Do you have any literature on the medication that I can read?

- Can I become addicted to this medication?

- What will happen to me, physically and psychologically, if I suddenly stop the medication on my own? What if I don't tell anyone I'm stopping the medication; what are the signs others can see that will tell them that I have stopped? What should these others do to help me if I stop taking the medication?

- At what point can the medication be discontinued? Is there a point after which the body becomes immune to the effects of the medication so that it ceases to be effective?

- How long does it take for the effects of the drug to leave the body? How long after the drug is discontinued should any dietary or alcohol restraints be observed?

- If this medication does not work, what other medications might be available?

Medication needs constant monitoring. Before the right dosage is established, you may need to telephone the psychiatrist several times. You will also need to call if the negative side effects are problematic or seem to be causing more hardship than is warranted by the positive effects of the drug.

For example, if you are sluggish or extremely tired all the time, are unable to concentrate, or have physical symptoms such as bleeding, muscle tremors, seizures, dizzy spells, hyperventilation, dark or discolored urine, rashes, inability to urinate, constipation, loss of menstrual period, severe headaches, vomiting or nausea, loss of sex drive, or other physical difficulties, you should call the psychiatrist right away. Similarly, if you still feel suicidal, homicidal, or self-mutilating, or if you develop hallucinations or delusions, or begin to feel hyperactive or out of control, call the psychiatrist immediately. If your call is not returned promptly, call again. Do not let these side effects go unattended.

Finally, be wary of any psychiatrist who does not seem familiar with the medication, who seems to discount your concerns, or who does not return your phone calls regarding questions about the medication or problems with it. If contacting the psychiatrist is always a problem, consider changing psychiatrists. However, you might want to discuss your decision with your therapist or support group first.

# Finding a Survivor Group

There is increased recognition today that people who have been traumatized or endured great losses can benefit greatly from participation in a support group. Groups for survivors of war, rape, and various forms of family abuse and for family members of persons who suffer from certain diseases, such as cancer, are becoming fairly common and thus are easy to find. Survivors of crime, natural catastrophes, vehicular accidents, and other forms of trauma and survivors and family members of certain types of illnesses may have a harder time finding a group.

To search for a group appropriate for you, consult the following resources:

- Your local library

- Your local (county or city) mental health or social services department

- Your local police department

- Local hospitals

- Local newspapers—survivor groups may be listed in the classified ads, in the community section, or in sections pertaining to family life and mental health

You may also want to check with the local chapter of the American Psychological Association, the American Psychiatric Association, or the National Association of Social Workers to see if someone there can help you locate a survivor group. A therapist with expertise in trauma may also be able to refer you to such a group. In addition, the following support groups and referral services may be helpful:

AA World Service (Alcoholics Anonymous), P.O. Box 459, Grand Central Station, New York, NY 10163; (212) 870-3400. Check local listings as well.

Al-Anon Family Group Headquarters and Alateen (both for the families of alcoholics), World Service Office, P.O. Box 862,

Midtown Station, New York, NY 10018; (212) 302-7240. Check local listings as well.

American Suicide Foundation, 1045 Park Ave., New York, NY 10028; (800) 531-4477.

Group Project for Holocaust Survivors and Their Children, 345 East 80th St., New York, NY 10021; (212) 737-8524.

Incest Survivors Anonymous, P.O. Box 17245, Long Beach, CA 90807; (310) 428-5599.

National Child Abuse Hotline, Childhelp USA; (800) 4-A-CHILD.

National Coalition against Domestic Violence, P.O. Box 18749, Denver, CO 80218; (800) 799-7233 or (303) 839-1852.

National Organization for Victims Assistance (NOVA), 1757 Park Road NW, Washington, D.C. 20010; (202) 232-6682.

National Self-Help Clearinghouse, 25 West 43rd St., Rm. 620, New York, NY 10036; (212) 354-8525.

Ray of Hope (for suicide survivors), P.O. Box 2323, Iowa City, IA 52244; (319) 377-9890.

Some support groups are led by professionals, others by survivors only. Some have a religious basis or are identified with a certain faith or denomination. Self-help survivor groups and church-led groups that do not employ professionals usually are free or charge only what is necessary to meet expenses. Survivor groups that are led by professionals vary in price. Some offer a sliding scale; others do not.

If you are in a twelve-step program such as Alcoholics Anonymous, Narcotics Anonymous, Overeaters Anonymous, Al-Anon, or Nar-A-Non, you might ask at your meetings whether anyone knows of a survivor group appropriate for you.

Also, if you have a physical or emotional problem related to the trauma—for example, if you lost a limb or developed some other physical or emotional problem such as depression—you might want to inquire (using any of the resources listed above) about survivor groups organized around your physical or emotional concerns, rather than the type of trauma you endured. For instance, if you developed an eating disorder as a result of your trauma, you may want to consider Overeaters Anonymous (OA) as well as professionally led groups. Similarly, if the trauma triggered, or worsened, a problem with alcohol or drugs, you may want to at least try some AA or NA

(Narcotics Anonymous) meetings. It is usually suggested that you go to at least six meetings before you decide whether the program fits your needs.

If you don't have any luck in finding a group that fits your needs or experiences, you might consider starting one. You can start by contacting a therapist or clinic specializing in stress or in trauma work to see if there is interest in helping to organize and direct a support group.

## Further Reading

The following publications offer further information that may be helpful in your search for help:

American Psychological Association. 1989. "If Sex Enters into the Psychotherapy Relationship." Write to Order Department, American Psychological Association, 750 First St. NE, Washington, D.C. 20002; or call (202) 336-5500.

Catherall, Don. 1992. "Seeking Professional Help: Finding the Right Therapist and the Right Treatment" in *Back from the Brink: A Family Guide to Overcoming Traumatic Stress*. NY: Bantam.

Stanford Friedman, Susan. 1979. *A Woman's Guide to Psychotherapy*. Englewood Cliffs, N.J.: Prentice-Hall.

# Appendix B

# Resources

This appendix lists two types of resources: (1) names, addresses, and/or telephone numbers of agencies and organizations that may be able to provide assistance of various kinds and (2) titles of books, pamphlets, newsletters, audiotapes, and other materials that might be of use to you in understanding trauma and healing from it, and in controlling symptoms and secondary problems.

These resources are listed alphabetically by the following topics:

- Alcohol and drug abuse

- Battering

- Child abuse

- Crime

- Depression

- Eating disorders and compulsive behavior

- Legal assistance

- Natural catastrophes

- Rape and sexual assault

- Relaxation and symptom-management

- Suicide

- Vehicular accidents

- War and combat

The organizations and materials listed here are by no means all the resources available. In fact, this list is only a beginning. In some categories there are hundreds of articles and books available; in others, unfortunately, there is very little. I encourage you to look beyond this list on your own. Spend some time at your local library, and ask the librarian for assistance if you need it. Also talk to other survivors and helping professionals to see what resources they can recommend.

# Alcohol and Drug Abuse

## Agencies and Organizations

If you suffer from alcoholism or drug addiction, you will probably need to go to a detox center, where you will receive the medical care you need as you go through withdrawal. Do *not* attempt to detox by yourself; withdrawal can lead to medical emergencies. Furthermore, since withdrawal tends to create the symptoms of depression, the process can be so painful that you may be tempted immediately to begin using your drug again to ease the emotional distress. In some clinics, antidepressants are given to ease the transition.

After you have successfully withdrawn from your drug, you need treatment that not only helps you abstain from your drug, but also offers insight into the reasons you needed it in the first place. Consider an inpatient or outpatient rehabilitation program that is specific to your drug. Some programs are free. Many programs, such as Alcoholics Anonymous (AA), Narcotics Anonymous (NA), and Cocaine Anonymous, include twelve-step meetings or will refer you to the local chapter of an organization that does.

You can obtain the names of treatment centers from the phone book, from hospitals, and from city or county mental health or social service agencies. In addition to local programs, there are specialized centers around the country. Names of these programs can be obtained from your doctor and/or therapist, from your local drug or alcohol-rehabilitation board or council, from a local hospital, or from twelve-step meeting members.

If you have been addicted for many years, don't be surprised if you need to enroll in treatment programs more than once to complete your healing. Nationwide, multiple hospitalizations are the norm, not the exception. Also, when you begin a program, be sure you receive a complete medical examination, as well as an evaluative interview for clinical depression. If you suffer from depression as well, your ability to stay clean and sober will be made that much more difficult.

Information about AA, Al-Anon, Adult Children of Alcoholics (ACOA), Cocaine Anonymous, NA, and Nar-Anon meetings can be obtained from your telephone directory or local library, or by calling the national offices of these organizations. See also the section "Finding a Support Group" in appendix A.

Al-Anon: (800) 356-9996

Alcoholics Anonymous World Service: (212) 870-3400

Narcotics Anonymous: (818) 773-9999

## *Books and Other Materials*

Many books, pamphlets, workbooks, and audio- and videocassettes on all issues related to alcoholism, drug addiction, and other forms of substance abuse are available through Hazelden Educational Materials, Box 176, Pleasant Valley Road, Center City, MN 55012. Call (800) 328-9000 for a free catalog. Some of the best of these materials are included in the following list.

Alcoholics Anonymous World Services. *The Big Book* and *The Twelve Traditions.* Available from Alcoholics Anonymous World Services, Box 459, Grand Central Station, New York, NY 10163.

Gorski, Terence. 1989. *Passages through Recovery: An Action Plan for Preventing Relapse.* Center City, Minn.: Hazelden Educational Materials.

Hughes, Richard, and Robert Brewin. 1979. *The Tranquilizing of America.* New York: Warner Books.

Johnson, Vernon E. 1983. *I'll Quit Tomorrow.* New York: Harper and Row.

Mann, Marty (ed). 1981. *Marty Mann Answers Your Questions about Drinking and Alcoholism.* New York: Holt, Rinehart and Winston.

May, Gerald. 1988. *Addiction and Grace.* Center City, Minn.: Hazelden Educational Materials.

Milam, James R., and K. Ketchan. 1981. *Under the Influence: Guide to the Myths and Realities of Alcoholism.* New York: Bantam Books.

Mumey, Jack. 1988. *Loving an Alcoholic,* New York: Bantam Books.

Nakken, Craig. 1988. *The Addictive Personality: Roots, Rituals, and Recovery.* Center City, Minn.: Hazelden Educational Materials.

Twerski, Abraham J. 1990. *Addictive Thinking: Why Do We Lie to Ourselves? Why Do Others Believe Us?*. Center City, Minn.: Hazelden Educational Materials.

Weil, Andrew, and Winifred Doren. 1981. *From Chocolates to Morphine: Understanding Mind-Active Drugs*. New York: Houghton Mifflin.

# Battering

## Agencies and Organizations

You can be directed to sources of help by courts, social service agencies, churches, battered women's shelters, or state chapters of the National Coalition against Domestic Violence. Call (303) 839-1852, the national office of the coalition, for information about your state chapter, or check your local phone directory. The organization also maintains an information line: (800) 799-7233.

You may also be able to get names and phone numbers of sources of assistance from your local police, library, community crisis center, or mental health hotline.

It may be helpful for you to contact the National Organization for Victim Assistance, 1757 Park Road NW, Washington, D.C. 20010; (202) 232-6682. This organization can provide crisis intervention, short-term counseling, medical and legal advice, and referrals to some eight thousand victim-assistance programs across the country, including battered women's programs and rape crisis centers.

You can also contact the National Domestic Violence Hotline, P.O. Box 7032, Huntington Woods, MI 48070; (800) 779-7233.

## Books and Other Materials

Martin, Del. 1981. *Battered Wives*. San Francisco: Volcano Press.

NiCarthy, Ginny. 1986. *Getting Free: A Handbook for Women in Abusive Relationships*. Seattle: Seal Press.

Walker, Lenore. 1979. *The Battered Woman*. New York: Harper and Row.

White, Evelyn. 1985. *Chain Chain Change: For Black Women Dealing with Physical and Emotional Abuse*. Seattle: Seal Press.

Zambrano, Myrna M. 1985. *Major Sola Que Mal Acompanada: Para la Mujer Golopeada/For the Latina in an Abusive Relationship*. Seattle: Seal Press.

# Child Abuse

## Agencies and Organizations

The National Child Abuse Hotline, run by Childhelp USA, provides on-the-spot telephone counseling to any child being abused (physically or sexually) and offers immediate assistance, information, and referrals to anyone concerned about abused children. Call (800) 442-4453. Childhelp's address is 1345 N. El Centro Ave., Hollywood, CA 90028.

For information and free literature on child abuse, you can also contact the National Council on Child Abuse and Female Violence, 1155 Connecticut Ave. NW, Suite 400, Washington, D.C. 20036; (800) 222-2000 or (202) 429-6695.

VOICES in Action is a national network of male and female incest survivors, local groups, and contacts throughout the United States that offers free referrals to therapists, agencies, and self-help groups endorsed by survivors. (VOICES stands for Victims of Incest Can Emerge Survivors.) VOICES also maintains a listing of more than a hundred confidential groups in which people who have survived particular types of abuse can write to each other. In addition, the group publishes a newsletter, holds an annual meeting, and offers training for group leaders. Write to P.O. Box 148309, Chicago, IL 60614; or call (312) 327-1500.

## Books and Other Materials

Numerous books, pamphlets, and workbooks on recovering from physical and/or sexual abuse are available from Hazelden Educational Materials, Box 176, Pleasant Valley Road, Center City, MN 55012. Call (800) 328-9000 for a free catalog.

Adams, Caren, and Jennifer Fay. 1989. *Free of the Shadows: Recovering From Sexual Violence.* Oakland, Calif.: New Harbinger Publications.

Bass, Ellen, and Laura Davis. 1998. *The Courage to Heal.* New York: Harper and Row.

Cambridge Women's Center. *For Crying Out Loud.* Available from Cambridge Women's Center, 46 Pleasant St., Cambridge, MA 02139; (617) 354-8807. Although this newsletter is written by and for women with histories of sexual abuse, the information it contains is relevant and helpful for male survivors as well.

Courtois, Christine. 1999. *Adult Survivors of Child Sexual Abuse*. Available from Families International, 11700 West Lake Park Dr., Park Place, Milwaukee, WI 53224.

Engel, Beverly. 1989. *The Right to Innocence: Healing the Trauma of Sexual Abuse*. New York: Ivy.

Farmer, Steven. 1989. *Adult Children of Abusive Parents*. Los Angeles: Lowell House.

Kunzman, Kristin. 1990. *The Healing Way: Adult Recovery from Childhood Sexual Abuse*. Center City, Minn.: Hazelden Educational Materials.

Lew, Mike. 1989. *Victims No Longer: Men Recovering from Incest and Other Sexual Abuse*. New York: Nevramont Publishing Co.

Matsakis, Aphrodite. 1991. *When the Bough Breaks: A Helping Guide for Parents of Sexually Abused Children*. Oakland, Calif.: New Harbinger Publications.

———. 1996. *I Can't Get Over It: A Handbook for Trauma Survivors*. Oakland, Calif.: New Harbinger Publications.

———. 1998. *Trust after Trauma: A Relationship Guide for Trauma Survivors and Those Who Love Them*. Oakland, Calif.: New Harbinger Publications.

National Center on Child Abuse and Neglect. "Everything You Always Wanted to Know about Child Abuse and Neglect." Available from the National Center on Child Abuse and Neglect, Department of Health and Human Services, P.O. Box 1182, Washington, D.C. Also available from the same address is a listing of free and low-cost pamphlets on child abuse and neglect.

Nice, Suzanne, and Russell Forest. 1990. *Childhood Sexual Abuse: A Survivor's Guide for Men*. Center City, Minn.: Hazelden Educational Materials.

Ratner, Ellen. 1990. *The Other Side of the Family: A Book of Recovery from Abuse, Incest, and Neglect*. Deerfield Beach, Fla.: Health Communications.

VOICES in Action. *The Newsletter*. Available from VOICES in Action, P.O. Box 148309, Chicago, IL 60614; (312) 327-1500. This newsletter for adult male and female incest survivors is provided as part of VOICES' annual $35 membership fee. It provides information, resources, book reviews, and writings by and for survivors. It is currently expanding to include more information on issues of male survivors.

# Crime

## *Agencies and Organizations*

Your area should have a victim-assistance center that can give you information about your legal rights and offer legal, financial, and psychological help. Usually these centers are listed under "Victim Assistance" in telephone directories. Addresses and phone numbers of these centers can probably also be obtained from the police, local social service agencies, your local legal aid society, or your local bar association. (If you were raped, see also the listings under "Rape and Sexual Assault" in this appendix.)

Many states provide financial assistance for certain types of crime victims. Each state varies in its qualifications and in the amount it offers for counseling, living expenses, medical help, funeral expenses for murder victims, rape evidence kits, legal fees, disability claims, and other kinds of assistance. Under certain circumstances, victims' families can obtain various types of help. This is most often the case for the families of murder victims.

If you were a victim of a crime while working on the job, you may qualify for worker's compensation. Inquire at your place of employment, your local office of the Department of Social Services, or your state worker's compensation board or office. Your employer may also offer various forms of assistance.

If you have become disabled due to the crime, you may be able to apply for Social Security benefits through the Social Security Administration. You may also be able to deduct losses from theft from your federal income tax. Obtain publication 547 from the Internal Revenue Service (by calling 800-829-3676) for a full description of the circumstances under which you can take such a deduction.

Sometimes insurance companies raise premiums or refuse to cover victims of a theft. The Federal Insurance Administration has a policy that will cover your residence no matter how many times you have been victimized. It is not available in all states, however. Write to Federal Crime Insurance, P.O. Box 6301, Rockville, MD 29850; or call (800) 638-8780.

You may also want to contact the National Organization for Victims Assistance (NOVA), a private, nonprofit organization of victim and witness practitioners, criminal-justice professionals, researchers, former victims, and others who are advocates for victims. Write to NOVA, 1757 Park Road NW, Washington, D.C. 20010; or call (202) 232-6682.

### Books and Other Materials

Bard, Morton, and Dawn Sangrey. 1986. *The Crime Victim's Book,* 2nd ed. Secaucus, N.J.: Citadel Press. This book is one of the best resources available for crime victims and their families. It contains an excellent description of the psychology of crime victims and explains in simple language how victims can work effectively to claim their rights within government and legal bureaucracies. It also provides an outline of typical court procedures.

National Criminal Justice Reference Service. "Report to the Nation on Crime and Justice: The Data." Available from National Criminal Justice Reference Service, Box 6000, Dept. F, Rockville, MD 20850. Ask for publication NCJ 87068. This report provides general information about crime and the criminal justice system.

NOVA. *Victim Rights and Services: A Legislative Directory.* Available from NOVA, 1757 Park Road NW, Washington, D.C. 20010; (202) 232-6682. This publication gives an overview of the federal and state victim rights and services legislation and victim-compensation measures currently in effect.

# Depression

### Agencies and Organizations

As has been said repeatedly in this book, if you have a clinical depression, you need to consult a therapist or other mental health professional experienced in treating people who suffer from depression. See appendix A for guidelines for finding such assistance.

### Books and Other Materials

Burns, David D. 1980. *Feeling Good: The New Mood Therapy.* New York: Signet Books.

Copeland, Mary Ellen. 1992. *The Depression Workbook.* Oakland, Calif.: New Harbinger Publications.

Presnall, Louis. 1973. *Search for Serenity.* Center City, Minn.: Hazelden Educational Materials.

———. 1985. *First Aid for Depression.* Center City, Minn.: Hazelden Educational Materials.

Rosellini, Gail, and Mark Warden. 1988. *Here Comes the Sun.* Center City, Minn.: Hazelden Educational Materials.

# Eating Disorders and Compulsive Behavior

## Agencies and Organizations

If you suffer from anorexia, bulimia, or compulsive overeating, you need to arrange a consultation with an eating-disorders specialist, who can advise you whether you need an inpatient or an outpatient program. If your weight is dangerously high or low, or if your eating disorder is making it impossible for you to function or has caused medical complications, you may need hospitalization.

In the past, most inpatient and outpatient units specialized in anorexia or bulimia, but today more and more clinics are accepting individuals who struggle with compulsive overeating or obesity. Furthermore, an increasing number of insurance policies are paying for hospitalization for eating disorders.

Whether you need inpatient or outpatient help, your therapy should have a dual focus: symptom management (eliminating the destructive eating patterns and replacing them with constructive ones) and insight therapy. Follow the guidelines in appendix A for finding a therapist or program. Overeaters might also consider attending Overeater's Anonymous meetings (listed in the phone directory) as well as being evaluated for depression.

Hospitalization is usually not advised for other forms of compulsive behavior, unless there are medical or life-threatening problems resulting from the compulsion. (In that case, the hospitalization would be for your medical problem, not the compulsion, per se.) For help in understanding and curbing your compulsive behavior, whether it surrounds gambling, spending, sexual activity, or other behaviors, you will need individual counseling with a counselor who specializes in addictions and compulsions (see the guidelines in appendix A for finding such a person). You may also want to consider participation in Gambler's Anonymous, Debtor's Anonymous, Sex Addicts Anonymous, or Sex and Love Addicts Anonymous; consult your phone directory for listings.

## Books and Other Materials

Alexander, Eliot. 1991. *Sick and Tired of Being Fat: A Man's Struggle to Be Okay*. Center City, Minn.: Hazelden Educational Materials.
Hollis, Judi. 1985. *Judi Hollis's Collection for Recovering Overeaters*. Center City, Minn.: Hazelden Educational Materials.

————. 1990. *Fat Is a Family Affair: A Hope-filled Guide for Family and Friends of Eating Disorder Sufferers.* Center City, Minn.: Hazelden Educational Materials.

L. Elizabeth (anonymous). 1987. *Listen to the Hunger: Why We Overeat.* Center City, Minn.: Hazelden Educational Materials.

Roth, Geneen. 1982. *Feeding the Hungry Heart: The Experience of Compulsive Eating.* New York: Signet.

Sandbek, Terence J. 1986. *The Deadly Diet: Recovering from Anorexia & Bulimia.* Oakland, Calif.: New Harbinger Publications.

Steketee, Gail, and Kerrin White. 1990. *When Once Is Not Enough: Help for Obsessive Compulsives.* Oakland, Calif.: New Harbinger Publications.

Waldrop, Heidi. 1990. *Showing Up for Life: A Recovering Overeater's Triumph over Compulsion.* Center City, Minn.: Hazelden Educational Materials.

# Legal Assistance

## Agencies and Organizations

If you need the assistance of an attorney but cannot afford the customary legal fees, you can search out sources of low-cost or even free legal aid. Many lawyers volunteer time doing *pro bono* work—work for which they don't charge. Contact the following sources and inquire about low-cost or free legal assistance for your particular legal problem: your local courthouse, state bar association, police department, local battered women's shelters and rape crisis centers, your local legal aid society, or the law school of a nearby university. These sources may also have literature they can send you.

In the telephone directory, look in the white or yellow pages under "Legal Assistance," "Lawyer Referral Services," "Legal Aid," and "Legal Services Plans," for listings. You may also want to look in the yellow pages under "Attorneys" or "Lawyers," scanning the ads for lawyers who have sliding-scale payment plans, who offer a half-hour or hour of free consultation, or who specialize in your problem area. Then call a few of the numbers you find. If one lawyer can't help you, he or she may be able to refer you to someone who can.

Also, lawyers will sometimes work on a contingency basis, which means that if you win your case they get a percentage of any award or settlement you receive. But if you lose your case, you don't owe your attorney any fees.

# Natural Catastrophes

## *Agencies and Organizations*

Each state has its own disaster relief agency or office of emergency assistance. States vary in the types of compensation and services they offer. Contact your local agency for specific information about your state.

If the President of the United States declares a disaster area, the services of the Federal Emergency Management Agency (FEMA) become available. These services include some grants and loans, as well as crisis counseling. A local center is set up to provide assistance in disaster areas. To apply for assistance, call (800) 462-9029. Also available is a publication titled "Disaster Assistance Programs: A Guide to Federal Aid in Disasters," as well as other pamphlets that outline the types of aid available.

The American Red Cross also provides assistance for disaster victims. Contact your local chapter for further information.

Unfortunately, to date little has been written about stress reactions to natural disasters. General readings on PTSD should be helpful.

# Rape and Sexual Assault

## *Agencies and Organizations*

Contact your local rape crisis center for information and support. If your area does not have a rape crisis center, see if there is a battered women's shelter available. You might also call your local social services department for assistance.

Some rape crisis centers offer free or low-cost individual or group therapy; some do not. Most such centers have the names of qualified therapists. However, even if a therapist comes highly recommended, be sure to check out the therapist's credentials. As is discussed further in appendix A, you should only work with a therapist who has expertise in the area of sexual assault and with whom you feel some emotional affinity and trust. The therapist's skills and experience are critically important in helping you to heal. However, equally important for your healing is that there be an emotional match between you and your counselor.

Also check victim-assistance centers and the other sources of assistance for victims listed above under "Crime." You may be able to receive financial help for counseling, medical problems, and any losses incurred as a result of the rape.

## Books and Other Materials

Copeland, Mary Ellen. 1992. *The Depression Workbook*. Oakland, Calif.: New Harbinger Publications.

Fay, Jennifer, and Caren Adams. 1989. *Free of the Shadows: Recovering from Sexual Violence*. Oakland, Calif.: New Harbinger Publications.

Ledray, Linda E. 1986. *Recovering from Rape*. New York: Owl Books, Henry Holt and Company.

Lew, Mike. 1988. *Victims No Longer: Men Recovering from Incest and Other Sexual Abuse*. New York: Nevramont Publishing Co. This book, the first of its kind, explains the problem of male sexual victimization in lay terms and provides first-person accounts as well as written exercises for male survivors.

McEvoy, Alan W., and Jeff B. Brookings. 1984. *If She Is Raped: A Book for Husbands, Fathers, and Male Friends*. Holmes Beach, Fla.: Learning Publications, Inc.

Warshaw, R. 1988. *I Never Called It Rape*. New York: Harper and Row.

# Relaxation and Symptom-Management

## Agencies and Organizations

Here are a couple of the many stress-related organizations that offer help:

International Society for Traumatic Stress Studies, 435 North Michigan Ave., Suite 1717, Chicago, Ill. 60611 (312) 644-0828.

Anxiety Disorders Association of America, 6000 Executive Boulevard, Rockville, Md. 20852 (301) 231-9350.

## Books and Other Materials

Benson, Herbert. 1975. *The Relaxation Response*. New York: Avon.

Bourne, Edmund J. 1995. *Anxiety and Phobia Workbook*, 2nd ed. Oakland, Calif.: New Harbinger Publications.

Davis, M., E.R. Eshelman, and M. McKay. 1995. *The Relaxation & Stress Reduction Workbook*, 4th ed. Oakland, Calif.: New Harbinger Publications.

Miller, Emmett. *Letting Go of Stress*. This audiocassette is available from Source, 945 Evelyn St., Menlo Park, CA 94025; (800) 528-2737 or (415) 328-7171 in California.

Nudzynski, Thomas. *Relaxation Training Program*. This three-cassette set is available from Guilford Publications, 72 Spring St., New York, NY 10012; (800) 365-7006 or (212) 431-9800 in New York.

# Suicide

## Agencies and Organizations

If someone close to you has committed suicide, you may benefit from participating in a grief-and-loss seminar, a bereavement group, or a special group for survivors of suicide. Many local hospitals, churches, and mental health agencies offer grief-and-loss seminars or groups. They may also be able to refer you to a grief counselor or a suicide survivor group in your area.

You can also inquire about survivor groups in your area from your local state or county mental health service agency, from your nearest suicide-crisis hotline, at local hospitals and churches, or from the following organizations:

The American Suicide Foundation, 1045 Park Ave., New York, NY 10028; (800) 531-4477. The American Suicide Foundation also offers referral services and lists of survivors groups sponsored by educational, religious, medical, and mental health institutions by state.

Ray of Hope, P.O. Box 2323, Iowa City, IA 52244; (319) 337-9890. There are chapters in the Midwest and in New York, New Jersey, and other states. This organization offers a referral service and publications for suicide survivors.

## Books and Other Resources

Alexander, Victoria G. 1991. *Words I Never Thought to Speak: Stories of Life in the Wake of Suicide*. New York: The Free Press.

Barrett, Terence. 1989. *Life after Suicide: A Survivor's Grief Experience*, Fargo, N.D. Prairie House.

Crook, Marion. 1988. *Teenagers Talk about Suicide*. Checktowaga, N.Y.: University of Toronto Press.

———. 1992. *Please Listen to Me: Your Guide to Understanding Teenagers and Suicide*, 2nd ed. Bellingham, Wash.: Self-Counsel Press.

Danto, Bruce L., et al. 1980. *Suicide and Bereavement*. Stratford, N.H.: Ayer Company Publishers.

Heckler, Richard A. 1994. *Waking Up, Alive: The Descent, the Suicide Attempt, and the Return to Life*. New York: Grosset-Putnam Books.

Robinson, Rita. 1992. *Survivors of Suicide*. North Hollywood, Calif.: Newcastle Publishing.

Ross, Eleanora. 1987. *After Suicide: A Unique Grief Process*. Iowa City, Iowa: Lynn Publications. To order, contact Ray of Hope, P.O. Box 2323, Iowa City, IA 52244; (319) 337-9890.

———. 1990. *After Suicide: A Ray of Hope*, 2nd ed. Iowa City, Iowa: Lynn Publications. To order, contact Ray of Hope, P.O. Box 2323, Iowa City, IA 52244; (319) 337-9890.

Wertheimer, Allison. 1991. *A Special Scar: The Experiences of People Bereaved by Suicide*. New York: Routledge.

# Vehicular Accidents

## Agencies and Organizations

You can contact your local Vet Center (see "War and Combat," below) to find the name of a therapist who is experienced in helping trauma survivors. Trauma-recovery clinics, rape crisis centers, and battered women's shelters may also be helpful in recommending specific counselors, and may have information about survivor groups. You might also want to telephone hospitals in search of a survivor group. As of this writing, however, survivor groups for accident survivors are rare. (See appendix A for more information on finding therapists and support groups.)

Unfortunately, to date little has been written about stress reactions to vehicular accidents. General readings on PTSD should be helpful.

# War and Combat

## Agencies and Organizations

Veterans can seek assistance at their closest Department of Veterans Affairs Medical Center (VAMC). Most of these centers offer counseling services for individual and family problems, as well as assistance and referral for alcohol and drug-related problems.

VAMCs are increasingly becoming aware of PTSD, and some offer both in- and out-patient group and individual therapy for veterans suffering from combat-related PTSD. Application for inpatient units can be made through the psychiatry or psychology services at your local VAMC, or through your local Vet Center.

Vet Centers may be listed in your telephone directory under "Vet Centers" or as "Veterans Outreach Centers." Vet Centers are small counseling clinics aimed at providing therapy, social services, employment assistance, and other types of services to Korean and World War II veterans and to all Vietnam-era veterans and veterans who served in war zones in Grenada, Lebanon, Panama, the Persian Gulf, and other conflict areas since the Vietnam War (and to their families).

The following veterans service organizations can also provide various forms of assistance:

American Legion, 1608 K Street NW, Washington, D.C. 20006; (202) 861-2700.

Blinded Veteran's Association, 477 H St. NW, Washington, D.C. 20001; (202) 371-8880.

Department of Veteran's Affairs, 1811 R St. NW, Washington, D.C. 20009; (202) 265-6280.

Disabled American Veterans, 807 Maine Ave. SW, Washington, D.C. 20024; (202) 554-3501.

Jewish War Veterans, 1811 R St. NW, Washington, D.C. 20009; (202) 265-6280.

Paralyzed Veterans of America, 801 18th St. NW, Washington, D.C. 20006; (202) 872-1300

Veterans of the Vietnam War, National Headquarters, 760 Jumper Rd., Wilkes-Barre, PA 18702; (717) 825-7215.

Vietnam Veterans of America, 1224 M St. NW, Washington, D.C. 20005; (202) 628-2700. Most states have local chapters.

## *Books and Other Materials*

Goodwin, Jim. "Continuing Readjustment Problems among Vietnam Veterans: The Etiology of Combat Related Post-Traumatic Stress Disorders." Available from Disabled American Veterans, P.O. Box 14301, Cincinnati, OH, 45213.

Hansel, Sarah, Ann Steidle, Grace Zaczek, and Ron Zaczek (eds.). 1995. *Soldier's Heart: Survivors' Views of Combat Trauma*. Luthersville, Md.: Sidran Press.

MacPherson, Myra. 1984. *Long Time Passing: Viet Nam: The Haunted Generation*. Garden City, NY.: Doubleday and Colk, Inc.

Mason, P.H.C. 1990. *Recovering from the War: A Woman's Guide to Helping Your Vietnam Vet, Your Family, and Yourself.* New York: Penguin Books.

Matsakis, Aphrodite. 1996. *Vietnam Wives: Women and Children Surviving Life with Veterans with PTSD*, 2nd ed. Lutherville, Md.: Sidran Press.

Robbins, Christopher. 1987. *The Ravens.* New York: Crown Publishers, Inc.

Sonnenberg, S., A. Blank, and J. Talbott. 1985. *The Trauma of War: Stress and Recovery in Vietnam Veterans.* Washington, D.C.: American Psychiatric Press, Inc.

# Appendix C

## Deep Breathing Techniques and Muscle Relaxation Exercises

Before you try to remember and write down the stressful or traumatic events you endured, consider doing some muscle relaxation exercises, deep breathing, or physical exercise—or some combination of these if that works better for you. The following sections offer some guidelines. You can use breath control or a modified form of muscle relaxation while writing in your journal in order to help you focus and keep your anxiety level at a minimum.

**A note of caution:** When you begin the muscle relaxation exercises suggested here or elsewhere, obtain the approval of your physician, psychiatrist, or other mental health counselor first. Your doctor or psychiatrist's consent is especially critical if you are on any type of medication. The lowered heart rate and increased oxygen flow induced by deep breathing or relaxation can interact negatively with certain medications. You need to check with your doctor to be sure that there will be no negative side effects for you. Whether or not you are on medication, do not attempt to do deep breathing or relaxation exercises for more than one hour.

For some people the relaxation exercises can bring forth intolerable memories. If this happens to you, stop immediately. If you suffer from multiple personality disorder, if you tend to use dissociation as a means of coping, or you've been told by a mental health professional that you dissociate frequently (even if you don't believe it), do not even begin the muscle relaxation exercises unless you've been given specific medical permission to do so. Also observe the other guidelines listed in the "Cautions" section of the introduction.

# Deep Breathing

Your degree of body tension is reflected in the way you breathe. When you're under stress, you breathe shallowly. You can learn to calm yourself by practicing deep breathing exercises. Deep breath increases the oxygen flow to your brain, which increases your capacity to think and concentrate and helps rid your body of many toxins.

The following exercises will be useful to you not only in dealing with triggers, but in any life circumstance in which you want or need to calm yourself. Two forms of deep breathing exercises are offered here: abdominal breathing and calming breath (Bourne 1990).

Try to practice one of the following techniques regularly. Five minutes a day is recommended. Once you've become comfortable with one of the forms, you can use it to combat stress, anxiety, and other PTSD symptoms. Continuing to practice either of these techniques will make it second nature. You will naturally breathe more deeply, which will promote feelings of relaxation and well-being.

## *Abdominal Breathing Exercise*

1. Note the level of tension you're feeling. Then place one hand on your abdomen right beneath your rib cage.

2. Breathe slowly and deeply through your nose into the "bottom" of your lungs—in other words, send the air as low down as you can. When you're breathing from your abdomen, your hand should actually rise. Your chest should move only slightly while your abdomen expands. (In abdominal breathing, the diaphragm—the muscle that separates the lung cavity from the abdominal cavity—moves downward, causing the muscles surrounding the abdominal cavity to push outward.)

3. Once you've taken in a full breath, pause for a moment, and then exhale slowly through your nose or mouth, depending

on your preference. Be sure to exhale fully. As you exhale, allow your whole body to just let go, and count one. (You might visualize your arms and legs going loose and limp like a rag doll.)

4. Take ten slow, full abdominal breaths. Try to keep your breathing *smooth and regular*, without gulping in a big breath or letting your breath out all at once. Remember to pause briefly at the end of each inhalation. Count to ten, progressing with each exhalation. The process should go like this: Inhale, pause, exhale, count. Inhale, pause, exhale, count. Inhale, pause, exhale, count. And so on up to ten. If you start to feel light-headed while practicing abdominal breathing, stop for thirty seconds, and then start up again.

5. Repeat the exercise if you wish by doing two or three "sets" of abdominal breaths, remembering to count up to ten for each set (each exhalation counts as one number). Five full minutes of abdominal breathing will have a pronounced effect in reducing anxiety or early symptoms of panic. Some people prefer to count backward from ten down to one on each breath. Feel free to do this if you prefer.

## Calming Breath Exercise

1. From your abdomen, inhale slowly to a count of five.

2. Then hold your breath to a count of five.

3. Exhale slowly, through your nose or mouth, to a count of five (or more if it takes you longer). Be sure to exhale fully.

4. Once you've exhaled completely, take two breaths in your normal rhythm, then repeat steps 1 through 3 in the cycle above.

5. Keep up the exercise for at least five minutes. This should involve going through *at least* ten cycles of in-hold-out. Remember to take two normal breaths between each cycle. If you start to feel light-headed while practicing this exercise, stop for thirty seconds and then start again.

6. Throughout the exercise, keep your breathing *smooth and regular*, without gulping in breaths or breathing out suddenly.

7. Each time you exhale, you may wish to say, "relax," "calm," "let go," or any other relaxing word or phrase silently to yourself. Allow your whole body to let go as you do this.

# Progressive Muscle Relaxation

Progressive muscle relaxation was developed over fifty years ago by Dr. Edmund Jacobsen as a means of deep relaxation. This technique can be especially effective if you feel anxiety physically, in the form of tightness in your neck, shoulders, back, jaw, or around your eyes, or if you experience high blood pressure, insomnia, muscle spasms, or headaches associated with tension.

Progressive muscle relaxation involves tensing and then relaxing sixteen different muscle groups. It takes only fifteen to twenty minutes to do the whole sequence and requires nothing more than quiet and enough space to comfortably sit or lie down. Unless you experience overwhelming negative thoughts during the exercise, or some of the muscles being used have been injured so that the exercises are painful, there should be no reason you cannot use this relaxation technique.

Here are a few general guidelines for preparing to do progressive muscle relaxation:

- Set aside enough time (you might need thirty minutes at first) at a certain time of day for doing the exercises. When you first get up, before going to bed, and before a meal are the best times. After eating is the worst.

- Make sure you're comfortable: the room should be a comfortable temperature, quiet, and free from interruptions; your clothing should not be restrictive; and your entire body needs to be supported. You can lie down, perhaps with a pillow beneath your knees for extra support. Or you can sit in a chair, but be sure your head is supported along with the rest of your body. (Sitting may be preferable if you feel unsafe lying down because of your trauma. Whenever and however you position yourself, be sure you feel safe.)

- Try not to worry or think about outside events. Put them away for the time being. Also, don't worry about your performance of the technique. The goal is relaxation here—it's not a competitive sport.

Aside from helping you cope with trigger situations, regular, daily practice of progressive muscle relaxation can have a significant beneficial effect on your general anxiety level. You can use the following exercises (from Bourne 1990) before, during, or after completing any of the written exercises in this book, or before, during, or after doing any other kind of work on the trauma, either in a group or in individual counseling.

The idea is to tense each muscle group hard (but not so hard that you strain) for about ten seconds, and then to let go of it suddenly. You then give yourself fifteen to twenty seconds to relax, noticing how the muscle group feels when relaxed in contrast to how it felt when tensed before going on to the next group of muscles. You might also say to yourself, "I am relaxing," "Letting go," "Let the tension flow away," or any other relaxing phrase during each relaxation period between muscle groups. Throughout the exercise, maintain your focus on your muscles. When your attention wanders, bring it back to the particular muscle group you're working on. The following guidelines provide detailed suggestions for doing progressive muscle relaxation the correct way:

- When you tense a particular muscle group, do so vigorously, without straining, for seven to ten seconds.

- You may want to count "one-thousand-one," "one-thousand-two," and so on, as a way of marking off seconds.

- Concentrate on what is happening. Feel the buildup of tension in each particular muscle group. It is often helpful to visualize the particular muscle group being tensed.

- When you release the muscles, do so abruptly, and then relax, enjoying the sudden feeling of limpness. Allow the relaxation to develop for at least fifteen to twenty seconds before going on to the next group of muscles.

- Allow all the *other* muscles in your body to remain relaxed, as far as possible, while working on a particular muscle group.

- Tense and relax each muscle group once. But if a particular area feels especially tight, you can tense and relax it two or three times, waiting about twenty seconds between each cycle.

Once you are comfortably supported in a quiet place, follow these detailed instructions.

1. To begin, take three deep abdominal breaths, exhaling slowly each time. As you exhale, imagine that tension throughout your body begins to flow away.

2. Tighten your fists. Hold seven to ten seconds, and then release for fifteen to twenty seconds. Use these same time intervals for all other muscle groups.

3. Tighten your biceps by drawing your forearms up toward your shoulders and "making a muscle" with both arms. Hold, and then relax.

4. Tighten your triceps—the muscles on the undersides of your upper arms—by extending your arms out straight and locking your elbows. Hold, and then relax.

5. Tighten the muscles in your forehead by raising your eyebrows as far as you can. Hold, and then relax. Imagine your forehead muscles becoming smooth and limp as they relax.

6. Tighten the muscles around your eyes by clenching your eyelids tightly shut. Hold, and then relax. Imagine sensations of deep relaxation spreading all around the area of your eyes.

7. Tighten your jaw by opening your mouth so wide that you stretch the muscles around the hinges of your jaw. Hold, and then relax. Let your lips part and allow your jaw to hang loose.

8. Tighten the muscles in the back of your neck by pulling your head back, as if you were going to touch your head to your back. (Be gentle with this muscle group to avoid injury.) Focus only on tensing the muscles in your neck. Hold, and then relax. Since this area is often especially tight, it's good to do the tense-relax sequence twice.

9. Take a few deep breaths and tune in to the weight of your head sinking into whatever surface it is resting on.

10. Tighten your shoulders by raising them up as if you were going to touch your ears. Hold, and then relax.

11. Tighten the muscles around your shoulder blades by pushing your shoulder blades back as if you were going to touch them together. Hold the tension in your shoulder blades, and then relax. Since this area is often especially tense, you might repeat the tense-relax sequence twice.

12. Tighten the muscles of your chest by taking in a deep breath. Hold, and then release slowly. Imagine any excess tension in your chest flowing away with the exhalation.

13. Tighten your stomach muscles by sucking in your stomach. Hold, and then release. Imagine a wave of relaxation spreading through your abdomen.

14. Tighten your lower back by arching it up. (You can omit this exercise if you have lower back pain.) Hold, and then relax.

15. Tighten your buttocks by pulling them together. Hold, and then relax. Imagine the muscles in your hips going loose and limp.

16. Tighten the muscles in your thighs all the way down to your knees. (You'll probably have to tighten your hips along with your thighs, since the thigh muscles attach at the pelvis.) Hold, and then relax. Feel your thigh muscles smoothing out and relaxing completely.

17. Tighten your calf muscles by pulling your toes toward you. (Flex carefully to avoid cramps.) Hold, and then relax.

18. Tighten your feet by curling your toes downward. Hold, and then relax.

19. Scan your body for any residual tension. If a particular area remains tense, repeat one or two tense-relax sequences for that group of muscles.

20. Imagine a wave of relaxation slowly spreading throughout your body, starting at your head and gradually penetrating every muscle group all the way down to your toes.

You might want to record the instructions for this exercise on an audiocassette to expedite your early practice sessions. Or you may wish to obtain a professionally made tape of the progressive muscle relaxation exercise. There are many of these available, some of which are to be played while you sleep. However, the sleep tapes have not been proven to be as effective, and are not practical for those who have trouble sleeping. Here are some books and tapes that help you practice active muscle relaxation:

Benson, H. 1975. *The Relaxation Response.* New York: Avon.

Bourne, Edmund J. 1995. *Anxiety and Phobia Workbook*, 2nd ed., Oakland, Calif.: New Harbinger Publications.

Davis, M., E.R. Eshelman, and M. McKay. 1995. *The Relaxation and Stress Reduction Workbook*, 4th ed. Oakland, Calif.: New Harbinger Publications.

Miller, Emmet. *Letting Go of Stress.* This audiocassette is available from Source, 945 Evelyn St., Menlo Park, CA 94205; (800) 528-2737 or (415) 328-7171 in California.

Nudzynski, Thomas. *Relaxation Training Program.* This three-cassette set is available from Guilford Publications, 72 Spring St., New York, NY 10012; (800) 365-7006 or (212) 431-9800 in New York.

# Appendix D

# Self-Assessment: Depression and Post-Traumatic Stress Disorder

## Depression

A severe clinical depression, in which you are barely able to talk, walk, and or function, is easy to identify. However, it's more difficult to tell the difference between feelings of sadness, frustration, and discouragement, which are a normal part of life, and mild or moderate clinical depression. One difference is that in clinical depression, the despondency lasts a long time or is cyclical: the depressed feelings may go away and then return later.

Some depressions are reactive, in that they arise in response to a specific set of stressful events. Others are considered chronic, in that they have lasted for over two years without a period of two months or longer of relief.

The following questions will help you determine whether you have experienced what is called a major depressive episode. They are adapted from *DSM-IV*. Jot down your answers in the margin or in your journal.

1. Have you ever suffered from a depressed mood that lasted at least two weeks?

2. Have you ever, for at least two weeks, suffered from a loss of interest in or an inability to experience pleasure?

If you answered no to both of these questions, then it is highly unlikely that you suffer from depression. However, if you answered yes to at least one of these questions, continue on.

3. Over the same two-week period, did you feel depressed most of the day, nearly every day, as noticed by yourself or by others? (Feeling depressed can also be expressed as irritability.)

4. Over the same two-week period, did you or others notice that you lost most of your previous interest or pleasure in all or almost all of your daily activities, nearly every day?

5. Over the same two-week period, did you gain or lose more than 5 percent of your body weight (when not dieting) or did you notice a major increase or decrease in your appetite?

6. Over the same two-week period, did you have insomnia or hypersomnia (sleeping a lot) nearly every day?

7. Over the same two-week period, did you feel fatigued and without energy nearly every day?

8. Over the same two-week period, did you feel hyperactive and agitated or the opposite, underactive and sluggish, nearly every day, as observed by others, not just yourself? (This question refers to physical sensations, not to emotional restlessness or sluggishness.)

9. Over the same two-week period, did you feel worthless or extremely guilty about relatively inconsequential matters nearly day?

10. Over the same two-week period, did you have trouble concentrating or thinking or suffer from indecision nearly every day?

11. Over the same two-week period, did you have recurring thoughts of death or suicide (with or without a specific plan), or did you devise a specific plan for killing yourself or attempt suicide?

If you have answered yes to at least five of these symptoms and you also meet the following two criteria, you are considered to have had a major depressive episode. First, these symptoms must have caused important problems in vocational, social, personal, and other areas of functioning. Second, none of the following conditions applies:

- An organic brain problem or other medical problem caused or maintained the symptoms.

- What you experienced was a normal reaction to the death of a loved one.

- You suffer from schizophrenia, schizophreniform disorder, delusional disorder, or psychotic disorder.

- The symptoms are the result of substance abuse or some other form of substance and medication.

If you have met the criteria for a major depressive disorder, do not despair. Depression is a highly treatable condition. Although our knowledge of it is still in its infancy stages, the last decade has seen a virtual explosion of interest in and research into depression. Improved treatment methods and many forms of effective medications exist that were not available ten to fifteen years ago.

The most important step you can take is to seek help. But don't just go to any counselor or psychiatrist: find one who specializes in depression. Depression will not go away by itself. It is likely to worsen over time, and you can become so depressed that you will be unable, or unwilling, to receive the help you need and deserve.

# References

Albeck, J. 1994. "Intergenerational Consequences of Trauma: Reframing Traps in Treatment Theory—A Second Generation Perspective," in *Handbook of Post-Traumatic Therapy*, Mary Beth Williams and John F. Sommer, Jr., Eds., Greenwood Press, Westport, Conn. pp 106–128.

American Psychiatric Association, 1994. *Diagnostic and Statistical Manual of Mental Disorders*, fourth ed. (DSM-IV). Washington, D.C.: American Psychiatric Association.

Aronfreed, J., et al. 1971. *Developmental Psychology Today*. Del Mar, Calif.: CRM Books.

Asch, S. 1955. "Opinions and Social Pressure." *Scientific American* 193: 31–35.

Ayto, J. 1990. *Dictionary of Word Origins*. New York: Little, Brown and Company.

Barnhard, C. (ed.) 1996. *The American College Dictionary*. New York: Random House.

Barocas, H., and C. Barocas. 1973. "Manifestations of concentration camp effects on the second generation," *American Journal of Psychiatry* 130, 7:820–821.

Bass, E., and L. Davis. 1988. *The Courage to Heal: A Guide for Women Survivors of Child Sexual Abuse*. New York: Harper and Row.

Bazyn, K. 1977. "Introduction," in Paul Tournier's *The Best of Paul Tournier*. New York: Inverson.

Beck, A. T. 1976. *Cognitive Therapy and the Emotional Disorders*. New York: International Universities Press.

Beck, A. T., and G. Emery. 1985. *Anxiety Disorders and Phobias: A Cognitive Perspective.* New York: Basic Books, Inc.

Beecher, H. K. 1946. "Pain in men wounded in battle." *Annals of Surgery* 123.

Ben Artzi-Pelossof, N. 1996. *In the Name of Sorrow and Hope.* New York: Alfred Knopf.

Bhatia, S., M. Khan, and A. Sharma. 1986. "Suicide risk: Evaluation and management." *American Family Physician* 34:3.

Blatt, Thomas Toivi. 1997. *From the Ashes of Sobibor: A Story of Survival.* Evanston, Ill.: Northwestern University Press.

Bourne, E, J. 1995. *Anxiety and Phobia Workbook,* 2nd ed. Oakland, Calif.: New Harbinger Publications.

Bowles, C. 1978. "Guilt: How it affects your patients, how it affects you." *Nursing Care* 12:10.

Brende, J. 1991. *A Workbook for Survivors of War.* Columbus, Ga: Trauma Recovery Publications.

Burger, D. 1977. "The survivor syndrome: A problem of nosology and treatment." *American Journal Psychotherapy* 31:238–251.

Call, E. (chair). 1995. "Efficacy of eye movement desensitization and reprocessing (EMDR) treatment for trauma survivors as measured by the Rorschach." Audiotape from the Treatment of Trauma: Advances and Challenges, the 11th Annual Meeting of the International Society for Traumatic Stress Studies, Boston.

Campbell, C. 1978. *Nursing Diagnosis and Intervention.* New York: John Wiley and Sons.

Campbell, J. 1988. *The Power of Myth.* New York: Doubleday.

Cascardi, M., and K. D. O'Leary. 1992. "Depression symptomatology, self-esteem, and self-blame in battered women." *Journal of Family Violence* 7:249–259.

Chapman, E. 1993. "The many faces of post-traumatic stress syndrome." *Journal of the American Institute of Homeopathy* 86:2, 67–71.

Courtois, C. 1988. *Healing the Incest Wound: Adult Survivors in Therapy.* New York: W.W. Norton and Company.

Daniele, Y. 1994. "As survivors age: Part 1." *Clinical Quarterly.* Menlo Park, Calif.: The National Center for Post-Traumatic Stress Disorder. 4:1–7.

Davis, L. 1990. *The Courage to Heal Workbook.* New York: Harper and Row.

Dimsdale, J. E. (ed.). 1964. *Survivors, Victims, and Perpetrators: Essays on the Nazi Holocaust.* Washington, D.C.: Hemisphere Publishing Corporation.

Epstein, H. 1979. *Children of the Holocaust.* New York: Putnam.

Figley, C. 1995. "Systematic traumatology: Family therapy with trauma survivors." Presentation at the Maryland Psychological Association. Rockville, MD, Dec.12.

Foa, E. B., G. Steketee, and B. Olasov-Rothbaum. 1989. "Behavioral/cognitive conceptualization of post-traumatic stress disorder." *Behavior Therapy* 20:155–176.

Freud, A. 1996. *The Ego and the Mechanisms of Defense*. New York: International Universities Press, Inc.

Freud, S. 1961. "The ego and the id," in *The Standard Edition of the Complete Psychological Works of Sigmund Freud* (Vol. 19), edited and translated by J. Strachey. London: Hogarth (original work published in 1923).

Freyberg, J. T. 1980. "Difficulties in separation and individuation as experienced by offspring of Nazi Holocaust Survivors." *American Journal of Orthopsychiatry* 50:87–95.

Garner, D. M., and P. E. Garfinkel. 1985. *Handbook of Psychotherapy for Anorexia Nervosa and Bulimia*. New York: The Guilford Press.

Giller, E. 1994. "Foreword," in *Catecholamine Function in Post-Traumatic Stress Disorder: Emerging Concepts*, edited by M. Murburg., Washington, D.C.: *American Psychiatric Press.*

Glover, H. 1985. "Guilt and aggression in Vietnam veterans." *The American Journal of Social Psychiatry* 5(1):15–18.

Glover, H. 1992. "Emotional numbing: a possible endorphin-mediated phenomenon associated with post-traumatic stress disorders and other allied psychopathologic states," *Journal of Traumatic Stress Studies*. Vol. 5:4, 643–676.

Golding, J. M., 1994. "Sexual assault history and physical health in randomly selected Los Angeles women." *Health Psychology* 13: 13–128.

Grinker R., and J. Spiegel. 1945. *Men under Stress*, Philadelphia: Blakiston.

Grossman, A. 1996. *On Killing: The Psychological Cost of Learning to Kill in War and Society*. New York: Little and Brown.

Grossman, A. 1998. "On killing." Presentation at Readjustment Counseling Service Region 1B, Baltimore, Md. July 22.

Hales, R., S. Yudofsky, and J. Talbott (eds.). 1994. *The American Psychiatric Press Textbook of Psychiatry*, 2nd ed. Washington, D.C.: American Psychiatric Press.

Harrison, G. B. (ed.). 1948. *Shakespeare: The Complete Works*. Harcourt, Brace and World, Inc.

Hayashi, I. 1997. "Impact of stress following a catastrophic urban disaster: 1995 Kobe earthquake." Audiotape, 97 ISTSS-47and 48, International Society for Traumatic Stress Studies, 13th Annual Meeting, Montreal, Canada.

Heckler, R. A. 1994, *Waking Up, Alive: The Descent, the Suicide Attempt, and the Return to Life*. New York: Grosset-Putnam Books.

Hendlin, H., and A. P. Haas. 1984. "Suicide and guilt as manifestations of PTSD in Vietnam combat veterans." *American Journal of Psychiatry* 148:589–591.

Henricks, R. 1994. "Great world religions: Beliefs, practices, histories; part four of five: Confucius, the Tao, the ancestors and the Buddha: The religions of China." Audio tape series: Superstar Teachers. The Teaching Company, 7405 Alban Station Court, A-107. Springfield, VA 22150–3418.

Herman, J. 1992. *Trauma and Recovery*. New York: Basic Books

Hollon, S. D., and J. Garber. 1988. "Cognitive therapy" in *Social Cognition and Clinical Psychology: A Synthesis*, edited by L.Y. Abramson. New York: The Guilford Press.

Horowitz, M. J. 1986. *Stress Response Syndromes*. North Vale, N.J.: Jason Aronson.

Hyer, Lee, et al. 1994. *Trauma Victim: Theoretical Issues and Practical Suggestions*. Muncie, Ind.: Accelerated Development.

James, B. 1994. "Trauma and the attachment relationship: Integration of theory, assessment, and treatment." Audiotape 94ISTSS-40, International Society for Traumatic Stress Studies, 10th Annual Meeting, Chicago, Illinois.

Janoff-Bulman R., and C. B. Wortman. 1977. "Attributions of blame and coping in the 'real world': Severe accident victims react to their lot." *Journal of Personality and Social Psychology* 35:351–363.

Jiang, W., B. Michael, D. Krantz, R. Waugh, E. Coleman, M. Hanson, D. Frid, S. McNutly, J. Morris, C. O'Conner, and J. Blumenthal. 1996. "Mental stress-induced myocardial ischemia and cardiac events." *Journal of the American Medical Association* 175:21.

Johnson, D. R. 1996. "Creating healing relationships for couples." Audiotape 96ISTSS-81, International Society for Traumatic Stress Studies, 12th Annual Meeting, San Francisco, CA.

Joseph, S. S., P. Hodgkinson, W. Yule, and R. Williams. 1993. "Guilt and distress 30 months after the capsize of the *Herald of Free Enterprise*." *Personality and Individual Differences* 14:27–273.

Kolb, L. 1983. "Return of the repressed: Delayed stress reaction to war." *Journal of the Academy of Psychoanalysis* 11:531–545.

Kollbrunner, J. 1996. "Is guilt the taboo of modern psychology?" *Support Care Cancer* 4:67–70.

Kubany, E. 1994. "A cognitive model of guilt typology in combat-related PTSD." *Journal of Traumatic Stress*, 7:3–19.

———. 1996. "Cognitive therapy for trauma related guilt." Audio cassettes 96 ISTSS-16, 25 and 26, 12th Annual Meeting, International Society for Traumatic Stress Studies, San Francisco, CA.

———. 1997. "Thinking errors, faulty conclusions, and cognitive therapy for trauma-related guilt." *National Center for Post Traumatic Stress Disorder Quarterly* 7:6–8.

Kubany, E., F. Abueg, J. Brennan, S. Haynes, F. Manke, and C. Stahura. 1996. "Development and validation of the trauma-related guilt inventory (TRGI)." *Psychological Assessment* 8:428–444.

Kubany, E., F. Abueg, W. Kilauano, F. Manke, and A. Kaplan. 1997. "Development and validation of the sources of trauma-related guilt survey: War zone version." *Journal of Traumatic Stress* 10: 235–258.

Kubany, E., and F. Manke. 1995. "Cognitive therapy for trauma-related guilt: Conceptual bases and treatment outlines." *Cognitive and Behavioral Practice* 2:27–62.

Kubler-Ross, E. 1981. *On Death and Dying*. New York: Alfred Knopf.

Kulka, R., W. Schlenger, J. Fairbank, B. Jordan, C. Marmar, and D. Weiss. 1990. *Trauma and the Vietnam War Generation: Report of findings from the National Vietnam Veterans Readjustment Study*. New York: Brunner-Mazel.

Krystal, H. 1971. "Trauma: Consideration of its intensity and chronicity," in *Psychic Traumatization*, edited by H. Krystal and W. Neiderland. Boston: Little, Brown.

Lewis, C. N. 1980. "Memory adaptation to psychological trauma." *American Journal of Psychoanalysis* 40:319–323.

Mahrer, A. (ed.). 1967. *The Goals of Psychotherapy*. New York: Appleton-Century-Crofts.

Marin, P. 1981. "Living in moral pains." *Psychology Today* Nov:69–79.

Matsakis, A. 1989. "The battle against obesity." Unpublished Paper.

———. 1994. *Post-Traumatic Stress Disorder: A Complete Treatment Guide*. Oakland, Calif.: New Harbinger Publications.

———. 1996. *I Can't Get Over It: A Handbook for Trauma Survivors*. Oakland, Calif.: New Harbinger Publications.

———. 1998. *Trust after Trauma: A Guidebook to Relationships for Survivors and Those Who Love Them*. Oakland, Calif.: New Harbinger Publications.

McKay, M., and P. Fanning. 1987. *Self-Esteem: A Proven Program of Cognitive Techniques for Assessing, Improving and Maintaining Your Self-Esteem*. Oakland, Calif.: New Harbinger Publications.

McNeil, D. E., C. Hatcher, and R. Reubin. 1988. "Family survivors of suicide and accidental death." *Suicide and Life-Threatening Behavior* 18:137–148.

Menchu, R., M. S. Miles, and A. S. Demi. 1992. "A comparison of guilt in bereaved parents whose children died by suicide, accident, or chronic disease." *Omega Journal of Death and Dying* 24:203–215.

Milgram, S. 1963. "Behavioral study of obedience." *Journal of Abnormal and Social Psychology* 67:371–378.

———. 1965. "Some conditions of obedience and disobedience to authority." *Human Relations* 18:57–75.

Mitchell, J. E., and E. D. Eckert. 1987. "Scope and significance of eating disorder.s" *Journal of Consulting and Clinical Psychology* 55(5):628–634.

Morin, R. 1998. "Hail to the philanderers-in-chief, unconventional wisdom." *The Washington Post* July 26, C5.

Murburg, M. (ed.). 1994. "Catecholamine function in post-traumatic stress disorder: Emerging concepts." *American Psychiatric Press*. Washington, D.C.

————. 1996. "Catecholamine in PTSD: The up, down, or sideways? Debate." Audiotape 96ISTSS-70, 12th Annual Meeting, International Society for Traumatic Stress, San Francisco, CA.

NCCAN (National Center on Child Abuse and Neglect). 1983a. "Child protection: A guide for state legislation." Washington, D.C.: U.S. Department of Health and Human Services.

————. 1983b. "Everything you always wanted to know about child abuse and neglect." Washington, D.C.: U.S. Department of Health and Human Services.

Neiderland, W. 1964. "Psychiatric disorders among persecution victims." *Journal of Nervous and Mental Disease* 139:458–474.

Niedenthal, P., J. Tangney, and I. Gavanski. 1994. "'If only I weren't' versus 'If only I hadn't': Distinguishing shame and guilt in counterfactual thinking." *Journal of Personality and Social Psychology* 67:585–595.

Opp, R. E., and A. Samson. 1989. "Taxonomy of guilt for combat veterans." *Professional Psychology: Research and Practice* 20(3): 159–165.

Pearlman, L. A. 1996. "Trauma and the fulfillment of human potential." Audiotape 96ISTSS-52, 12th Annual Meeting, International Society for Traumatic Stress Studies, San Francisco, CA.

Perry, B. 1994. "Psychophysiological effects of childhood trauma: Influence on development." Audiotape 94 ISTSS-103, International Society for Traumatic Stress Studies, 10th Annual Conference, Chicago, IL.

————. 1996. "Neurobiology sequelae of childhood trauma: PTSD in children," in *Catecholamine Function in PTSD: Emerging Concepts*, edited by M. Michele Murburg. Washington, D.C.: American Psychiatric Press.

Pittman, R. K., and S. P. Orr. 1990a. "The black hole of trauma." *Biological Psychiatry* 26:221–223.

————. 1990b. "Twenty four hour urinary cortisol and catecholamine excretion in combat-related post-traumatic stress disorder." *Biological Psychiatry* 27:245–247.

Rader, D. 1996. "There had to be something more out there—An Interview with Priscilla Presley." *Parade Magazine*, Feb:6–7.

Resick, P. 1994. "Cognitive processing therapy (CPT) for rape-related PTSD and depression." *Clinical Quarterly*, Summer/Fall.

Resick, P., and M. K. Schnicke. 1992. "Cognitive processing therapy for sexual assault victims." *Journal of Consulting and Clinical Psychology* 60:748–756.

————. 1993. *Cognitive Processing Therapy for Rape Victims: A Treatment Manual*. Newbury Park, Calif.: Sage Publications.

Robertson, W. J. 1994. "The concept of guilt." *Journal of Psychosocial Nursing* 32:15–18.

Rosenheck, R., and P. Nathan. 1985. "Secondary traumatization in the children of Vietnam veterans with post-traumatic stress disorder." *Hospital and Community Psychiatry* 36(5):538–539.

————. 1986. "Impact of posttraumatic stress disorder of World War II on the next generation." *The Journal of Nervous and Mental Disease.* 174(6):319–327.

Seltzer, F. 1994. "Trends in mortality from violent deaths: Suicide and homicide, United States, 1960-1002." *Statistical Bulletin of the Metropolitan Insurance Company* 75:2, April-June.

Shatan. C. 1973. "The grief of soldiers: Vietnam veterans self-help movement." *American Journal of Orthopsychiatry* 43:640–653.

Shay, J. 1994. *Achilles in Vietnam.* New York: Atheneum Press.

Shovar, G. P. 1987. "Medical professionals," in : *PTSD: A Handbook for Clinicians,* edited by T. M. Williams. Cincinnati, Ohio: Disabled American Veterans.

Sigal, J., and V. Rakoff. 1971. "Concentration camp survival: A pilot study of effects on the second generation." *Canadian Psychiatric Association Journal* 16:393–397.

Smyth, L. 1994. *The Cognitive-Behavioral Treatment of Anxiety Disorders.* Havre de Grace, Md: RTR Publishing Company.

Spaccarelli, S. 1994. "Stress, appraisal, and coping in child abuse: A theoretical and empirical review." *Psychological Bulletin,* 116:340–362.

Staats, A. W. 1975. *Social Behaviorism.* Homewood, Ill.: Dorsey Press.

Staudacher, C. 1987. *Beyond Grief: A Guide for Recovering from the Death of a Loved One.* Oakland, Calif.: New Harbinger Publications.

————. 1991. *Men and Grief: A Guide for Men Surviving the Loss of Loved One.* Oakland, Calif.: New Harbinger Publications.

Suhr, M. 1986. "Trauma in pediatric populations." *Advanced Psychosomatic Medicine* 16:31–47.

Sun, L. 1998. "Tiananmen Square leader feels 'moral guilt' over crackdown's toll." *The Washington Post.* April 24:A-3.

Swanson, J. 1995. "God and His prophet: The religion of Islam." Audiotape. The Teaching Company, 7405 Alban Station Court, A-107, Springfield, VA.

Terr, L. C. 1983. "Time sense following psychic trauma: A clinical study of ten adults and twenty children." *American Journal of Orthopsychiatry* 53:244–261.

Tournier, P. 1977. *The Best of Tournier.* New York: Harper and Row.

van der Kolk, B. A. 1988a. "The biological response to psychic trauma," in *Post Traumatic Therapy and Victims of Violence,* edited by Frank Ochberg. New York: Brunner/Mazel Publishers.

————. 1988b. "The trauma spectrum." *Journal of Traumatic Stress* 1:3.

————. 1990. "Symposuim on PTSD." Presented at the Anxiety Disorders Association of America, 10th National Conference, Bethesda, MD.

————. 1994a. "Biological basis of traumatic memory." Audiotape 94-ISTSS-65, International Society for Traumatic Stress Studies, 10th Annual Meeting, Chicago, Ill.

————. 1994b. "Neurobiology of trauma." Audiotape 94 ISTSS-72, International Society for Traumatic Stress Studies, 10th Annual Meeting, Chicago, Ill.

————. 1996a. "Brain imaging studies in PTSD." Audiotape, 95ISTSS-96, International Society for Traumatic Stress Studies, 12th Annual Meeting, San Francisco, CA.

————. 1996b. "The body keeps the score: Approaches to the psychobiology of PTSD," in *Traumatic Stress: The Effects of Overwhelming Experience on Mind, Body, and Society,* edited by van der Kolk, B. A., A. McFarlane, and L. Weisaeth. New York: Guilford Press.

van der Kolk, B. A., and C. P. Dicey. 1989. "The psychological processing of traumatic experience: Rorschach patterns in PTSD." *Journal of Traumatic Stress* 2:259–274.

van der Kolk, B.A., D. Pelcovitz, S. Roth, F. Mandel, A. McFarlane, and J. Herman. 1996. "Dissociation, somatization and affect dysregulation: The complexity of adaptation to trauma." *American Journal of Psychiatry* 153(7):83–93.

Walker, L. 1979. *The Battered Woman.* New York: Harper and Row.

Wiesel, E. 1960. *Night,* translated by S. Rodway. New York: Hill and Wang.

Williams, C., and T. Williams. 1987. "Family therapy for Vietnam veterans," in *Post-Traumatic Stress Disorders: A Handbook for Clinicians,* edited by T. Williams. Cincinnati, Ohio: Disabled American Veterans.

Williams, T. 1987. "Diagnosis and treatment of survivor guilt," in *Post-Traumatic Stress Disorders: A Handbook for Clinicians,* edited by T. Williams. Cincinnati, Ohio: Disabled American Veterans.

Wilson, R. R. 1987. *The Body's Emergency Response: Breaking the Panic Cycle for People with Phobias."* Washington, D.C.: Anxiety Association of America.

# Also by Aphrodite Matsakis

## TRUST AFTER TRAUMA

*A Guide to Relationships for Survivors and Those Who Love Them*

Step-by-step exercises help readers manage emotions, handle unresolved issues, and end self-perpetuating cycles of withdrawal and isolation.
*Item TAT Paperback $15.95*

## I CAN'T GET OVER IT

The second edition of this groundbreaking work guides readers through the healing process of recovering from PTSD one step at a time.
*Item OVER Paperback $16.95*

## WHEN THE BOUGH BREAKS

Provides the information parents need to identify sexual abuse, deal with the reactions of others, and help children cope and heal.
*Item BOU $14.95*

## POST-TRAUMATIC STRESS DISORDER

This guide for professionals includes a variety of techniques balancing symptom management and emotional control with work aimed at reexperiencing feelings and healing the effects of trauma.
*Item CANT Hardcover $49.95*

Call toll-free 1-800-748-6273 to order. Have your Visa or Mastercard number ready. Or send a check for the titles you want to New Harbinger Publications, 5674 Shattuck Avenue, Oakland, CA 94609. Include $3.80 for the first book and 75¢ for each additional book to cover shipping and handling. (California residents please include appropriate sales tax.) Allow four to six weeks for delivery.

Prices subject to change without notice.

# Some Other New Harbinger Self-Help Titles

*Claiming Your Creative Self: True Stories from the Everyday Lives of Women*, $15.95
*Six Keys to Creating the Life You Desire*, $19.95
*Taking Control of TMJ*, $13.95
*What You Need to Know About Alzheimer's*, $15.95
*Winning Against Relapse: A Workbook of Action Plans for Recurring Health and Emotional Problems*, $14.95
*Facing 30: Women Talk About Constructing a Real Life and Other Scary Rites of Passage*, $12.95
*The Worry Control Workbook*, $15.95
*Wanting What You Have: A Self-Discovery Workbook*, $18.95
*When Perfect Isn't Good Enough: Strategies for Coping with Perfectionism*, $13.95
*The Endometriosis Survival Guide*, $13.95
*Earning Your Own Respect: A Handbook of Personal Responsibility*, $12.95
*High on Stress: A Woman's Guide to Optimizing the Stress in Her Life*, $13.95
*Infidelity: A Survival Guide*, $13.95
*Stop Walking on Eggshells*, $14.95
*Consumer's Guide to Psychiatric Drugs*, $16.95
*The Fibromyalgia Advocate: Getting the Support You Need to Cope with Fibromyalgia and Myofascial Pain*, $18.95
*Healing Fear: New Approaches to Overcoming Anxiety*, $16.95
*Working Anger: Preventing and Resolving Conflict on the Job*, $12.95
*Sex Smart: How Your Childhood Shaped Your Sexual Life and What to Do About It*, $14.95
*You Can Free Yourself From Alcohol & Drugs*, $13.95
*Amongst Ourselves: A Self-Help Guide to Living with Dissociative Identity Disorder*, $14.95
*Healthy Living with Diabetes*, $13.95
*Dr. Carl Robinson's Basic Baby Care*, $10.95
*Better Boundaries: Owning and Treasuring Your Life*, $13.95
*Goodbye Good Girl*, $12.95
*Being, Belonging, Doing*, $10.95
*Thoughts & Feelings, Second Edition*, $18.95
*Depression: How It Happens, How It's Healed*, $14.95
*Trust After Trauma*, $15.95
*The Chemotherapy & Radiation Survival Guide, Second Edition*, $14.95
*Surviving Childhood Cancer*, $12.95
*The Headache & Neck Pain Workbook*, $14.95
*Perimenopause*, $16.95
*The Self-Forgiveness Handbook*, $12.95
*A Woman's Guide to Overcoming Sexual Fear and Pain*, $14.95
*Don't Take It Personally*, $12.95
*Becoming a Wise Parent For Your Grown Child*, $12.95
*Clear Your Past, Change Your Future*, $13.95
*Preparing for Surgery*, $17.95
*The Power of Two*, $15.95
*It's Not OK Anymore*, $13.95
*The Daily Relaxer*, $12.95
*The Body Image Workbook*, $17.95
*Living with ADD*, $17.95
*When Anger Hurts Your Kids*, $12.95
*The Chronic Pain Control Workbook, Second Edition*, $17.95
*Fibromyalgia & Chronic Myofascial Pain Syndrome*, $19.95
*Kid Cooperation: How to Stop Yelling, Nagging & Pleading and Get Kids to Cooperate*, $13.95
*The Stop Smoking Workbook: Your Guide to Healthy Quitting*, $17.95
*Conquering Carpal Tunnel Syndrome and Other Repetitive Strain Injuries*, $17.95
*An End to Panic: Breakthrough Techniques for Overcoming Panic Disorder, Second Edition*, $18.95
*Letting Go of Anger: The 10 Most Common Anger Styles and What to Do About Them*, $12.95
*Messages: The Communication Skills Workbook, Second Edition*, $15.95
*Coping With Chronic Fatigue Syndrome: Nine Things You Can Do*, $13.95
*The Anxiety & Phobia Workbook, Second Edition*, $18.95
*The Relaxation & Stress Reduction Workbook, Fourth Edition*, $17.95
*Living Without Depression & Manic Depression: A Workbook for Maintaining Mood Stability*, $18.95
*Coping With Schizophrenia: A Guide for Families*, $15.95
*Visualization for Change, Second Edition*, $15.95
*Angry All the Time: An Emergency Guide to Anger Control*, $12.95
*Couple Skills: Making Your Relationship Work*, $14.95
*Self-Esteem, Second Edition*, $13.95
*I Can't Get Over It, A Handbook for Trauma Survivors, Second Edition*, $16.95
*Dying of Embarrassment: Help for Social Anxiety and Social Phobia*, $13.95
*The Depression Workbook: Living With Depression and Manic Depression*, $17.95
*Men & Grief: A Guide for Men Surviving the Death of a Loved One*, $14.95
*When Once Is Not Enough: Help for Obsessive Compulsives*, $14.95
*Beyond Grief: A Guide for Recovering from the Death of a Loved One*, $14.95
*Hypnosis for Change: A Manual of Proven Techniques, Third Edition*, $15.95
*When Anger Hurts*, $13.95

Call **toll free, 1-800-748-6273,** to order. Have your Visa or Mastercard number ready. Or send a check for the titles you want to New Harbinger Publications, Inc., 5674 Shattuck Ave., Oakland, CA 94609. Include $3.80 for the first book and 75¢ for each additional book, to cover shipping and handling. (California residents please include appropriate sales tax.) Allow two to five weeks for delivery.

*Prices subject to change without notice.*